Teaching Creative
and Critical Thinking

Teaching Creative and Critical Thinking

An Interactive Workbook

MARJORIE S. SCHIERING

ROWMAN & LITTLEFIELD
Lanham • Boulder • New York • London

Published by Rowman & Littlefield
A wholly owned subsidiary of The Rowman & Littlefield Publishing Group, Inc.
4501 Forbes Boulevard, Suite 200, Lanham, Maryland 20706
www.rowman.com

Unit A, Whitacre Mews, 26-34 Stannary Street, London SE11 4AB

Copyright © 2016 by Marjorie S. Schiering

All rights reserved. No part of this book may be reproduced in any form or by any electronic or mechanical means, including information storage and retrieval systems, without written permission from the publisher, except by a reviewer who may quote passages in a review.

British Library Cataloguing in Publication Information Available

Library of Congress Cataloging-in-Publication Data

Names: Schiering, Marjorie S., 1943– author.
Title: Teaching creative and critical thinking : an interactive workbook / Marjorie S. Schiering.
Description: Lanham : Rowman & Littlefield, [2016] | Includes bibliographical references and index.
Identifiers: LCCN 2016009082 (print) | LCCN 2016017155 (ebook) | ISBN 9781475819618 (cloth : alk. paper) | ISBN 9781475819625 (Electronic)
Subjects: LCSH: Creative thinking—Study and teaching. | Critical thinking—Study and teaching. | Creative teaching.
Classification: LCC LB1062 .S336 2016 (print) | LCC LB1062 (ebook) | DDC 370.15/7—dc23
LC record available at https://lccn.loc.gov/2016009082

∞™ The paper used in this publication meets the minimum requirements of American National Standard for Information Sciences—Permanence of Paper for Printed Library Materials, ANSI/NISO Z39.48-1992.

Printed in the United States of America

Contents

Foreword, *Drew Bogner, PhD, President of Molloy College*	vii
Preface	ix
Acknowledgments	xi
Introduction	1

SECTION 1: LEARNING-THROUGH-PLAY — 3

Overview	3
Explaining and Defining Creativity: Creative Cognition	3
Explaining Creative Cognition and Metacognition: Critical Thinking	4
Two Processes of Creativity	4
Explaining the Acronyms and Basics of the IM and IBR	5
Possible IM Components and IBR Activities	6
Advantages of IM and IBR for Academics and Socialization	6
Continuation and Culmination of Advantage Points	8
IM or IBR as Learning Centers	8
IM or IBR as Alternative Means of Assessment	9
Reciprocal Thinking Phases (Schiering, 1999)	9
Reviewing the Cognitive Collective	9
Reciprocal Thinking Phases: Overall Definition	9
Teaching Thinking and the IBR	10
Thinking Complexity	11
Connecting Creative Cognition to Constructing IBR Pages	13
Connecting Creative Cognition to Playing the IBR Pages	13
Effects and Affects of IM and IBR	13

SECTION 2: THE IM AND IBR WITH FOUR INTERACTIVE RESOURCES — 15

Introduction, *Louis Laupheimer*	15
Overview	16
Project- and Performance-Based Instruction	16
A Narrative: IM, A Learning Center, and the IBR, *Amanda Lockwood*	34
Summary	36

SECTION 3: CREATIVE COGNITION, CRITICAL THINKING AND METACOGNITION — 37

Overview	37
Interactive Activities to Make and/or Play	39
Reciprocal Thinking Phases Skills: Identification and Application for Fifteen Activities from Section 3, *M. Schiering*	138
Learning Standards for Twenty-Three Activities from Section 3, *Nicole Diblasio*	140
Addendum to Section 3 Activities: Kicking It Up a Notch, *Joshua Schiering*	151

SECTION 4: IM AND IBR: SUMMING UP THE METHOD AND STRATEGY — **155**

   Overview — 155
   Creative Cognition's IBR: Leadership Building: Matthew Schiering — 155
   The IBR for Review or Introduction to a Piece of Literature — 156
   The IBR for a Review or Introduction to a Thematic Unit of Study — 156
   Example of an IBR: *The Gruffolo*: A First-Grade IBR, *Elizabeth Struzzieri* — 157
   Intertwining Creativity and Innovation for Classroom Success: The IBR as Inspiration for Learning Achievement, *Dr. Laura Shea Doolan* — 191
   IBR and IM within and beyond the College Classroom — 192
   Author's Closing Thoughts — 195

   References — 197

   About the Author — 201

Foreword

How do people learn and what is the best way to teach? These are the essential questions that every teacher contemplates and the questions that animate the work of Marjorie Schiering. I know this from my earlier collaboration with her on the book we coauthored entitled, *Teaching and Learning: A Model for Academic and Social Cognition*.

In that book, we explained the cognitive theories that help one answer these questions and began the conversation on the methods a teacher can use to be most effective in teaching the diversity of students in the classroom.

In *Teaching Creative and Critical Thinking: An Interactive Workbook*, Schiering continues the conversation focusing specifically on the practicalities of teaching, sharing with the reader the techniques she has developed during her many years as a classroom educator.

The products of these techniques, many of which have been created by our education students, are often displayed on our campus. When I talk with the teacher candidates who created them, they tell me how each worked, transforming the learning environment for their student learners where they are participating in teaching.

We know that good teaching is infectious and draws from the excitement of the teacher. During our many hours working together on our collaborative book, I learned about these techniques and they changed how I taught. I was inspired to rework my Modern Japanese History course to be more experiential and explorative. My hope is that this book will inspire you as well, allowing you to reflect on how you teach.

Drew Bogner, PhD, President of Molloy College

Preface

WHERE DOES CREATIVITY BEGIN? WHEN DOES IT START? ARE YOU A CREATIVE COGNITION/THINKING INDIVIDual? If yes, then how are you creative? And, why do you suppose you have this ability? If your answer is "No," then why do you suppose that is the case? These four questions are the ones I pondered when writing this workbook, and also when asking others to make contributions to it—contributions representing their creativity for others to engage in and enjoy through experiential self-educating.

In the early years of my teaching at the first- through sixth-grade levels conscious thought was given about how I wanted to teach, how to make lessons interesting for student learners. I realized that open-ended assignments, whether inside or outside of the classroom, provided ample opportunity for one's imagination to be put into play/learning-through-play. That's all well and good, but how does that figure into the barrage of state and national tests students, let alone teachers or those in other fields of work, must take to qualify for initial positions or advancement?

Is it just open-ended assignments that bring about success? Certainly not! But the by-products of this type of assignment are using one's imagination, acceptance of one's work by self or others, use of socialization skills, collaboration and teamwork, and the development of self-empowerment and self-efficacy—and the benefit list continues.

The key to a methodology laden with interactive and creative cognition being employed in learning and resulting in doing well on tests is: Ready? Here it is: *We remember that which made a significant impact on our lives.* In the late 1930s this was referred to as experiential learning by John Dewey. In the 1990s the title was changed to constructivism. However, both concepts remain the same in that one constructs meaning from experience. The Interactive Method (IM) exemplified in this workbook incorporates both the aforementioned ideas with involvement in learning through one's creativity by learning-through-play.

Example: Today, at the very beginning, the Interactive Method might be a four-year-old coming over to a friend's house and playing teacher, cars, school, house, that first video game or app that he/she used on the phone, or a conversation at home, or some "fun" thing that was done in school. It's that last one of these listed things-to-do upon which this workbook focuses. Having one imagine for the purpose of creating something, impacts memory acquisition and retention. It just does—because whatever was done had meaning for the individual and sometimes that includes entire groups of them.

Later, when formal schooling begins, what is retained most frequently is that which, once again, made an impression on us. It could be a social situation. The key factor is being involved in the learning and teaching (oneself or others) process. When there's role playing in third grade or in a college classroom the material is retained due to the impact of the dialogue, the involvement of being part of the experience, whether as an observer or participant.

Think for a moment of the first time you rode a bicycle, experienced a special holiday celebration, a vacation, going to a friend's house, being outside enjoying a game on the sidewalk, being in a park. Or in later years, think about the first time driving a car, moving away from home to your own place, relationships. Each of these may be recalled with some detail, depending on their level of significance in your life.

That "making learning memorable," involving conscious knowing of what one is thinking, is what this interactive workbook addresses, as does the book upon which it is based: *Learning and Teaching Creative Cognition: The Interactive Book Report.* Both deal with learning-through-play, with the content for this workbook delivered in four specific parts. Following is an overview of sections 1–4 of this workbook.

Section 1: A definition of creativity and, subsequently, creative cognition, along with two types of creative processes begin the section. Then there are explanations of the IM, and the Interactive Book Report (IBR). The latter of these later serves as the vehicle for section 4 of the workbook. The IBR as an alternative means of assessment is also addressed. Academic and socialization advantages of the aforementioned methodology and accompanying activities are provided. The concept of Learning Centers being made of IBR pages is given attention, and "The Reciprocal Thinking Phases" of cognition and metacognition are examined for the *teaching of thinking and developing thinking skills*. The bottom lines for teaching thinking and developing skills are: (1) preparing one to be successful with learning standards, as well as with (2) application and implementation in learning-through-play as the *vehicle* of student-learner achievement, and (3) self-efficacy and empowerment are improved as one comes to see him/herself as an achieving individual both academically and socially. This first section closes with the "Effects and Affects of the IM and IBR."

Section 2: This section of the workbook first provides information about the IM and IBR being project- and performance-based instruction. Such methodology involves the student learner, regardless of age or grade level. Retention of material is at a zenith with this type of instruction. Photographs of four interactive instructional resources for learning-through-play are provided, as well as the uses, materials needed for its construction, and step-by-step directions for the making of the educational learning tool. Each activity is designed to be self-corrective. Templates are provided at the close of the section. These templates and pictures of the four interactive resources serve as viable reference points. A few closing remarks by teacher Amanda Lockwood addressing the use of the IM in a Learning Center and the IBR come directly before the summary of the section.

Section 3: This is the largest section of this interactive workbook. It begins with an explanation of project- and performance-based activities that compose the heart of this workbook. These activities were designed by student learners, teacher candidates, preteens, and teens along with a few parents, as well as by professionals who have been teaching for some time. These activities include directions for making and playing the activity and often what Reciprocal Thinking Phases skills (Schiering, 1999) are employed. In some cases, the creators of an activity have included learning standards that apply to it. Following the activities, Nicole DiBlasio shows how twenty-three of the activities in this section apply to Common Core learning standards. Nearly every activity in section3 has a sample of the completed activity in a photo or illustration provided. An addendum to this section, "Kicking It Up a Notch" by Josh Schiering, gives a good example of taking the concepts even further.

Section 4: An overview of the section is provided, with the Interactive Book Report and/or interactive instructional resources as leadership-building activities. Ideas for this section are from businessman Matthew Schiering. Next is a review of steps to be taken for making an IBR on a piece of literature and thematic unit of study. Then, Elizabeth Maria Struzzieri reformatted and modified a complete IBR to demonstrate the construction and use of this learning-through-play endeavor. Elizabeth's original work was done with classmate Giana Schenone in early 2015. A narrative titled "Intertwining Creativity and Innovation for Classroom Success: The IM and IBR as Inspiration for Learning Achievement" is provided by Dr. Laura Shea Doolan. The IBR and IM within and beyond the college classroom come before the author's closing statement.

You are invited to keep in mind that any of the pages you see in this section or the preceding ones, topic-wise and/or involvement-wise, may be used for a Learning Center, and surely as an alternative means of assessment when individuals demonstrate playing the page effectively.

(The beauty of having the IBR pages being self-corrective ones is that if errors are made, the student is the first to know and can deal with relearning in preparation for a formalized test, or later demonstrating his/her knowledge of the material by playing the page as an alternative means of evaluation of student comprehension.)

Acknowledgments

First I thank my husband, George, who tirelessly devoted his time to photocopying activities, making PDF files, making copies of the manuscript with and without figures and photos. He literally spent a good deal of time preparing the pages of sections 2 and 3 of this workbook. Frankly, had it not been for his steadfast determination regarding the transference of documents, this workbook may not have been completed. He also made interactive resource templates and established the "work-in-progress" website www.creativecognition4U.com.

Then, previous to that, there are two individuals who most profoundly influenced the writing of *Teaching Creative and Critical Thinking: An Interactive Workbook*. They are both PhD's, but in different areas. First, Drew Bogner, the president of Molloy College.

One day in the hallway waiting for the elevator across from his office he noticed my roll-cart loaded with Interactive Book Reports (IBR). Now, he could have walked on by, given a nod or not. But instead, he stopped and he asked me what these notebooks were. I answered his query with a detailed explanation. Albeit this was more information than he wanted, nonetheless he listened. He did that and then consciously thought as he mentioned how he'd never seen anything like these IBRs. His words pretty much were, "I like what I'm seeing. You ought to do something with that. These are really good."

What he'd done was stimulate my own interest and curiosity, as leaders and good educators often do without even thinking about it. His intuition, firmly grounded, brought me food for thought, as this initial interest helped formulate an answer to "what to do."

Fast-forward a year or more and there comes into view/play, another individual. This is Tom Koerner, PhD. He's a person whom happenstance presented to me. His publishing insight, based on knowledge and foresight, after seeing several Interactive Book Reports, resulted in his saying: "You ought to write a book and workbook on that, show examples, provide designs, discuss the relevance of the students being involved in their learning."

Okay, maybe that wasn't word for word what he said, but Tom had firmly encouraged me and subsequently planted an idea, which took hold by bringing the IM and IBR to light. The predecessor to this workbook, *Learning and Teaching Creative Cognition: The Interactive Book Report* would not exist if not for Tom's encouragement and guidance. As time passed, his associate, Carlie Wall, also gave of her time and expertise to assist me in that book coming to be, and this present book as well.

Overall, the appreciation of these individuals is given attention now because they came along at a time when their insight and ability to be active listeners, formulate ideas, pay attention, provide encouragement, and be positive began the work on this Interactive Workbook.

The idea of the IM began at the start of my teaching career and the implementation of the IBR happened toward the latter years. Acknowledgment is therefore given to those thousands of individuals who either used the IM for learning or made IBRs and passed them along or showed me that creative thinking may be developed, shared, enhanced, or basically established through being engaged in the learning process.

Over the years of my career I spent a good portion of my teaching in the North Rockland Central School District. My last ten years there were at the Stony Point Elementary School. The third through fifth graders who participated in Student Council and also those in Schiering's fifth-grade class practiced the interactive method of learning and teaching others, as well as one's self.

In 1998 and 1999, the student learners in my fifth-grade class made IBRs and entered them in the NYS Earth Day Competition. Coming in second and first place, respectively, they contributed to the furtherance of the IM and IBR during my college teaching career. The cooperation of teachers and students alike from Stony Point Elementary School is sincerely acknowledged. Their contribution to the overall philosophy of this book was encouraged by their participation in learning-through-play.

ADDITIONAL ACKNOWLEDGMENTS

Diane Fornieri is given acknowledgment for her help with the *Teaching and Learning: A Model for Academic and Social Cognition* book from 2011. Nick Simone is acknowledged for making a Word document from a PDF; and IT persons Ben Sales, Joseph Kuczyk, Dennis Neary, Dave Friedrich, Kevin Cooper, and Kevin Milella for their continual assistance with computer-related endeavors. And then there are the teacher candidates, teachers, and student learners who contributed to the pages of this workbook. Among them, two are singled out for their extra assistance. First is Nicole DiBlasio, who, in many cases, provided the Common Core learning standards applied to the workbook's activities, as well as coauthored an activity. Louis Laupheimer is credited with providing the Introduction to the second section of this workbook and activity pages as well. This newly certified teacher and teacher candidate, respectively, came forward to contribute these additional components of the workbook and their interest and dedication is sincerely appreciated. Elizabeth Maria Struzzieri is given acknowledgment for her contribution of *The Gruffolo* IBR, and Jennifer Botte for sharing the work she did with her fifth graders creating IBRs in small groups. Then there is Rickey Moroney, who assisted with photographing teacher-candidate IBR pages to be inserted into section 3. Anthony Marino is mentioned for contributing through his teaching and postdoctoral work to this book and the previous one as well with his design of the Reciprocal Creative Thinking Process graphic organizer. Joan Byrne is mentioned for her collaboration on The Linear Creative Process.

Last but not least I recognize my friend Angela Sullivan, who called so many times to say "Keep up the good work, you can do this." So too are our children and their spouses acknowledged, as they have been my touchstones for so many things and years: Matt/Maddy, Alyssha and Paul Miro, Joshua and Katie, Jolie, Mara, and Dave Moore, Seth and Carolina.

SPECIAL ACKNOWLEDGMENT

As in the previous book, Eileen Chapman is acknowledged with gratitude for her transcribing the book's content, addressing photocopying corrections to text structure, formatting, and being available for a myriad of other technological components including the separation of figures into folders. Her allegiance to this project knew no limits. She's a colleague who over the years became a friend and came to know the substance of my work as being a worthwhile endeavor. Thank you, Eileen, hardly seems adequate, but shall have to suffice in that you are remarkable in your steadfastness for helping others, not necessarily as a titled "teacher," but one who teaches nonetheless through example and camaraderie.

Introduction

IM AND IBR SUCCESS: A PERSONAL PERSPECTIVE: JENNIFER BOTTE
IN THE PRECURSOR TO THIS BOOK, LEARNING AND TEACHING CREATIVE COGNITION: THE INTERACTIVE BOOK *Report* the beginning sentence states: "Does anything new exist in teaching or learning? In 2015 it hardly seems possible." Well, two years ago Jennifer Botte, a former teacher candidate from an integrated language arts and reading class I was teaching at Molloy College put the IBR into her classes' daily routine. When she did that, something *new* was created, because it was her students and they were new to the concepts of the IM and IBR. *Most anytime there's something new introduced to the recipients of information, the possibilities of creativity and learning something different or differently is experienced.*

Jennifer stated: "I was using project and performance work for my thirty-one fifth graders. However, these were highly structured activities. I remembered Dr. Schiering using her invention of *The Interactive Book Report (IBR)* and the explanation of the *Interactive Method (IM)* of learning and teaching. So, I started to rethink the tight parameters on assignments I gave: 'Create this or that, use this material, make it this size, here's who you're going to work with and this is approximately how long it will take.'

"Now, with the idea of using the IBR, I decided to think of projects as 'skeletons' where students would fill in all the necessary parts to make it come alive! I provided the support frame, which I see as my responsibility. But, I gave learners full access to everything else and I hoped that would spark a new insurgence of excitement for everyone.

"I introduced the IM and the IBR on Body Systems and the class was self-separated into five groups, each with the assignment to create an IBR on a particular body system, such as, respiratory, skeletal, and so forth. Several weeks later, with a lot of collaborative work going on in our classroom, the IBRs were completed. It was then that I discovered the following:

1. Children had been working at home on some pages with designing and creating pages during their "free" time.
2. When the IBRs were done the students loaned them to each other.
3. Students learned from one another, as opposed to a book, or video.
4. The class came together as a community of learners.
5. They had fun making the IBRs and playing the pages of one another's creations.
6. They tested themselves to see what was retained and discovered that it was almost everything!
7. They LOVED teaching their classmates through the use of their particular body-system IBR.
8. Parents were fascinated with the games their children developed and commented positively on this IBR activity."

TWO LONG ISLAND SCHOOLS: NYS ENVIRONMENTAL CONSERVATION CONTEST
A year before Jennifer's experience, a group of students from a Floral Park, Long Island, school and the Lexington School for the Deaf entered the NYS Environmental Conservation Contest addressing the topic of sustainability. They did this with interactive instructional resources placed on posters they'd made. A new category was instituted, as no one on the Environmental Contest Committee had ever seen an interactive poster, and here were over fifty of them out of two thousand entrants in the contest. That's pretty impressive; to change the categorical qualifications of a state contest.

The students came in first through third place in their category with an honorable mention as well. Those attending the award ceremony in the fall of that year said that they would never forget this experience and would use the interactive resources forever. The book *Learning and Teaching Creative Cognition: The Interactive Book Report* has chapter 20 devoted to the "study" that resulted from this aforementioned experience.

Many teacher candidates, while making the IBR, have mentioned that using the IBRs Reciprocal Thinking Chart to identify what cognitive and/or metacognitive skills were used when playing a particular page resulted in their knowing how to teach thinking. This information, brought to job interviews, resulted in their obtaining the sought-after teaching position. One teacher, using her IBR as a prototype in 2008 in her North Carolina classroom had her students make IBRs on various pieces of literature. Because of this endeavor and use of the IM she received the Teacher of the Year award.

In terms of teacher candidates, perhaps most impressive is that by using the Reciprocal Thinking Phases skills by way of knowing what you're thinking, passing the state tests for reading is doable. That's because these tests call for recognizing and knowing, when reading a paragraph or set of passages, that test takers are identifying, recognizing analyzing, discerning, problem solving, risk taking, prioritizing, and the like and are able to answer questions involving these cognitive and metacognitive skills.

Now, as this book's author and one of the contributors to the pages that are playable, you're invited to play the pages of this workbook and share them, make some of your own design, spread the word about the IM and the IBR. Or you might separate the pages into *Learning Centers* or interactive resources used as, at the very least, alternative means of assessment. This means if the child plays-the-page successfully, he or she may be evaluated by the level of success. Don't be surprised if it's 100 percent, because by being involved in the learning the retention of information is very great.

Most importantly, enjoy this book by learning-through-play! And be sure to visit www.creativecognition4U.com to view videos of interactive activities and other ideas for either the IBR or the IM of learning and teaching.

BOOK'S AUDIENCE

This book is for you! And, it's for all those students who wrote or commented on how the learning-through-play experience impacted their lives in a positive manner. It's about how the creativity involved in the IM and IBR was being part of "who one is" as naturally as awakening in the morning. And it's for all those who want to develop learning situations that engage the individual as well as whole groups in appreciating the wonderment of discovery—the mind's ability to imagine, create, and think effectively and to identify thinking skills "in-play." Doing thus equates with this book's contents being a primary benefit to best practice when teaching and learning at any grade level: elementary, middle, high school or college, and beyond.

AUTHOR'S PHILOSOPHY AND BOOK INFORMATION

Teaching and learning are reciprocal processes. What we learn becomes who we are and influences how we conduct ourselves and think about ourselves. Learning-through-play/interactive and collaborative means of instruction are the most engaging and enjoyable ways to learn, as well as the best ways to assure retention of information, enhance thinking skills, and stimulate imagination for creativity. That's a huge statement, but the research I and others have conducted and/or the experiences we've had, which for me is nearly fifty years, attests to learning that involves the student, at whatever grade level, resulting in retention of presented material.

About ten years ago a friend of mine went back to college after a forty-three-year hiatus. He had to take a foreign language and was concerned about learning vocabulary. One of the activities in this workbook involves making a Flip-Chute and then creating cards for it. This friend learned his vocabulary words, perfectly, and passed the Foreign Language course with flying colors. And for his daughter who was a freshman in college and whom he had advised using this device, the outcome was the same.

The author's philosophy includes what we think and feel becoming what we say and do. Consequently, our lives are very large conversations, in general. The material in this book is a result of so many conversations. Thus, the pages in section 3 are those of teacher candidates, student learners, and teachers, as well as parents. Regardless, the book is written and designed through practical examples of IBR pages to engage you in knowing about your thinking so you will grow and go with that awareness—then share it by using these playable pages with others who will benefit from this knowledge.

SECTION 1

Learning-through-Play

OVERVIEW

This rather expansive first section of the interactive workbook addresses learning-through-play, and the reader should note two factors: (1) There is no age limitation to learning-through-play. (2) We remember that which made an impression on us, and learning using an interactive means of instruction creates memories that are retained for future use in and outside the academic arena.

A definition of what it means to be creative and have creative cognition follows. Then, two figures are presented that relate to types of creative processes. These are given attention so one might have an idea of how sequential and organized or simultaneous use of one's imagination may be. Neither process is more important or right than the other; rather, they simply exist as possibilities.

From this point the book explains the Interactive Method (IM) of learning and teaching, which is followed by the Interactive Book Report (IBR) connected to the concept of self-learning. The IBR pages, of this overall learning/teaching strategy, are self-corrective for student empowerment and self-efficacy, as well as self-correction, and as an alternative means of assessment.

Advantages of the aforementioned IM and IBR for academics and socialization are given attention. The concept of Learning Centers being made of IBR pages is addressed along with *The Reciprocal Thinking Phases: Cognition and Metacognition* for application and implementation in learning-through-play.

(The following information in this first section of the workbook comes from *Learning and Teaching Creative Cognition: The Interactive Book Report* [Schiering, Rowman & Littlefield, 2015].)

EXPLAINING AND DEFINING CREATIVITY: CREATIVE COGNITION

"Synonyms for the word 'creative' explode from the computer's thesaurus with words like 'original, imaginative, inspired, artistic, inventive, resourceful, ingenious, innovative, and productive' listed. These are cognitive or thinking skills that one needs to convey the simple definition of just one word! Confusion may follow, as each word does have a meaning of its own. However, cognition/thinking-development, in terms of one's being 'creative,' revolves around using imagination and being inventive in varied ways.

"This process of creativity, in turn, requires reflecting on what one is thinking—metacognition. Creativity may be looked at as an aspect of personality that is characterized by novel and appropriate ideas and processes. The idea of teaching through the use of applying interactive instructional techniques, a system of teaching, referred to in this book as an Interactive Methodology (IM), and the product addressed as the Interactive Book Report (IBR), allow for this application of inventive differentiated thinking in abundance. Linda Neiman (2012), founder of Creativity at Work, a consulting, coaching, and training alliance, says that creativity is the act of turning new and imaginative ideas into reality and involves thinking and producing. 'If you have ideas and don't act on them, then you are imaginative, but not creative,' she states.

"Creativity involves all individuals whether teachers or students, at any age or grade level. It applies to most fields of work or play. It may be located in one's home, in a group setting, or pretty much anywhere at any time. Creativity is a defining force in the shaping of identity as there's a person's drive to be different and special. Psychologists define this facet of personality as the need for uniqueness. 'In one way or another, we are all unique, and so let's examine this uniqueness in a general context and then move to specifics. In order to do this examination, one must know that creative cognition is thinking that's creative, as cognition is a synonym for thinking'" (Schiering, 2015).

"Creative Cognition is Creative Thinking" (Schiering, 2012)

EXPLAINING CREATIVE COGNITION AND CREATIVE METACOGNITION: CRITICAL THINKING

"Creative cognition and metacognition (higher-order) thinking are exhibited by an individual's thinking resulting in a new idea, the ability to manipulate humor to design a joke, artistic or literary work, painting or technological innovation, which has been accomplished in an original manner. You may question if this new thing must have the components of an actual object... something materialistic that has been produced? The answer I would think is that creativity is represented by an idea as much as something to manipulate. The key factor is that what has been created has not been present anywhere, previously.

"One is actively, mentally, and/or physically involved in cognitive processes that include all varieties of cognitive and metacognitive/higher-order thinking skills. It's when one actually does what he/she has imagined and designed, or uses this creation for physically or mentally designing something that hasn't been presented that creativity is exhibited. The going forth and 'doing' the creation (self-actualizing) is the highest metacognitive process' (Schiering, 1999)."

Critical thinking is involved in creativity as one examines the process of creating something. This scrutiny involves analyzing the process and evaluating the finished product. A few pages from here the Reciprocal Thinking Phases' skills are explained and defined to emphasize the concept of critical thinking being an integral part of creative thinking. *When one is teaching creativity, so too is critical thinking involved.*

"*Creativity ideas may come from varied media formats or be displayed that way. Nonetheless, this new thing that has been realized is just that, 'new.' Not just new to you, but new in general. One's imagination made it possible to exist in the empirical, heuristic, experience-based realm*" (Schiering, 2000–present).

Overall, this section's terms are original, inventive, resourceful, and exhibit rather ingenious thinking. The thinking involves some of the following skills: organization, evaluation, advanced decision making and problem solving, reflection, and self-actualization. The skills are evidenced when designing and making interactive instructional resources for an IBR, which comprises section 2 of this workbook.

TWO PROCESSES OF CREATIVITY

Linear Creative Process

Do you know how you are creative? One process of creativity may be done in a linear fashion. In that case, the thinking is sequential and progressively orderly. There is no going back and forth, but a movement from one component to another. The following flow chart solidifies terms associated with creative processes/stages as follows, because each stage leads to the next one: (1) Image(s) and/or ideas/conceptualizations lead to (2) Imagining(s), (3) bringing forth memories, (4) visualizing and discerning these impact on (5) a sensory response or trigger which would lead to (6) inventions, (7) decision making/critiquing the creative idea, which leads to (8) problem solving, that culminates with (9) creating, as the "final" stage. This process is sequential. One goes from "Images" to "Creating" with seven processes in between these (Schiering and Byrne, 2013).

The Creative Cognition Process: Linear Design

Images/Ideas → Imaginations → Bringing-forth Memories →

Visualizations → and discernment → Sensory responses →

Inventions → Decision-making and → Critiquing →

Problem Solving → Creating

Figure 1.1. The Creative Cognition Process: Linear Design (Schiering and Byrne, 2013)

Reciprocal Creative Process

You may be one who processes creativity in a simultaneous manner. If so, then you'd be using a reciprocal process. "There would be a back-and-forth between each of the numbered Linear Creative Cognition Process stages. Subsequently, as with most things we experience, there is 'reciprocity' within and between these ways of thinking creatively, or otherwise. Furthermore, there may be additional thinking skills, such as persistence and modifications being made as one is involved in creating.

"When modifications are addressed this is usually for one's verifying his or her creation and then possibly changing it from the original idea. The main point is that there is no specific order for the creativity, other than beginning with one's ideas. Discussing this concept of 'reciprocity of creative cognition' with Schiering providing the terms/skills within figure 1.2, Dr. Anthony Marino graphically designed the figure, which is titled: *The Reciprocal Creative Cognition Process.*

(Note that in figure 1.2, The Reciprocal Creative Process has all terms/skills originating with the center oval section of IDEAS. Then, all the other sections, as well as Images and Inventions are connected one to the other.)

The reciprocity of creativity is a back and forth, a within and between way of thinking.

EXPLAINING THE ACRONYMS AND BASICS OF THE IM AND IBR (SCHIERING, 2015)

"You may be looking at these acronyms and wondering what they are and if there's a difference between them. If you are, then the answers would be that the *IM* stands for the *Interactive Methodology,* which is a means of learning and teaching that addresses one's doing 'hands-on' type of work and also being creatively involved in the cognitive/thinking process. The IBR frequently accompanies or is part of this methodology, and it is a learner self-constructed binder-style book used as a specific strategy for learning.

"Its pages are interactive instructional resources/educational games that address the topic of a unit of study or a book read. Learners make the IBR working alone to design, imagine, create the pages, or work with a partner

Note that in Figure 1.2: The Reciprocal Thinking Process that all processes originate with the center oval section of IDEAS. Then, the other sections, as well as Images and Inventions are connected one to the other. The reciprocity of creativity is a back and forth, a within and between way of thinking.

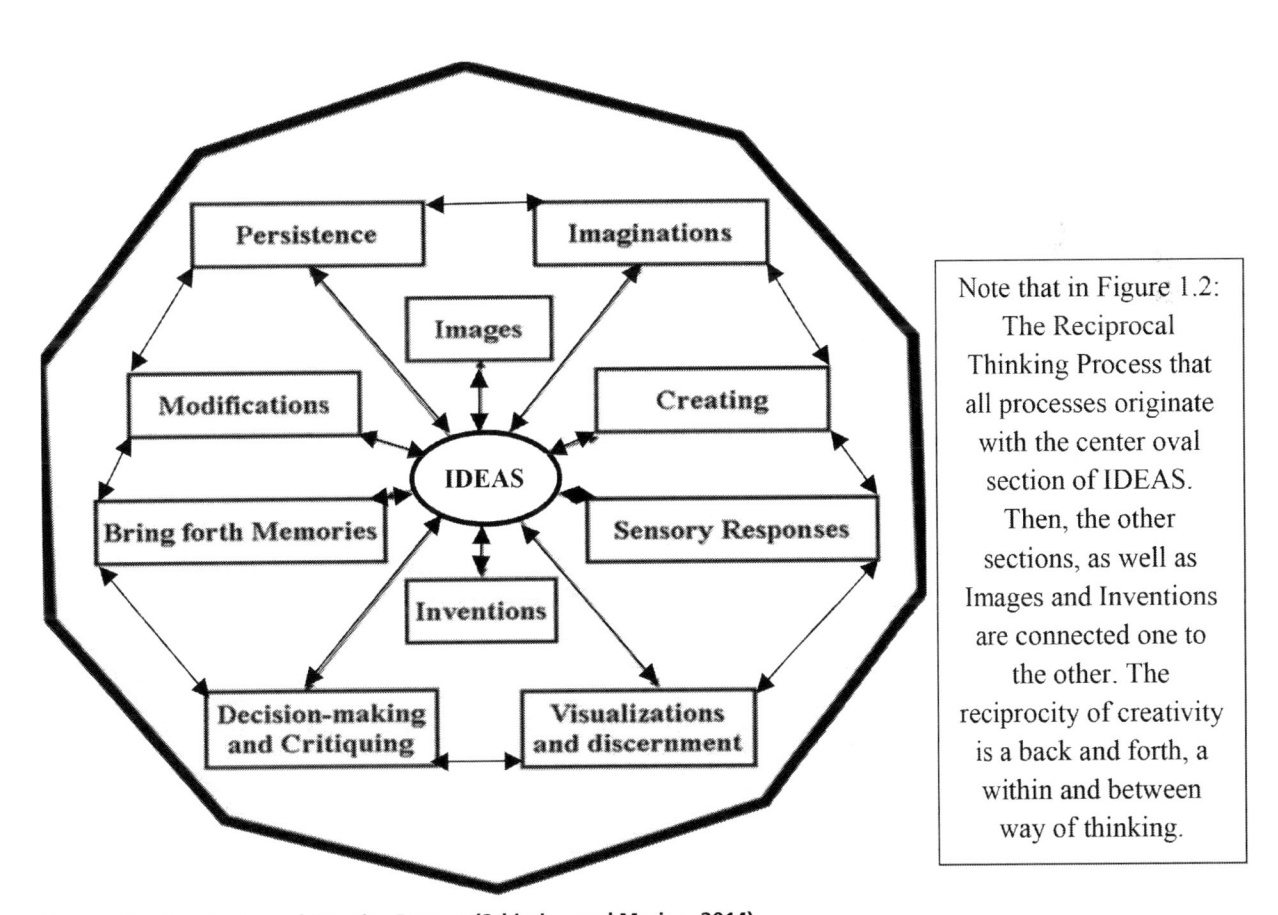

Figure 1.2. The Reciprocal Creative Process (Schiering and Marino, 2014)

Learning-through-Play

or in small group format to do this. Each page of the IBR's activities is self-corrective, or has an example of the completed page. And, the pages may be used as an alternative means of assessment. This is accomplished by the page-players being successful with comprehension of the material presented and evidenced by this success with correct answers.

"When referencing a methodology, as with the IM, there's a lot to consider. Most importantly this is to realize that a method is 'how' something is done. In this case, the IM is a creative cognition interactive means of learning and/or teaching. With a bit of detail, the IM's approach involves a student or one who's learning through inventing for the purposes of being creative, sharing ideas, exchanging visions, and engaging participants in the process of information retention" (Schiering, 2015).

POSSIBLE IM COMPONENTS AND IBR ACTIVITIES

"The IM may involve role-playing, puppetry, or personally made educational games, including floor and wall games. What's frequently evident is that there's a presentation of work, such as a project made for display or sharing. Dance and art may be part of these IBR page activities, or three-dimensional mazes, dioramas, diagrams, drawings, and technology, which are used as tools to assist with these constructions. However, the main components require tactile/kinesthetic as well as auditory and visual involvement in learning with use of any or all of the four modalities at the same time.

"As stated earlier, this IM of learning and teaching, as well as the IBR itself, requires, as a key component, CREATIVITY. There's the use of one's cognition to produce evidence regarding thinking skills such as, *Basic awareness*, *Critical analysis*, and *Metacognitive Processes* (higher-order thinking) skills of evaluation, advance decision making, reflection, and self-actualization, to name just four of these."

ADVANTAGES OF IM AND IBR FOR ACADEMICS AND SOCIALIZATION (SCHIERING, 2015)

Explaining "Advantage"

"What does it mean to have an advantage? Some might say it's simply a benefit or having a lead over something else, and they'd be correct. Realizing that the IBR involves learning and teaching that is interactive serves as the center point of the advantages or "pluses" regarding this endeavor. The following five areas are addressed as being gains of this project for learners and teachers alike at any grade or age level. Following this listing there are over fifteen continuing upsides of the IM and IBR listed.

IBR Advantage Point 1: Preferred Groupings

"If you're one who prefers working alone or with another, or in small groups, or like being on a team, your preferences are met with the IBR. Any grouping is possible for the making of this instructional resource. Things to remember about this IBR include that educational game pages are self-corrective. Then, with ideas put in place, the images are brought forth to creation for playing-the-pages, as one would play a game. This is done, topic-wise, to review a piece of literature, as much as serving as an introduction to those who've not read the book.

"Or, the IBR may address a thematic unit of study. Whichever, it is interdisciplinary in that there needs to be at least one interactive page involving reading, English language arts, math, science, and social studies. Those pages may be made in any group or singularly. The pages are bordered and titled with attractive lettering and design. Titles should mention the discipline being addressed. Then, the pages may be different colors or the same, but there needs to be something eye-catching in the overall makeup of the page."

IBR Advantage Point 2: Convenience and Engagement

"The IM may be used every day in the classroom or wherever one is trying to learn new or formerly presented material. The IM is an interactive way of learning and teaching. It may also be used once a week or a few times a month, or once in a while for most of a semester or throughout the year. Primarily, this decision depends on the one using the methodology and the appropriateness of the IBR for learning new material or reviewing something already presented. The idea is to use the IM and IBR whenever it's handy or expedient, as it's quite open-ended . . . you use the method and the book when it's appropriate, in your opinion, to use them. The big thing is . . . you decide if it works for you and if, as a teacher, it works for your class, by showing them how this method is practiced and the IBR is made for teaching oneself for learning and retention of what's been learned!

"One other thing is that this book addresses the idea that creative cognition is developed, as well as enhanced by making an IBR. It is! But, one should also know that the IM involves "engagement" in learning and the pages of the IBR individually adhere to learning and teaching interactively whether or not in a book format. The pages may be separate projects connected to new or formerly presented parts of a curriculum at any age or grade level.

"Additionally, these interactive pages of an IBR involve learning and teaching being intertwined with the roles of teacher being connected to those of the learners. As Delialioglu and Yildirim (2007) stated, 'Students are more engaged when the instruction increases the contact between student and teacher, provides opportunities for students to work in cooperation, encourages students to use active learning strategies, provides timely feedback on students' academic progression, requires students to spend quality time on academic tasks, establishes high standards for acceptable academic work and addresses different learner needs in the teaching process.'

"With the pages of the IBR being self-corrective, the instant feedback on one's academic acuity is clearly provided. Additionally, the active engagement of one's mind is predominant as the inventiveness and creative thinking, and imagination incorporation abound."

IBR Advantage Point 3: Belonging/Classroom Community

"The IBR gives an opportunity to have classroom togetherness. This 'sense' or feeling of 'joining' is primarily due to the individuals in the class working on the IBR project. There is a common goal of creating the IBR. Even if one is working to design a page without the help of others, the final product is entered in the book with all the other pages.

"This 'sense of belonging' occurs with each learner's different abilities and areas of interest being appreciated for the common good of the practiced IM. There's an emotional component of enjoying what one's creating, collectively. The making of an IBR meets and then, when completed, fulfills this emotional component of togetherness."

IBR Advantage Point 4: Reflective Practitioners and Socialization

"As the page or pages of an IBR are being made, there is ongoing reference back to personal experiences regarding the topic that is addressed. There's recalling whether it's from a specific happenstance or situation, or one read, or shared as an experience that someone else had. This reflection and practice of it is done through use of memory, and, if working on a page with another or others, there's shared reflection. These recollections help to form ideas for creation of pages and, of course, the socializing that occurs when there is sharing of thoughts and ideas, perhaps opinions, judgments, and feelings as well. The final result is collaboration.

"A portion of learning in a classroom or really in/at anyplace is that it's a social experience, which involves 'thinking about one's own thinking' (Olsen, 1995, pp. 130–38). Subsequently, the creators of the IBR are socializing reflective practitioners. This reflective partitioning means looking back to influence what exactly one is presently, actively 'doing.' And, with learners cooperating with one another to create pages for this book, there's ongoing communication. As we already know, learning is not just an academic experience, as there's interaction between individuals with discussion on the contents of the IBR, conversations.

"When working with others, the idea of using one's imagination to create leads to discourse, both verbally and nonverbally. Conversations tend to expand from the topic of the IBR to daily thoughts, ideas, opinions, and sometimes judgments and feelings. Meaning and perspectives are shared. Information is exchanged and problems are solved in a cooperative manner (Glatthorn, 1995). This process takes place in the classroom and wherever learning occurs, which is pretty much everywhere!

"Perspectives about self emerge as the IBR is being created. Since learning is frequently a reflective practitioner process, as stated previously, sharing is colored by individual perspectives, including perspectives about self and others. These come to be recognized as the composition surrounding the 'social' part of learning."

IBR Advantage Point 5: Cooperation

"The IBR instructional style and the strategy call for learners' cooperating and doing this through discussing, conversing, sharing, prioritizing, examining, evaluating, deciding, informing, synthesizing, conjuring, realizing, risk-taking, comparing and contrasting, classifying, recalling, inventing, imagining, designing, and creating activities to facilitate learning. The IBR reporting style calls for cooperation being an intrinsic part of the methodology and creation of pages for learning-through-play. 'With the use of the interaction and acceptance through cooperation, as well as creative thinking ideas regarding one's self and others, the IBR learning community is one that is most favorable for those involved. It's not just cooperation, but a comfort zone.'"

CONTINUATION AND CULMINATION OF ADVANTAGE POINTS

(1) Learners, teachers, all those involved in the IM or making of an IBR have the opportunity to talk WITH one another, as opposed to talking at someone or to others. The key expression is talking "with" because there's collaboration, and sharing. (2) Individuals, partnerships, or small groups are contributing participants in their own learning-through-play using imagination. (3) Proud ownership of work is evidenced along with empowerment and self-efficacy. (4) Retention of material is evidenced, due to experientialism/constructivism and alternative means of assessment. (5) The nuts and bolts of the IBR revolve around the use of auditory, visual, tactile, and kinesthetic instructional resources being designed and constructed, thus thoroughly involving a sensory-motor approach to learning. The neuroplasticity of the brain is therefore evidenced. (6) IBRs may be done individually or provide opportunities for conversation and collaboration, subsequently, enhancing "social cognition." (7) A positive classroom atmosphere is created. (8) Self-valuing is clearly evident. (9) Being a reflective practitioner is emphasized. (10) Work is project- and performance-based with evidence of the completed work being provided in a touchable format. (11) Thinking skills are finitely addressed. (12) No judgments are passed on the quality of work. (13) There's a digesting of one's thought processes and those of others as different IBR pages are "played." (14) State Common Core learning standards of project- and performance-based learning is provided through evidence of the IBR. (15) Sharing ideas brings forth trust. (16) Students are teaching and learning from other student-learner endeavors/IBRs and the teacher acts as a facilitator, with indirect instruction the mainstay.

Special Consideration

The use of the method by creating an IBR relating to a piece of literature or a thematic unit of study is time consuming. It's a project for inside and outside of school. If done at home and used to assist you in a specific subject, the making of interactive instructional resources requires concentration. While I personally do not see this as a downside, the fast-paced everything-must-be-done-now society in which we live might define this IBR learning and teaching strategy differently.

Biggest Advantage

Important to remember: "If you're the user of this Interactive Method and ultimately the *designer* and *creator* of an IBR, then you are the owner. Once you are in possession of something, it's yours, you created it, and your invention becomes valuable because it is of your own making" (Schiering and Marino, 2014; 2015).

IM OR IBR AS LEARNING CENTERS

Over the past two decades the idea of in-class Learning Centers has come to the foreground. These accompanied or followed the concept of project- and performance-based work, which Common Core standards emphasize these past few years. Consequently, one of the ideas of the IBR is to not use it in book format, as explained earlier, but rather take an activity from it and make it into a Learning Center.

In my fifth-grade classroom beginning in the later part of the 1990s we had Learning Centers based on interactive learning. Subsequently, there was a science section with every student or partnership making such things as Electro-Boards, Wrap-Arounds, puzzles and/or Task Cards, Pic-A-Dots, and board and/or floor games on a different topic in a particular discipline. These aforementioned were activities related to the Dunn and Dunn Learning Style Model for use of tactile/kinesthetic modalities. We'd have a forty-five-minute time slot that would be "Interactive Resources Exchange Time." Basically, what this meant was sharing what the student learners or partnerships had made with their classmates so learners were teaching other learners through the use of these educational games. The Dunn's Learning Style Model (1992) and subsequent attention to the use of varied perceptual preferences for learning are evidenced in section 2 with four interactive resources attributed to their Learning Style Model.

The aftermath of this use of educational games was that the students were empowered, learned from one another, had fun, were fully engaged, and appreciated classmates' work. Ultimately, no one learns the same way as another, so these IBR pages, converted into Learning Centers, provided opportunities to select your first, second, third, and so on way of learning. Audiotapes were made and later CDs, PowerPoints were created and used as well. Students' imaginations provided games that were not just tactile and kinesthetic, but involved auditory and visual perceptual preferences as well. Perhaps a word search was designed or crossword puzzle, *Jeopardy*-style game, or math periscope. The class determined their own learning process or selected the one that worked best for him/her and enjoyed this "special" time of the day. (Sections 2 and 3 of this book have ideas for IBR pages and Learning Centers.)

IM AND IBR AS ALTERNATIVE MEANS OF ASSESSMENT

Several times thus far you have read the words "alternative means of assessment." First it's important to know what is meant by assessment or evaluation. Traditionally, this is a set of questions and answers that may be in the following formats: multiple-choice, short answer, fill-in-the-blank, column-matching, or small/short essay.

The IM and IBR, conversely to this traditional mode of evaluation, calls for learners to engage themselves in learning by being involved in educational game playing and/or constructing. How one does the evaluation is through observation. This may be by separating the known from the unknown in a series of activities, or an authority figure observing the learner's ability to process information, store it, and manipulate or create it to his/her advantage for retention of curriculum.

RECIPROCAL THINKING PHASES (SCHIERING, 1999)

Ever wonder how to teach thinking or know when it's being taught? The IBR pages serve as a constant for the teaching of thinking through realization that specific cognitive and metacognitive skills are being utilized when a page is played. *The Reciprocal Thinking Phases* are presented in figure 1.3 with an explanation and definition of each Phase and skill on the following three pages.

In section 3 where there are examples of IBR pages, the where and how of the Reciprocal Thinking Phases' cognitive and metacognitive skills utilized for fifteen different activities are provided. When *The Phases* graphic organizer is utilized one comes to self-understanding of what creative cognition skills are used to either make the IBR activity or play the page involving this interaction. These may or may not be recorded.

Some of this discernment and deciding may be up to one's conjecture, but after recognition of the definition of each skill a comprehension of each skill readily comes to mind. The definitions of cognitive skills that appear on the *Reciprocal Thinking Phases Chart* are included in this section of the workbook.

Reciprocal Thinking and Feelings are the thoughts, ideas, opinions, judgments, and emotions individuals have, which result in a continual structuring and restructuring of their reality—beliefs and values upon which we take action. This is accomplished through personal and shared reflection. In some instances, it's important to note that thinking and feelings are so interwoven it's difficult to separate one from the other.

REVIEWING THE COGNITIVE COLLECTIVE

Human beings think as well as feel. The result is that this unity of thinking and feeling happens within the classroom, as well as outside it. Throughout a person's day, individuals move between varying cognitive processes and emotions. As teachers, we must address this natural progression and interplay by recognizing, first, that they occur, and, second, that in order to be effective teachers or human beings, we must know how this process happens and attend to it. *The Cognitive Collective is the interplay between and within an individual's or whole group's thinking and feelings.*

RECIPROCAL THINKING PHASES: OVERALL DEFINITION

The reciprocity of thinking refers to the ongoing exchange of comprehension that forms memory. This exchange occurs within and between the Phases of *Beginning Awareness, Critical and Creative Thinking,* and *The Metacognitive Processes.*

What you are thinking may not be what I am thinking, but awareness of what is transpiring cognitively, empowers learners and teachers alike. This empowerment happens while providing self-efficacy. Knowing what one is thinking helps to clarify learning with the individual's acknowledging the finite identification of the cognitive and metacognitive processes being experienced at any time.

RECIPROCAL THINKING PHASES
COGNITION and META-COGNITION

PHASE ONE
BEGINNING AWARENESS AND ACKNOWLEDGING

Recognizing

Realizing

Classifying

Comparing

Contrasting

Our thoughts, ideas, opinions, judgments and feelings impact "who" we are as learners. Joined, these form the "Cognitive Collective."

PHASE TWO
CRITICAL AND CREATIVE THINKING

Prioritizing
Communicating
Inferring
Predicting, Inventing
Generalizing
Sequencing
Initial deciding
Initial Problem-solving

PHASE THREE
META-COGNITIVE PROCESSES

Evaluating, Critiquing, Collaborating, Tolerating, Advanced-deciding and Problem-solving, Organizing, Risk-taking, Analyzing, Synthesizing, Recalling, Reflecting
Self-actuating

What are you thinking?

(Schiering, © 1999)

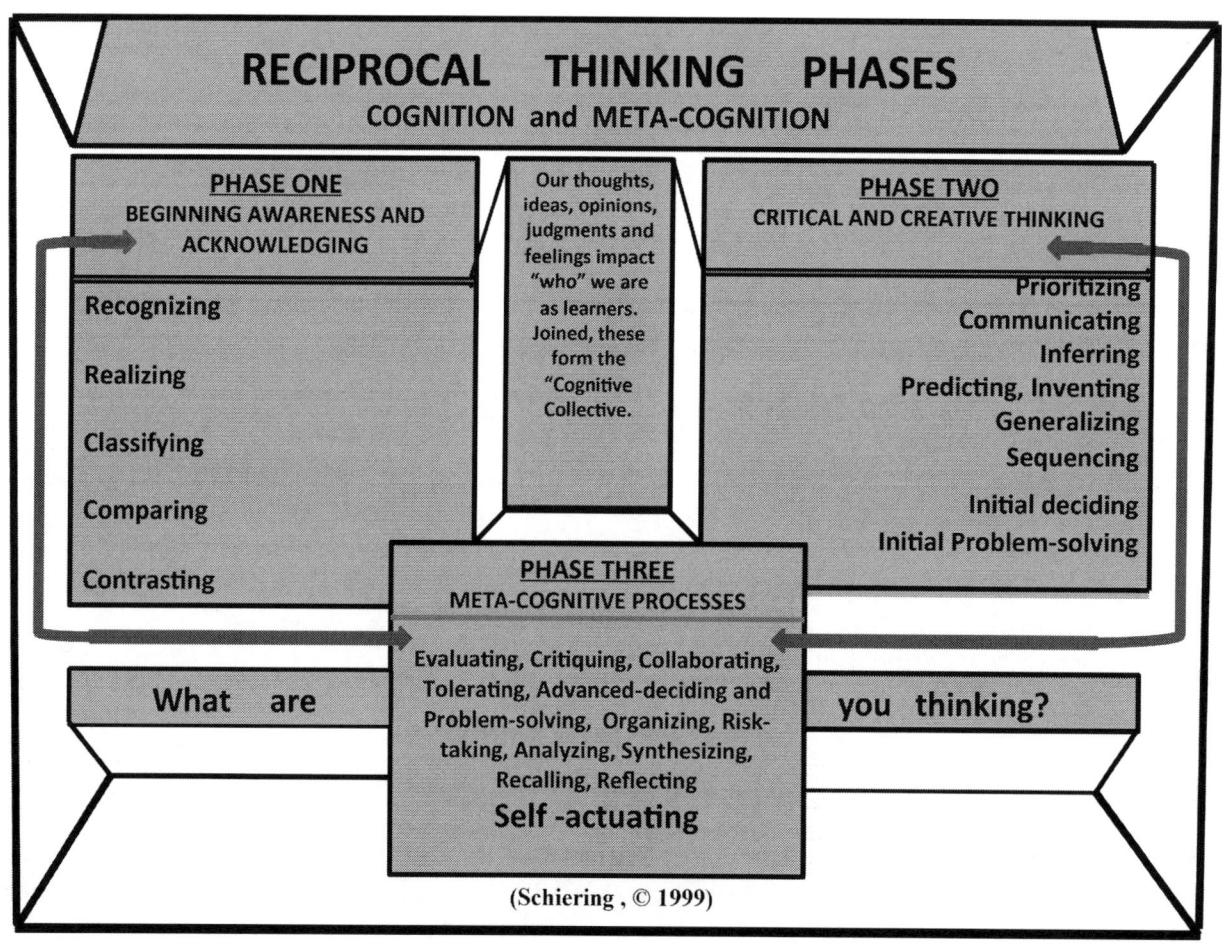

Figure 1.3. Reciprocal Thinking Phases: Cognition and Meta-cognition

The use of the word *Reciprocal* in the title "Reciprocal Thinking Phases" demonstrates that the processes of cognition and metacognition are occurring simultaneously, as opposed to being developmental with one evolving from the other. The use of the word "Reciprocal" emphasizes that thinking is ongoing and conducted within and between the Phases. The movement between and within Phases is occurring naturally, as one does not purposefully go from one thinking skill to another; it just happens. In the IBR, the beauty of these named and defined skills is in the identification of what one is thinking.

I think, therefore, I am.

TEACHING THINKING AND THE IBR

With respect to the IBR, the acknowledgment of one's thinking, the realizing of this thinking makes it possible to create interactive pages that are designed to facilitate one's imagination and make or even invent interactive instructional resources/education games. But, most importantly, the designer is aware of what is being thought when a page is played, and this is done through comprehension of the definitions and practical applications of the skills. Creative cognition is evidenced when the pages are designed and created and later learning-through-play occurs to solidify the IM and practical use of the IBR, whether in book format or in a Learning Center as described earlier.

Comprehension is occurring continuously and providing this skill through analysis, evaluation, comparing and contrasting, prioritizing, and self-actuating to name a few cognitive functions. Overall, comprehension is done by realizing the differences between types of thinking.

THINKING COMPLEXITY

"Thinking occurs in varying phases of complexity that are reciprocal in nature with the individual moving seamlessly between and among them. Each individual's thinking can be characterized by a number of specific cognitive skills that can be identified by individuals. This being the case, one can hone and develop these skills, identifying when he or she is using each and becoming more proficient in its usage.

Tasks for the learner and the teacher, therefore, would seem to be attending directly to helping one 'know what he/she is thinking,' helping each learner to identify when he or she is using a particular skill and assisting them in developing mastery over it." (Bogner, 2008; 2011)

Explaining Phase One: Basic Awareness and Acknowledging
This first Phase involves skill development relating to fact finding and ordering techniques that include initial classifying and cause the learner to start making connections to personal experiences and those presented orally or in written formats. Learners are able to respond to various stimuli in conversations, as well as configure answers to literal comprehension questions with accuracy. This Phase takes into consideration an individual's earliest forms of awareness.

Explaining Phase Two: Critical and Creative Thinking
This Phase involves the transcendence and inclusion through movement from and within one's beginning awareness. Learners process skills through visualizing and verbalizing the connections they have made from personal prior experiences and/or read material or verbalizations of others. It can be determined that the combination of critical and creative thinking relies on past awareness to construct new meaning. The learner may hypothesize, imagine, or visualize making connections from his/her own experiences or reading material for applied comprehension. Subsequently, determining outcomes from actions taken provides a comprehensive set of thoughts for initial problem solving and/or decision making.

Explaining Phase Three: Metacognitive Processes
This Phase occurs when the thinking goes beyond the cognitive and the learner actually knows what he or she wants to realize—exhibiting a control over his or her intake of material. There is critiquing accompanied by self-actuation through evaluation and synoptic-exercises (general and summative overviews) occurring. There is a realization of action or actions that need to be taken to facilitate the acquisition of knowledge. Metacognition is domain dependent as it is instantiated (firmly grounded) in a context or learning task (Tobias and Everson, 1995).

This being grounded refers to learning that addresses a specific subject area and refers to students working in a format that is structured and sequential. Abedi and O'Neil (1996) defined metacognition as consisting of strategies for planning, monitoring or self-checking cognitive/affective strategies, and self-awareness.

The result of learners and teachers' identifying and implementing the higher-order thinking skills in Phase Three is clearly evident in the area of implied comprehension with regard to their ability to ask and answer this type of question. This is where the answer is made obvious through conjecture or context clues that lead one to think that a specific answer is viable. An example would be a sentence about seeing a dog's footprints on the sand. It's implied that previously this animal had walked on the sand, because of these footprints. Implied comprehension is based on context clues or illustrative material being presented in auditory, visual, tactile, or kinesthetic formats.

Definition of Cognitive and Metacognitive Skills: Phase One

1. *Recognizing* helps a person to be aware of or identify things from previous experience and also to acknowledge something as being new to the one doing the recognizing.
2. *Realizing* focuses on the skills that help a person make real and to comprehend the importance of something that one did not know previously.
3. *Classifying* refers to arranging things into groups according to established criteria, for example, to arrange by age, height, color, type of clothing, or some category.

4. *Comparing* includes examining or judging between two or more things in order to show how they are similar.
5. *Contrasting* focuses on the difference between two things or more. When you combine comparing and contrasting there is discernment, a distinguishing between one thing and another, or perhaps one idea from another as to differentiate and perceive.

Definition of Cognitive and Metacognitive Skills: Phase Two

1. *Prioritizing* deals with or lists something in order of its importance.
2. *Communicating* refers to the exchange of information or conversation with other people by using words, signs, or writing and to express your thoughts or feelings clearly so other people understand them.
3. *Inferring* is the formation of opinion based on the information one has previously experienced, or indirect evidence being present.
4. *Active listening* addresses one's being attentive to the point of not just hearing what is being conveyed, but also examining it mentally in order to respond beyond repeating one's words.
5. *Inventing* is to discover, think up, devise or fabricate in the mind, think out, produce something new, or originate through experiment.
6. *Predicting* relates to the formation of an opinion that something will happen before it actually is a reality or has occurred.
7. *Generalizing* refers to forming an opinion after considering a few examples of it.
8. *Sequencing* is a series of related events, actions, or the like that happens or is done in a particular order, and placing it in specific orders.
9. *Initial Deciding* is beginning choice or judgment about something involving choice and/or resolution.
10. *Initial Problem solving* is beginning thought, dealing with and/or providing explanation about a difficult situation or person. It is finding the correct answer to a question, or the explanation for something that is difficult to comprehend.

Definition of Cognitive and Metacognitive Skills: Phase Three

1. *Evaluating* has to do with judging or determining the quality of something, as to assess or appraise its worth.
2. *Organizing* is to make into a whole with unified and coherent relationships or to arrange thoughts in an orderly fashion and is sometimes referred to as a person's being logical or sequential.
3. *Critiquing* refers to the formation of a thought or judgment as to whether something is good, bad, or somewhere in between those two places. Critiquing may also be an opinion that's given and connotes whether something is favorable, unfavorable, or possesses both of these components.
4. *Collaborating* is to work together with another person or group in order to achieve or produce something.
5. *Tolerating* concerns the pattern of recognizing and respecting behavior that is not pleasant, or not to be interfered with, allowed, or permitted without bringing comment.
6. *Advanced deciding and problem solving* involves the processes of reaching a high degree or level of difficulty with respect to choice, judgment, explanation, and/or resolution to a situation. Such thinking is accomplished by providing clarification about a tough or challenging situation. Or, it could be with respect to a person and finding the correct answer to a question, or the elucidation of something that is complicated, intricate, or complex to comprehend.
7. *Risk taking* is the action requiring grabbing a chance without knowing the outcome of that action or verbalization.
8. *Analyzing* concerns the careful examination of something in order to comprehend it. It concerns also the examination of thought and feeling components to ascertain their general composition for comprehension of them.
9. *Synthesizing* is to form by bringing together separate parts of a situation in a concise manner.
10. *Advanced Problem solving* relies on in-depth remembering or bringing to mind of a read, heard, visualized, or experienced situation.
11. *Recalling* involves bringing back to one's mind something from the past, as in reference to a memory, whether from a moment earlier or longer expanse of time in order to address a situation that requires a decision.
12. *Reflecting* is to realize something after thought or contemplation.
13. *Self-actuating* has to do with one's self going forward and taking action; doing something as opposed to remaining sedentary. What Are You Thinking?

CONNECTING CREATIVE COGNITION TO:

Constructing the IBR Pages

When making pages for the IBR one wants to recognize, using the *Phases* graphic organizer, what creative and critical cognition skills were involved in making the page. Looking at each section of the graphic organizer, examining each skill, the person making the page practices attention, orientation, and decision making with the use of his/her memory. These are utilized with discernment to determine which skills are being applied to the making of the IBR page. These may be listed or mentally noted. By listing or noting, the designer and maker of the page is teaching and learning by him/herself which creative cognition abilities are being present and utilized. This happens for each of the *Phases'* skills as the activities are imagined, designed, and constructed.

CONNECTING CREATIVE COGNITION TO PLAYING THE IBR PAGES

One of the major principles of the IM (interactive methodology) presented in this workbook is to realize what one is thinking through cognitive awareness, to be able to recognize and give attention to what's happening when a particular page of the IBR is being played after it has been made. Subsequently, when playing a page, or before that when designing the page, the individual, using the Phases' skills, is teaching him/herself thinking.

EFFECTS AND AFFECTS OF IM AND IBR

The purpose for this section regards how ideas might come to you about creativity being (1) personally empowering, (2) a means for building community, (3) knowing about one's character, and/or (4) creating if not concretizing friendships. The overall effect and affect of the IM and IBR touch on individuals' and groups' emotional security. The four numbered items most likely result in stabilizing an individual's view of himself/herself to the point of being an individual who, through self-actualization, realizes self-reliance as well.

Effects

First, let's take a moment and examine the definition of the word *effect*. You've probably heard it often enough in relation to the word "cause." An example might be that *because* of the loud sound, a person jumped-up when the book fell on the floor. The effect was the jumping-up of the person when this happened. In order for there to be an "effect" on a situation or someone, there needs to be an understanding of the means to realize a *consequence* or *achievement* or to *make something happen*, as to *bring it into being*.

Examples would be: (1) The *effect/result* of the IM caused learners to realize their creativity was part of their ability to imagine and invent. (2) The *effect* of their imagining and inventing resulted in bringing into being pages of the IBR for learning-through-playing. (3) Another *effect* of the IM and IBR is that others learned when playing the pages of the book and retained information, simultaneously. (4) The *effect* of the method and strategy, together, made an *impression* on all who experienced it. This was formidable and became part of one's lifelong learning.

Overall, the effect of the experience was that memory was utilized through reflection and recalling, which are part of the metacognitive processes. The interconnection of one's reciprocity of thinking and encountering the IM and IBR may well determine the significance of the learning situation's being most positive when one is engaged in it.

Affects

There's much to be related about the *affect* of the IM and IBR. The word "affect" means the emotional impact of something on oneself. When referring to the emotional impact of this method and strategy, the first thing that comes to mind is realizing the magnitude and differences of feelings about one's own creativity abilities, as evidenced in the IBRs I've seen over the past twenty-plus years.

Learners, and we're all learners, are affected by circumstances encountered each day. Some cause more of a reaction than others, but regardless of this, the reaction results in knowing about ourselves or those experiencing our response to the IM and IBR. Let's say you're using the IM to design and then create an IBR. If one is working with a few people on this project there needs to be cooperation and collaboration to which there is an emotional response—and affect.

Learning-through-Play

There is a sense of accomplishment when using the IM way of learning and teaching is realized along with the making of an IBR, as the participants have been immersed in conversation. By having this continual or ongoing communicating of ideas and feelings about the project, there comes a comprehension of "who" one is as a learner and possibly a teacher as well.

Definitely, there is an overall sense of self-worth and empowerment when experiencing the method and strategy of the IM and IBR. Individuals come to know that each one is capable of giving to others only that which one has for him or herself. With the use of the aforementioned these affective–emotional impact qualities include, but are not exclusive to, having for oneself and others *respect, caring, trustworthiness, fairness, kindness,* and *being responsible*. In summation, these feelings form the affect of the IM and IBR.

SECTION 2

The Interactive Method (IM) and IBR with Four Interactive Resources

INTRODUCTION BY LOUIS LAUPHEIMER

I am a student at Molloy College in my fourth year of studying to become an educator. During my introduction to higher education I have seen and observed many methods of what's called "best practice" in learning and teaching. However, the overall impression I have had is that interactive learning is a highly effective way to learn and instruct. Why? You may ask, and I'd reply that *today's world is about creation and innovation, and educator's innovation is interactive learning.* For example, technology, as we now know it for communication and new ideas being presented to connect us globally, as well as in a classroom, has been a stronghold for at least a decade. Situational learning that involves role play and educational gaming are part of classroom activities and commercial enterprises.

Although my time in the classroom has been short, I have made clear and distinct observations. First is that the type of school district is inconsequential, as are the types of students in that district when it comes to responses to interactive methods (IM) being practiced. Everyone, including the teachers, enjoys interactive learning. Through my time in the classroom I tried to capture as much as possible not only about teaching methods, but also about effective learning. I observed the students and saw what interested them and what made them want to learn. Students experiencing interactive learning, most often and frequently 100 percent of the time, reacted positively.

My overall observation is that regardless of the school district or types of students in it there's enjoyment in interactive learning, primarily due to involvement in it. This probably doesn't surprise you, but for someone being in the midst of their teacher training it is like an "ah ha" moment. I look at it this way: even as adults we have the desire to be a part of something, to have a positive reaction to or with something. As a child, middle grade learner, high school, or college person that desire for wanting to be involved/engaged in what's occurring, as opposed to being an observer, could move from desire to "need."

For example, a very popular growing phrase today is "get involved." This can be said about college, a social issue, and work, or as a matter of fact, most anything. Getting involved is being interactive, so why shouldn't we always be striving to get our students involved in learning? Is it too much work? Are people disinterested," I've questioned. Who knows? But if those are some factors, this book will make it very easy for them to realize the "interaction" of interactive learning not being work, but fun.

I was told by a professor once "a good teacher is one who shares their ideas." As a result I'm sharing about what I know regarding interactive learning and teaching. I'm doing this because, for one thing, I've noted that students learn differently from one another, and the amount of interactivity is relative to each child. So, at the very least there should be some amount of interplay in a classroom setting, some amount of interaction, and that may be creative interaction. When I observe this as a teacher I get to know my students, and that's important. It's an idea emphasized in all of my method classes. Think of this interactive learning idea also being a "tool" used to involve learners and teachers in realizing topics, and retaining information because of that interaction.

If you could think back to how you were taught at any grade level, what would you say caused you to "learn" what was presented? Most likely that lesson stuck with you because you were somehow involved with it, personally. Now I am not saying that every single thing you do in the classroom should be interactive every second of the day, but in my teacher-trainee perspective, the main points should be. I say that because you want learners to be involved and *learn by doing.* Bottom line: a person/learner/teacher walking away with some information and comprehension rather than nothing is a "slam dunk."

Let this book serve as a guide into the interactive method of learning with suggestions from Interactive Book Report (IBR) pages used for Learning Centers. Doing so, you may find, expands and opens your own mind to this type of method and the pages in this section and the next one that refer to varied types of classroom learning activities.

For those who have already embraced the IM philosophy I invite you to use this workbook as a resource. I cannot stress enough how important this topic of interactive, creative, and personal involvement in learning impacts education. Fulfillment is experienced in a way that provides people a way they prefer to learn or in other words "if children do not learn the way we teach, then we must teach them the way they learn" (Rita Dunn, 1992). Now, I'd add to that the concept that learning by experiencing is a process that will make that learning enjoyable, and something enjoyed is something recalled, remembered, and likely shared with another to help him/her learn.

The IM is a pass-along . . . as giving or *paying it forward*.

OVERVIEW

This section of the workbook provides an explanation of how the IM and IBR are project- and performance-based forms of instruction. Then, photographs of varied interactive instructional resources often associated with the Interactive Book Report (IBR) are presented. These are followed by uses of this activity and materials needed to construct it. Then, instructions are given for making this creative project designed for learning-through-play. Each activity is designed to be self-corrective and has templates at the section's end that may be cut out and used for making the activities represented in the photos or figures.

After these activity information sections there's a Tri-fold Board photo and accompanying narrative by former teacher candidate Amanda Lockwood. The commentary is on how she used this interactive instructional resource for instructing her young preschool student learners on word families, such as the "at" family with bat, cat, etc., on the Tri-fold Board. This last photo gives you the opportunity to envision how an IBR page, or in this case taking an IBR page and making it into a Learning Center, works in the classroom.

PROJECT- AND PERFORMANCE-BASED INSTRUCTION

The IM and IBR are examples of project- and performance-based instruction, as learners work for reasonably long periods of time to research, investigate, imagine, and then respond to a question or assignment. The content is significant, as thinking skills are addressed along with problem solving and decision making. Learning standards at the state and national levels are given attention through this instructional method, due to in-depth inquiry, student engagement, use of resources, and collaborating on answers to questions.

There's a need-to-know driving component when creating the IBR pages using the IM, and later when playing-the-pages. Such activity stimulates one's curiosity that results in open-ended questions and examination through evaluation of what's being constructed. The products to be made involve making choices, and in many cases all the skills listed on the Reciprocal Thinking Phases, as noted by the definition in section 1 are utilized at some point when using the IM and making an IBR or taking a page from it for a Learning Center.

The types of creative processes, as addressed in the first section of this workbook, are utilized during and after IBR construction. The work that is done is continually presented with others playing the pages or adding to them with their own ideas. This type of interaction brings about the implementation of *students teaching students* for these project and performance-based learning endeavors. Four activities, each one followed by an illustration of it and in some cases its separate components, appear on the following pages. (This "Activity" material is from *Learning and Teaching Creative Cognition: The Interactive Book Report*, chapter 16.) The activities in section 2 may be seen as a how-to-make demonstration at the website: creativecognition4u.com.

Flip-Chute Holder and Cards: Question-In and Answer-Out Activity

Flip-Chute (F.C.) Uses: This is one of the most often used and beneficial self-corrective interactive resources for tactile learners. This particular learning game is designed to assist students in gleaning information by placing a question/answer card in the top slot and receiving an answer in the bottom one, as the card flips over going through the chute. The upper right corner of the card is notched and this is where the question goes. When the card goes through the chute the answer appears, and one notices that the notch is on the bottom right side. That is because when the card was made the answer was placed on the card by turning it upside-down.

The student has control of this device. The learner determines when to let go of the card, while saying the answer, and the card goes through the chute. A pile of correct answer cards is made, as well as one of incorrect answers, with the latter being revisited until mastery is achieved. This learning device is appropriate for all age/grade levels. College students have been successful in learning foreign language vocabulary, while elementary students have found the F.C. instrumental in learning their multiplication tables.

Suggestions for F.C. cards with answers on the flip side include vocabulary with definitions, fraction pictures like one-quarter of a pie on one side and the fraction (¼) stated on the reverse side. Another use is identifying story characters and their quotations, cause and effect, and even fill-in-the-blank for vocabulary or sentence structure, synonyms and antonyms, or parts of speech. Another idea is to have a picture on the front/top side of the card with the word on the flip side. Or, one might have consonant blends on one side with the word "clown" and the "cl" letters underlined with a picture of a clown on the flip side of the card. Photo 2.1 is the Flip-Chute and Figure 2.1 shows the Flip-Chute cards.

Flip-Chute and F.C. Cards: Materials: Half-gallon milk or juice container, two 5 × 8 inch index cards, 1-inch wide masking tape, ten 2 × 2½ inch cut index cards, razor cutter or X-Acto knife or box cutter, scissors, 12-inch ruler, and contact paper and thematic stickers for container decoration.

Flip-Chute and Flip-Chute Card Construction Directions:

1. Pull open the top of the milk or juice container;
2. Cut the side fold of the top portion down to the top of the container;
3. On the front face measure down from the top 1½ inches and then 2½ inches and draw a horizontal line that is ¼ inch in from each side;
4. Cut out that opening with the box cutter (razor knife or X-Acto knife), and repeat the same procedure at the bottom on the container;
5. Using your 5 x 8 index cards, measure one with 6½ inches long by 3½ inches wide, and using the other card, measure 7½ inches long by 3½ inches wide, and then cut out these pieces;
6. Score the longer card ½ inch up from the bottom and the shorter card ½ inch up from the bottom and ½ inch down from the top;
7. Insert the smaller strip into the lower opening, and attach it with masking tape to the upper part of the lower opening and lower part of the upper opening. It should form the letter *C* backwards, if one is looking at it from the side;
8. Insert the longer strip with the scored part going over the lower part of the bottom opening and taping this. The upper portion of the strip is taped to the back of the container. At this point, you now have the chutes in place.
9. Using one of the 2 × ½ inch cutouts, put a notch in the upper right corner and write on the card a math equation, such as 2 × 2; now turn the card upside down so the notch appears in the lower right corner, and write the answer to the equation.
10. Place the Flip-Chute card into the upper slot of the Flip-Chute. This step is done by having the equation showing with the notch in the upper right corner of the card. The card will flip over once it's placed into the upper opening/chute, and the answer to the equation will appear in the bottom slot of the Flip-Chute. Make as many cards as you choose, and have students make these in any discipline. With every student having his/her own set of cards and Flip-Chute, each student may switch cards with a classmate to learn new material or review previously presented topics. Laminating the Flip-Chute cards is recommended as they'll last longer. See Figure 2.1.

See number 10 under Flip-Chute and Flip-Chute Card Construction Directions and then refer to Photo 2.1 and Figure 2.1 for illustrations of these items.

Pic-A-Dot: Select the Right Dot for Answer: Holder and Cards

Pic-A-Dot: Uses: This is a multiple-choice type of interactive self-corrective learning tool. A question or problem is posed, and then three answers are available. A pointed object, such as a pen or golf tee, is placed in the opening of the selected answer. If the card slides out, then the answer is correct; if not, then another try is deemed necessary for this self-corrective tactile game. The same types of uses as were mentioned for the Flip-Chute apply to this interactive resource with the difference mainly being the concept of three possible answers and students' having to make a choice regarding the correct one. Laminating the Pic-A-Dot Cards is recommended.

Photo 2.1.   Flip-Chute

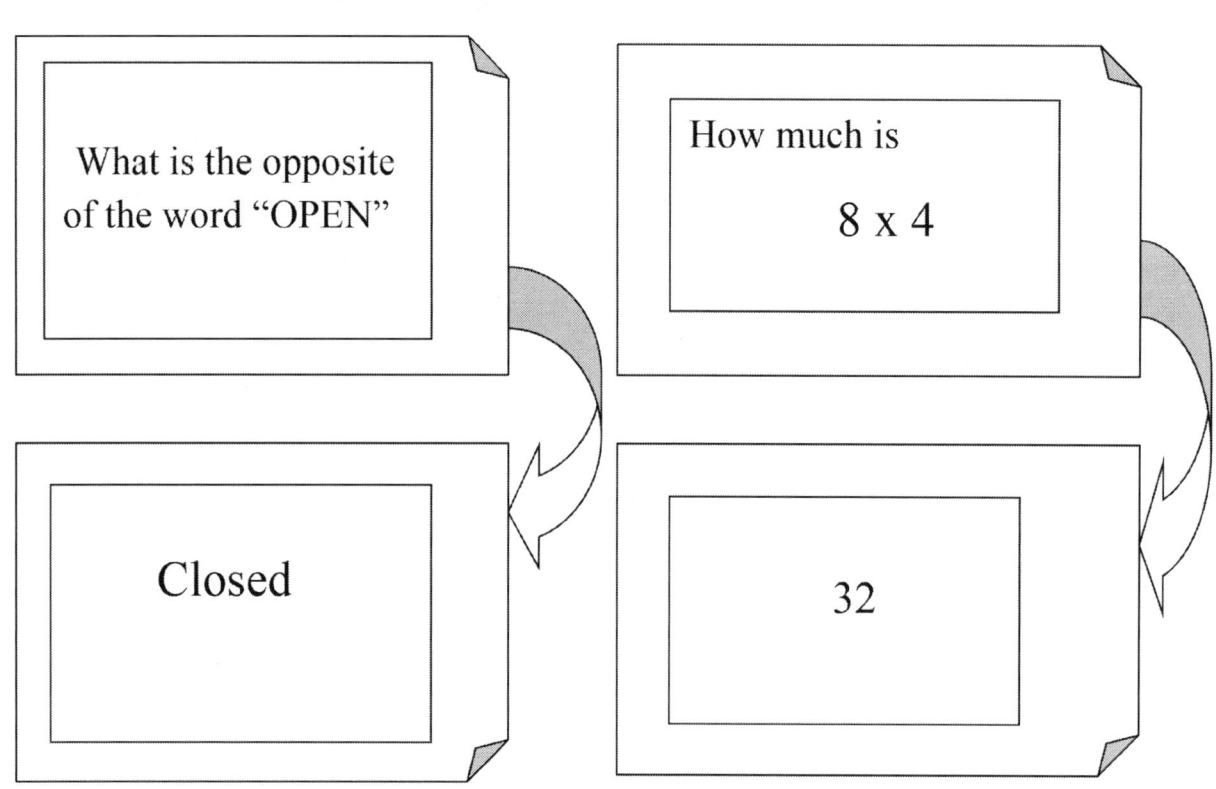

Figure 2.1.   Flip-Chute Cards: Question In: Answer Out

18   SECTION 2

Pic-A-Dot Holder and Cards: Materials: One two-pocket folder, fifteen 5 × 8 index cards, one-hole hole-puncher, masking tape, 12-inch ruler, and scissors.

Pic-A-Dot Holder and Pic-A-Dot Cards: Construction Directions:

1. Using a two-pocket folder, cut this in half, vertically, down the center;
2. Choose one half of the folder, and place the other half off to the side;
3. Addressing the pocket, use your ruler to measure and mark ½ inch in from each side and 2½ inches down from the top of the pocket. Cut out this U-shaped section (see photos for visuals of areas to be cut out);
4. From the bottom of the pocket, measure and mark upward 1 inch and 2 inches and ½ inch in from each side. Cut out this rectangle;
5. On the bottom strip of the pocket, punch one hole on the left, middle, and right side;
6. Place one 5 x 8 inch index card in the pocket. Trace the top opening outline, and each of the hole-punch circles. Remove the index card from the pocket and punch the holes out. But, for where you will place the correct answer, punch the hole out all the way to the bottom of the card. (This is the Pic-A-Dot Holder);
7. Place the index card back in the folder. In the outlined open space at the top, write a question. Example: The boy had four apples that cost one dollar each. He bought two more for one dollar each. How much did he spend on apples in all?
8. Just above the hole-punch areas write three answers. Example:
   $3.50 $5.00 $6.00
9. Insert the golf-tee and /or pen point into the hole that has the correct answer and pull the top of the card. If it easily slides out, then the correct answer has been selected;
10. Make as many Pic-A-Dot cards as you choose, and have students make these in any discipline. With each student having his or her own Pic-A-Dot holder and cards, students may switch cards with a classmate to learn new material or review previously presented topics.

Photo 2.2. Pic-A-Dot Holder

Below is a learning-style Pic-A-Dot Card outside the folder. The answer can be easily seen as the whole/dot to be picked when the card is pulled will slide out for the first choice.

The second strand of the Learning Styles Model has the elements of motivation, persistence, responsibility and structure. This strand is called . . . . . .

Emotional   Responsible   structure

Alexa Alongi (2013) made a Pic-A-Dot for the book Charlotte's Web. An example card appears below that is inside the holder. When a pointed object is placed in the third dot area the card, when pulled on, will slide out of the holder.

In *Charlotte's Web* by E.B. White the main characters are _____

| Turtle & Dog | Wilber & Fern | Charlotte & Wilber |

Photo 2.3. Pic-A-Dot Cards

Math Wrap-Around: Matching Questions and Answers

Wrap-Around: Uses: This tactile/kinesthetic self-corrective device is a matching game with questions on the left side of a paper and answers on the right side. However, answers are not placed directly across from the questions or statements. The size of the paper may vary. This interactive resource may be used for vocabulary with definitions and for matching characters with their statements/quotes.

It may also address identifying parts of speech, noun-verb agreement, singular and plural verb forms, math equations and answers (as seen in photo 2.4 by Jessica D'Amprisi), math word problems involving multiple computation skills, English or another language's word opposites, colloquiums, or foreign-language vocabulary words with the other side being the English vocabulary words. Laminating the Wrap-Around is recommended for cleanliness and durability.

Wrap-Around: Materials: One piece of cardstock paper (8½ × 11), scissors, 12-inch ruler, yarn (or string or ribbon) of a color contrasting with the paper, and dark-color magic marker.

Wrap-Around: Construction Directions:

1. Using the ruler, create a 1-inch margin around the cardstock paper;
2. Place a topic title on the top margin, such as "English/Spanish Wrap-Around";
3. Select the vocabulary or other criteria for the left-hand side and make a notch on the outside edge next to this word;
4. Select the vocabulary word definition, or the same word in another language, or other criteria for the right side "answer." Be sure the match is not directly across from the word or what you have on the left side;
5. Notch the cardstock paper on the outside edge of the right side;
6. Placing a hole at the top center of the cardstock paper, string a 3½-inch piece of yarn through this and knot at one end;
7. Swing the yarn in back of the board and into the first notch;
8. Put the yarn into the notch on the right side that provides the answer/match for the first notch on the left side. Swing the yarn around back, and go to the second notch on the left side, as the process is repeated;
9. When finished, trace the back of the card stock where the yarn appears. Use a marker or pen to do this. Now, undo the wrap;
10. The students wrap the yarn beginning with the first left notch, to the correct answer on the right side until the Wrap-Around is completely wrapped. This is a self-corrective activity because the student turns the Wrap-Around over and checks to see if the marked lines match where the yarn is located.

Electro-Boards: Making Connections

Electro-Board: Uses: This is a very popular self-corrective tactile and/or kinesthetic interactive instructional resource. It's kinesthetic when it's made poster-board size. One of the most interesting things is that this interactive instructional resource does not have a specified order for the match that's to be created. The connection between the question, such as a vocabulary word and its definition, may be anywhere on the Electro-Board.

Naming parts of an object, such as a flower, house, car, or animal, may have the part listed on the bottom of the Board and a drawing of the object on the top portion. The student uses a light-type continuity tester and places one end on the question and the other on the thought-to-be answer. If the light glows, the correct answer has been selected, and if not then it's time to try again.

Such things as math problems in addition, subtraction, multiplication, division, and word format; English vocabulary and definitions; or English words matching with objects or foreign-language words of the same object; Spanish or any other language/English vocabulary; identification of systems such as respiratory and circulatory; or sequences of events such as lifecycle of a butterfly or frog or stages of human development might be topics for the Electro-Board. Photos 2.5a and b and 2.6 show Electro-Boards.

Electro-Board: Materials: Poster board, colored markers, aluminum foil, hole-punch, ¾-inch masking tape, continuity tester, and scissors.

Electro-Board: Construction Directions:

1. Begin with two pieces of poster board of exactly the same size and shape;
2. Section the left side of the Electro-Board to correspond to the number of questions you will be asking. Section the right side similarly for the answers;

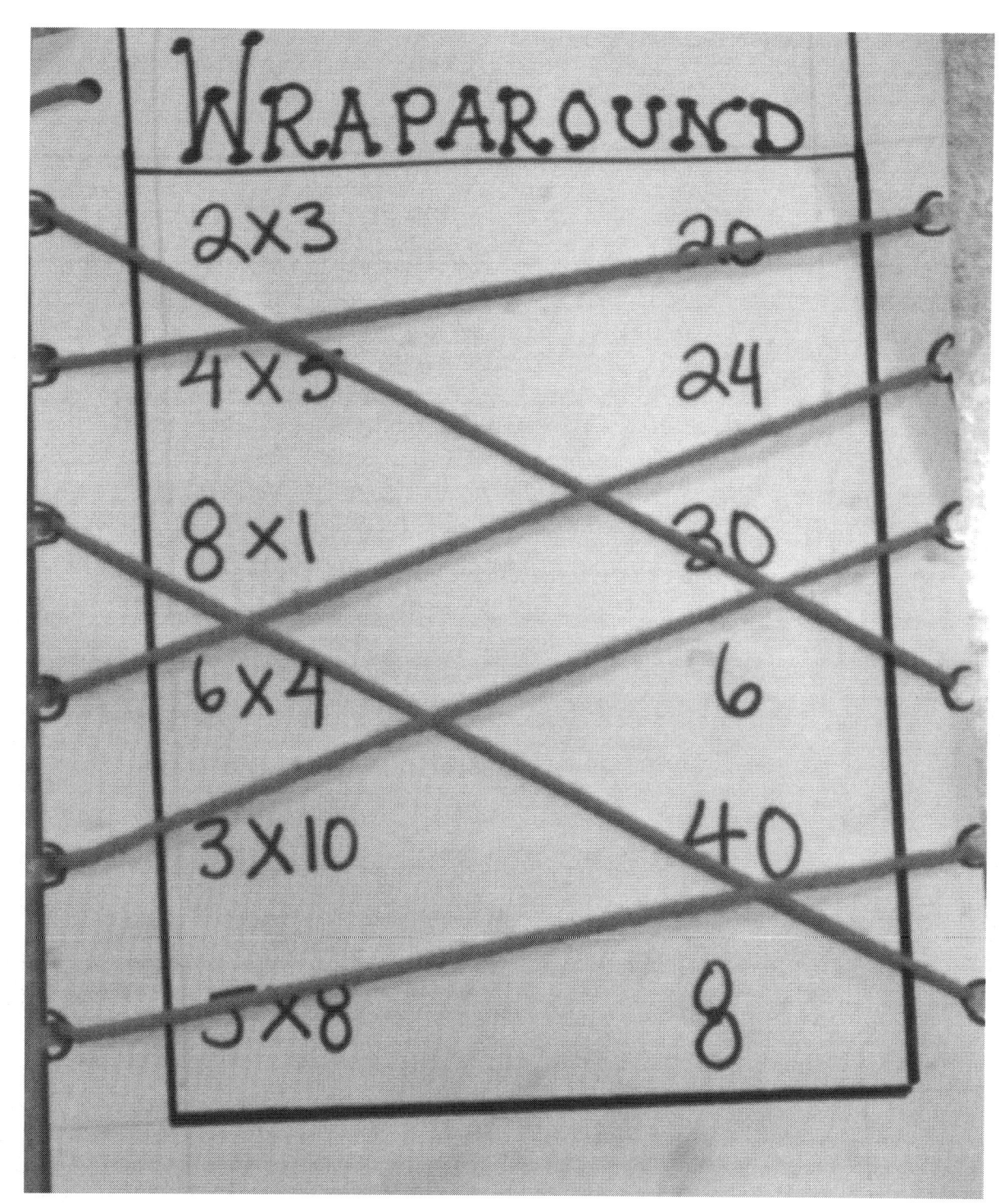

Photo 2.4. Wrap-Around by Jess D'Amprisi

22 SECTION 2

3. Using the hole-punch, make one hole at the point where each question will appear on the left side of the poster board, or randomly. Corresponding holes should be placed where the answers will appear;
4. Print the questions and answers on the poster board next to the punched holes. If you desire, a brass fastener may be placed in the punched holes with the wings on the reverse side opened fully. Answers should not be directly across from the questions;
5. Turn the poster board over. Place a ¼-inch-wide strip of aluminum foil in a line, connecting a question with the correct answer. The foil should begin at the hole for the question and end at the hole for the answer. Cover the foil strip with ¾-inch masking tape so that there is no foil (brass fastener) exposed;
6. Using a light-style continuity tester purchased in a hardware or automotive store, check the circuit by touching the aluminum foil hole and/or the brass fastener with the clip on the question or what's on the left side of the Electro-Board. Then, place the pointed end of the continuity tester on the thought-to-be answer on the Electro-Board. If the light lights up you've selected correctly.

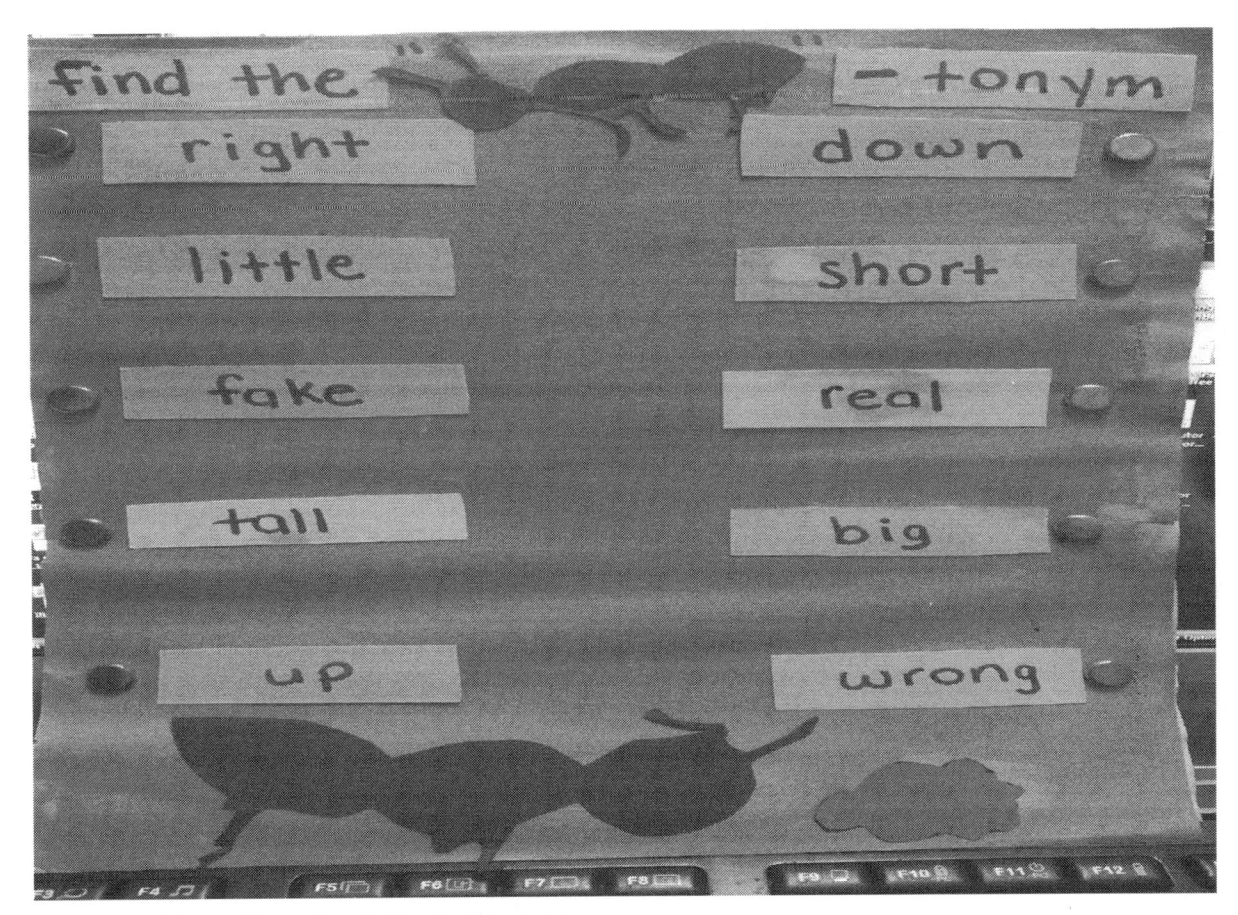

Photo 2.5a. Vertical Electro-board (Martika Mondesir)

The Interactive Method (IM) and IBR with Four Interactive Resources

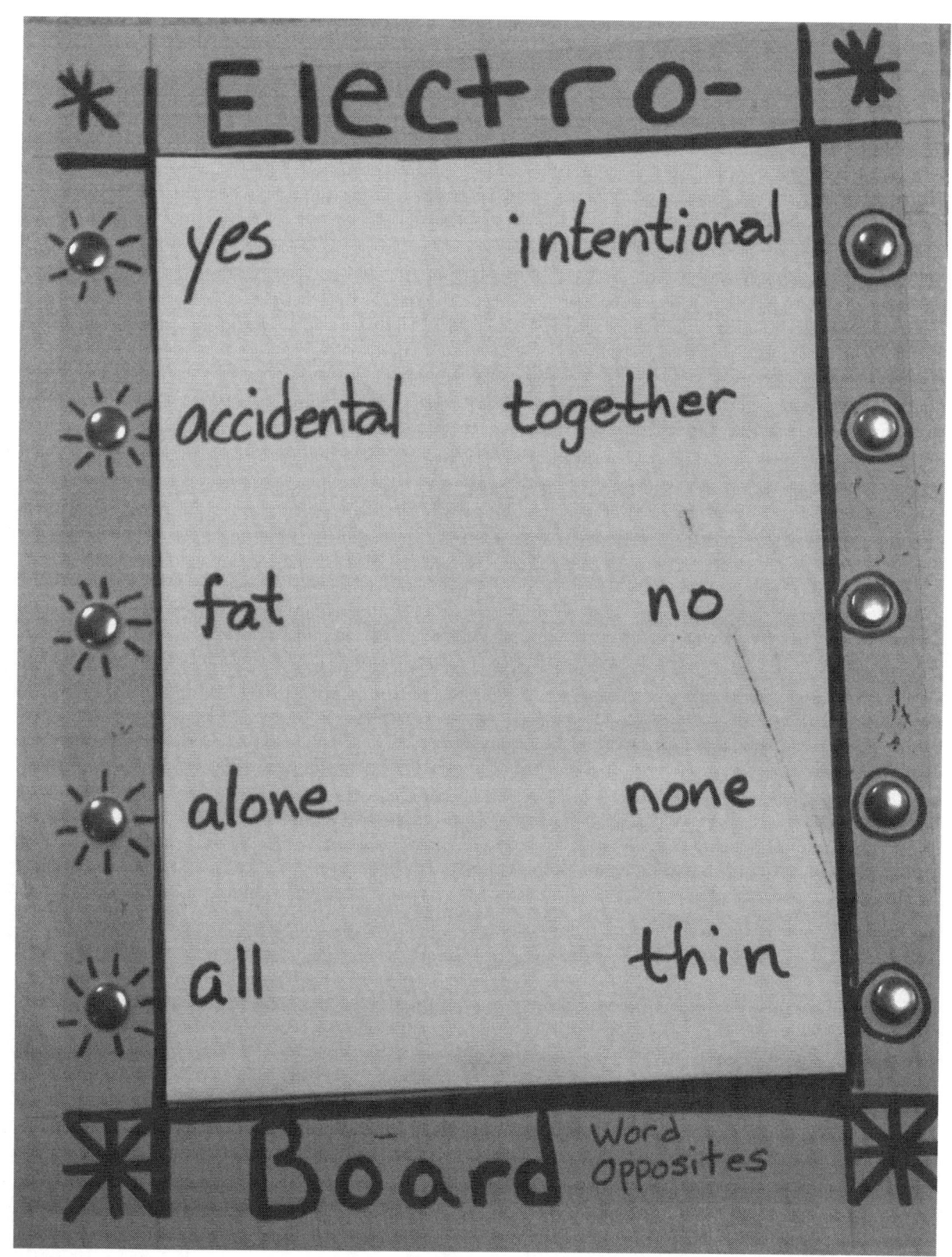

Photo 2.5b. Antonym Electro-board (Dominique Capolongo)

Let's Light Up the Empire State Building!

- The antenna broadcasts all television programs and FM radio stations in the New York Metropolitan market.

- The Empire State Building has 102 floors, with 1,860 steps from street level to the 102nd floor. The r 86th floor and 102nd floor Observatories offer the two highest vantage points in Manhattan

- The building took only 1 year and 45 days from April 7, 1930 to March 31, 1931. This is the fastest construction to date for a project of its scale.

- The Empire State Building's tower lights, illuminated to commemorate holidays, events and special causes. The tower lights are illuminated daily from sunset until 2 a.m

- Standing 1,454 feet above midtown Manhattan, the Empire State Building is considered the "World's Most Famous Office Building," and was recently named "America's favorite building" in a poll conducted by the American Institute of Architects.

- The Empire State Building has been "home" to some of the most famous movies, including King Kong, Elf, and of course James and the Giant Peach.

Photo 2.6. Electro-board Empire State Building: Jackie Gelbart & Nicole DiBliasio

Flip Chute Template

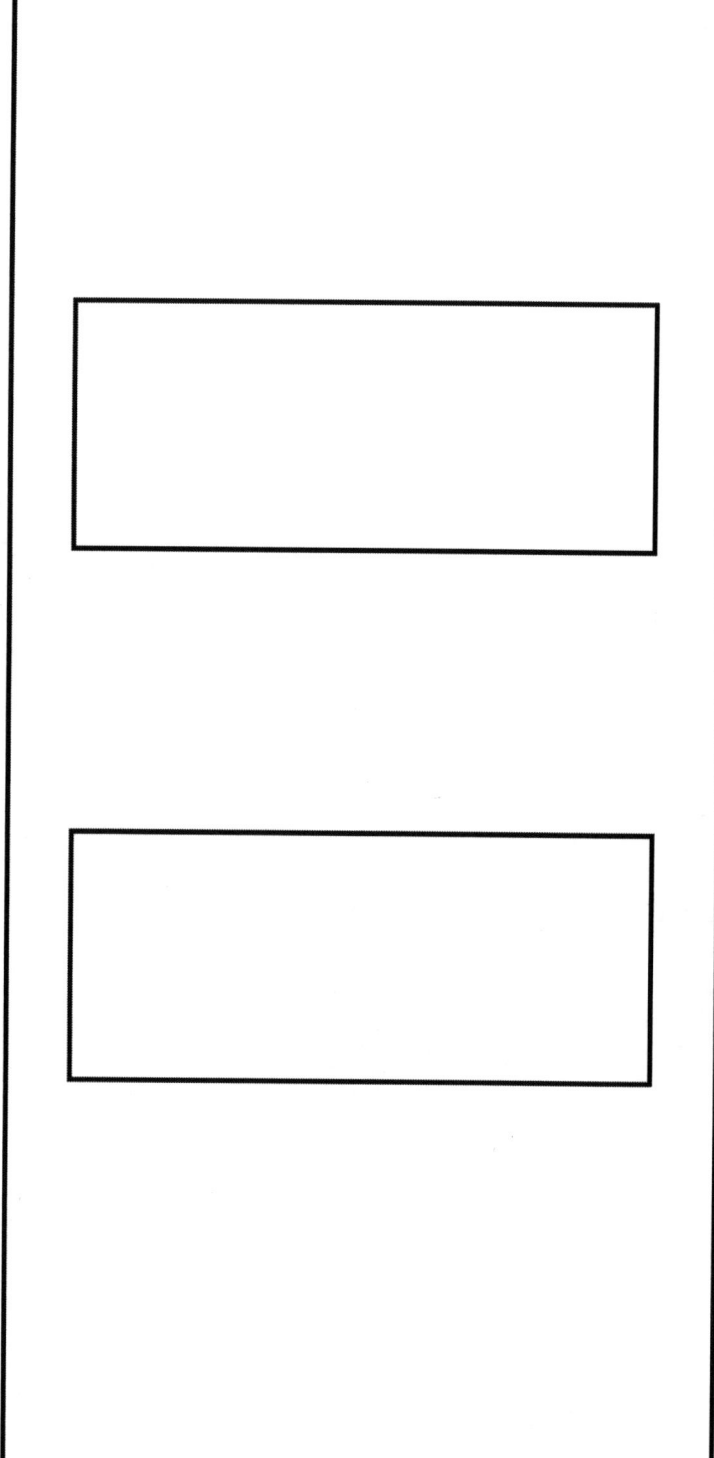

Figure 2.2. Flip Chute Template

Large Chute

Small Chute

Figure 2.2. (continued)

Flip Chute Cards

Question goes here

Answer goes here

The Interactive Method (IM) and IBR with Four Interactive Resources

Pick-A-Dot Visual Template

Enlarge to size

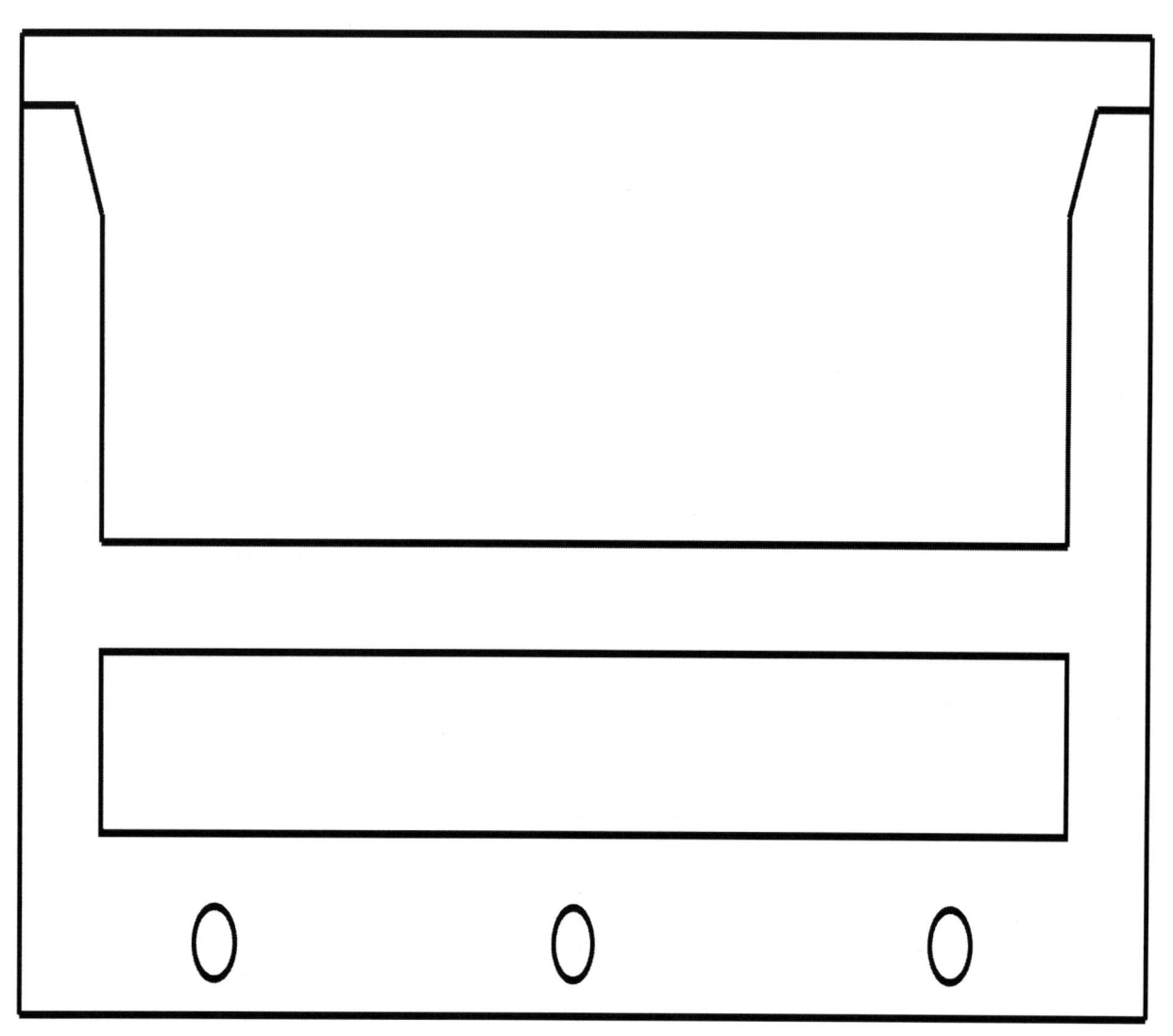

Figure 2.3.   Pick a Dot Visual Templates

Pick-A-Dot Cards Visual Template

Enlarge to size

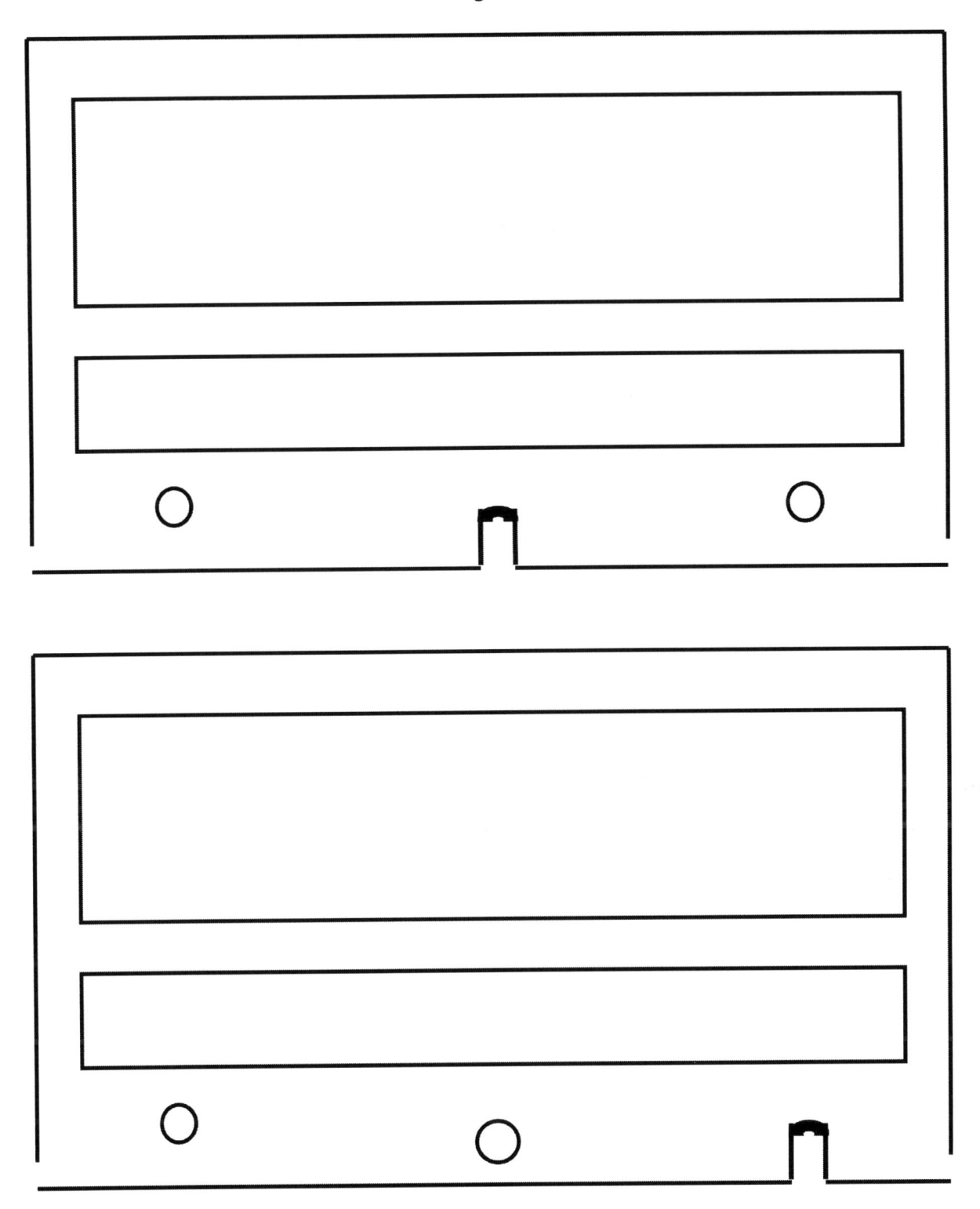

The Interactive Method (IM) and IBR with Four Interactive Resources

Wrap Around Visual Template

Enlarge to size 8 ½ X 11 Card Stock

QUESTION		ANSWER
QUESTION		ANSWER
QUESTION	Keep in mind not to put answers directly across from questions.	ANSWER
QUESTION		ANSWER
QUESTION		ANSWER
QUESTION		ANSWER

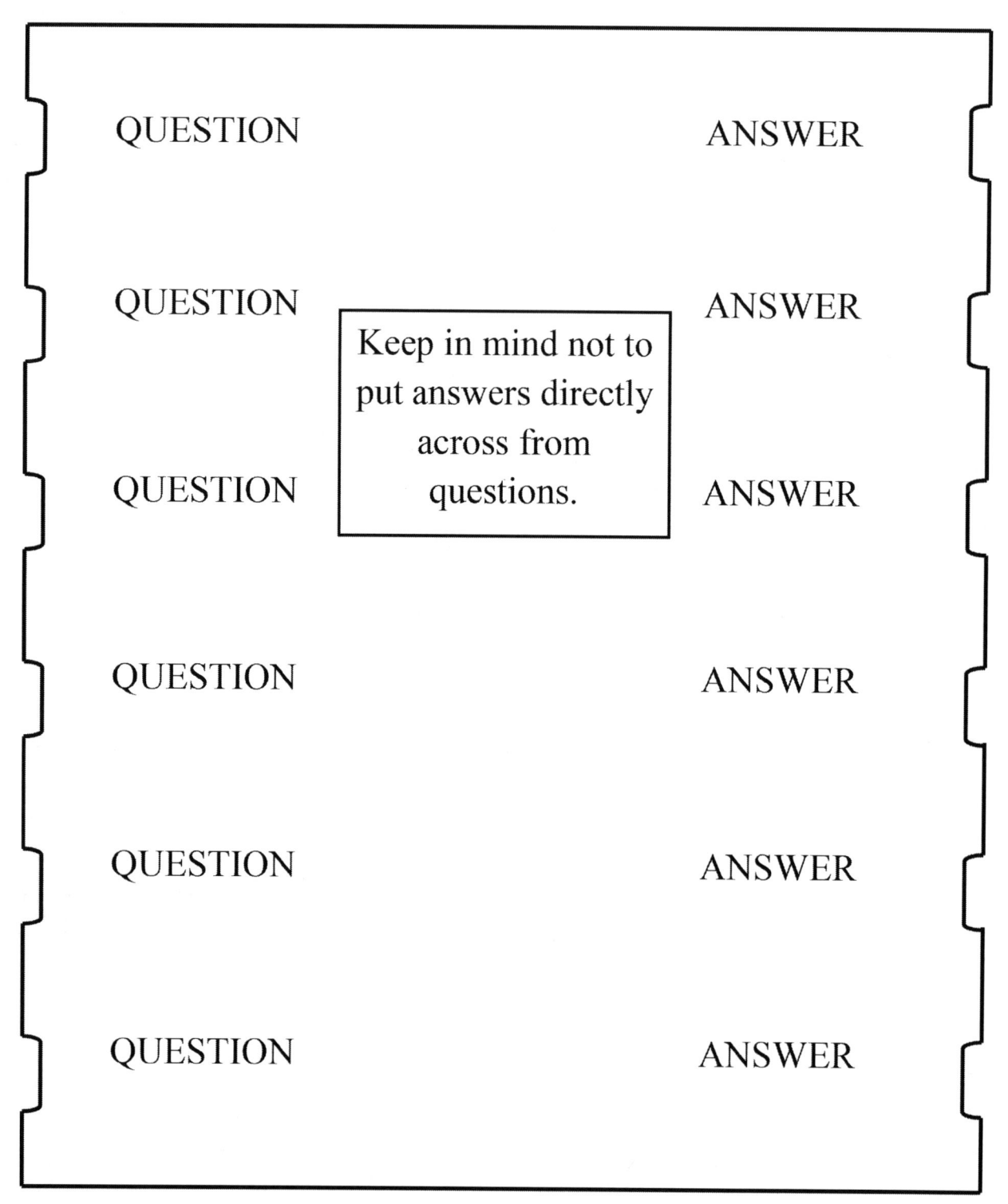

Figure 2.4. Wrap Around Visual Templates

32   SECTION 2

Electro Board Visual Template

Enlarge to size 8 $^{1/2}$X 11 Card Stock

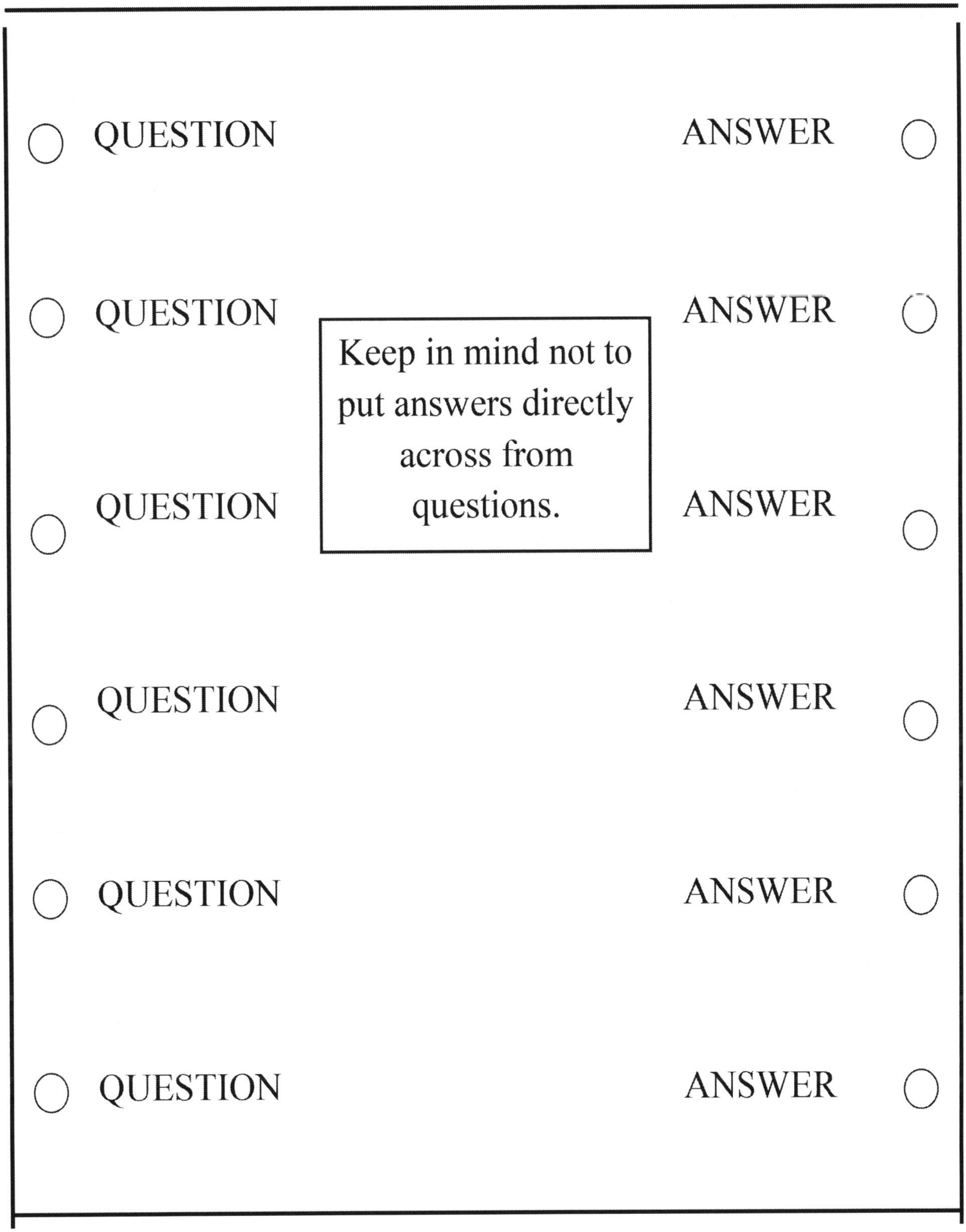

○ QUESTION   ANSWER ○

○ QUESTION   ANSWER ○

> Keep in mind not to put answers directly across from questions.

○ QUESTION   ANSWER ○

○ QUESTION   ANSWER ○

○ QUESTION   ANSWER ○

○ QUESTION   ANSWER ○

Figure 2.5. Electro Board Visual Template

A NARRATIVE: IM, A LEARNING CENTER, AND THE IBR, BY AMANDA LOCKWOOD

"The IM was practiced by me when I made a *Word Family Board* for teaching phonics to my student preschoolers. I wanted them to discover word families like the 'at, op, an' ones. The idea was to have them recognize that each of them belonged to a family and words could too. There were different members of a family, but the family name was like the ones mentioned previously in this paragraph. So, there could be a cat in the 'at' family, a mop in the 'op' family, and a pan in the 'an' family.

"In our Integrated ELA and Reading class at Molloy (EDU. 506A), we divided into partnerships to research and create an information packet and tri-fold brochure, then gave a demonstration lesson on a reading method. Dr. Schiering explained how difficult phonics can be for some children, having to sequence and connect letters and sounds. However, she said, 'When you make the connection to a family, you have an identification place for the children and that makes it personal.'"

Amanda continues, "On both outside flaps of the Tri-fold Board are pictures of things that belong in the Word Family Houses of at, en, op, in, un, and an. Two examples include the number 10 for the 'en' family and a picture of a top for the 'op' family. In the middle of the Tri-fold Board there's the Word Family House, which is a drawing of a house and the name of the family on the roof. A blank space in front of the family name is left for students to Velcro the letter that makes a word and that word is the family member. (Alphabet letters are used as the first name of the family member, so that 'c' is the first name of one of the 'at' family names, which when blended is 'cat'.)

"There's also a space for the picture of that family member. Or, for my Board, I had the pictures go on the bottom of the house at the frontdoor mat. I used creativity and creative cognition in the overall design of the Board and, of course, when making this activity by drawing the house and adding detail to the windows, the bushes, and/or chimney.

"The reaction of the students when first seeing the *Word Family Board* was amazing as they said, 'Wow, who made that, Ms. Lockwood?' When they discovered it was me they commented on how I put a lot of work into the Board, how it was awesome and beautiful. They wanted to use it right away. Even my older students saw the creativity and work I put into it. I think some of them may be proud of me by being creative and using it in my teaching. This opens up a whole other world for these students. Most of the time students only get excited by using technology, an iPad or Smart Board.

"Designing and constructing this Tri-fold Board required the use of technology, but then took a step back, because after it was completed no technology was needed to "play" with it. It is just as interactive as a Smart Board, even more so, because the students can physically touch, remove and replace the letters and pictures, and move them around to different locations instead of moving pictures on a board. The Tri-fold is three-dimensional! The students love the interaction of coming up to the Tri-fold Board, which is kinesthetic involvement, and then tactile involvement when making a decision about which letter goes where, and which picture represents that family member.

"As a child I was very creative, or I always tried to be; I remember that I could not draw beautiful pictures, as I wasn't born with that natural talent. I have always appreciated and sometimes felt jealous of people who were born with the ability to draw anything, easily. I think that with some things I may be a perfectionist, which might hinder my creativity by thinking my work is inferior, or I am not good enough. In elementary school my favorite special subject was art. I loved going and creating something new, because I found 'Creative Cognition' to be very RELAXING for me!

"Maybe because of my reaction to creativity, I want my students to appreciate it or find it enjoyable. I think it can be a huge help in learning. I'm an English Second Language teacher and with students creating something without words I find it comforts them, because the language barrier is not in art. Also, when creating worksheets, PowerPoints, or Smart Board lessons for my students, I always include some graphic or animation to help get their brain stimulated.

"As for the IBR, it was a big project when I was in college and it challenged me. I thought about designing pages and making the pages attractive with borders that were colorful. I stretched my thinking to be imaginative and inventive. Some things I kept just as I had them and some things I changed. What really matters is that I grew from this experience in realizing that there are many ways to do a project and I know this because I saw so many of my classmates' IBRs and they were all different.

Photo 2.7. Word Family House. (Lockwood, 2012).

Photo 2.8. Amanda's Student Using Tri-fold Board

The Interactive Method (IM) and IBR with Four Interactive Resources   35

"I don't mean different because they used a different book, but different because of the way the pages were to be played and the overall design. Creativity takes many forms and I think it's important to let children use their imaginations to develop their thinking skills and be part of something instead of apart from it" (Lockwood 2010). Photo 2.8 is of a student using the Word Family Tri-fold Board."

SUMMARY

This section of the Interactive Workbook has provided hands-on guides for project and performance-based instruction. The Interactive Method and Interactive Book Report types of activities enable you, with the photos and figures, to have a basic idea of their function as learning and teaching devices.

The methodology involves the student learner, regardless of age or grade level being personally involved in learning, gaining experiences upon which to build future references. It was explained that retention of material is at a "zenith" with this type of instruction, because a person recalls most readily that which he/she was involved. Maybe that is what's most important about this section of the interactive workbook, that you know being engaged in one's learning brings forth memories a very long while later, thus causing retention of presented material. The teaching and learning tools or strategies for the IBR are only a few of the ones that may be created, but it is that creative process, whether Linear or Reciprocal that involves the learner and develops one's creativity to be used again another day throughout one's life.

SECTION 3

Playing-the-Pages Activities

OVERVIEW

On the following pages are activities learners may "play" or in some cases "create" in order to play. The purposes of this section are to help students to learn about the topic being addressed, to collaborate with others, to create community, to be aware of thinking skills for each activity, and to enjoy the learning experience.

An overall idea of these interactive pages is for one to analyze and reflect on the IM and IBR while being involved in the processes of the Cognitive Collective (i.e., Reciprocal Thinking Phases: cognition and metacognition). This workbook serves as a guide to using your own imagination or developing another's through being engaged in the learning process: *learning-through-playing.*

Very important: This workbook is designed to be used as a prototype for creating interactive instructional resources to be used in an IBR or to learn about a topic of interest or one that's being assigned for study. The topic may or may not be one previously addressed in a learning setting, wherever that may be. The IBR and/or the interactive instructional resources used in it or for a learning center serve as much as an *introduction* to a piece of literature as it does a *review* of it. Also, the material may provide an introduction to a topic/thematic unit of study or review of it.

The authors of these forthcoming activities are primarily former teacher candidates from Molloy College in Rockville Centre, New York, with an addendum by Josh Schiering, vice president of Linx Summer Camp and Enrichment Center. Each activity has the author's name on it under the title. You are invited to not just play these activities, but in some cases make them. Or you may pick your favorite ones and try doing them in your classroom or at home. Each of the activities has construction directions. In most cases the page has an illustration of the finished product for reference.

This section of the workbook is the interaction portion. The activities call for constructing game boards and other tools for learning. Many activities are geared for preschool through grade seven student-learners. Some are at the high school and college levels. Regardless, use your imagination and make the activities applicable for the learning level you want to address. Activities involve:

1. Cutting and pasting
2. Drawing
3. Constructing a figure and/or creating a floor game
4. Designing and making graphic organizers
5. Getting materials for sequencing or solving problems
6. Role-playing a situation
7. Using the Internet for information gathering to be synthesized and used on a Story Board
8. Doing a Web quest
9. Creating and solving three-dimensional puzzles
10. Creating puppets and accompanying theater

Reciprocal Thinking Phases: At the end of this section there is a listing of fifteen activities followed by the specific Reciprocal Thinking Phases skills that are used when playing that page. *The reason this is done is to solidify your awareness, realization, and recognition of how the IBR teaches thinking and what thinking skills are being taught!* An example might be for the Geometrical Sailboat activity: *Recognizing* the six geometrical shapes and *Comparing* and *Contrasting* these while *Prioritizing* and *Organizing* the shapes into a sailboat, as well as *Predicting* the overall design that will be produced when the shapes are put together. You may find more cognitive and/

or metacognitive skills that are being utilized when playing the pages in an IBR and that's a good thing, as you become aware that thinking may be limitless.

Common Core standards: Also at the end of the section is a list of twenty-three of the activities with examples of at least two Common Core learning standards that are evidenced when playing the page. But if you examine them, these standards are applicable to most of the activities and may only need a specific grade level attached. These standards were attributed to the activities by teacher Nicole DiBlasio.

An addendum to the section titled "Kicking It Up a Notch!" is provided by Joshua Schiering, vice president of Linx Summer Camps and Enrichment Center in Wellesley, Massachusetts. This activity deals with six steps with six questions one might ask to make a project spectacular.

INTERACTIVE ACTIVITIES TO MAKE AND PLAY

1
"THINGS WE LIKE": A QUILT
M. Schiering

Materials: Large baggies (gallon size), duct or masking tape that's decorative or a solid color, drawing paper to fit in the baggies, crayons or markers, tally sheet.

Directions: This is an activity for several persons or an entire classroom of student-learners. A Smart Board list is made of things that are liked, serving as a class poll/vote tally sheet. Then, hand-made drawings or computer-generated clip art pictures are used for showing the listed items. This could be one's family, friend, pet, vacation spot, food item, etcetera. Tape the baggies together along the sides and bottom of the baggies on the *front side only*. Place drawings in the baggies *on the back side*, with one picture/drawing to a baggie. Now, hang up your Things We Like Quilt as a wall decoration.

Figure 3.1. Things-We-Like Quilt

Playing-the-Pages Activities   39

2
BIODEGRADABLE OR NOT? ELECTRO-BOARD
Julia Nackenson and Jessica Hurley

Materials: Crayons and/or computer-generated pictures, poster or foam core board, brass-fasteners, masking tape, aluminum foil, continuity tester.

Directions: Gather or make pictures of things that are biodegradable or not biodegradable. Using poster board or large foam core board, as well as the directions for making an Electro-Board (see section 2), put about fifteen pictures of things that are and are not biodegradable on the left side of the board. Place the words *biodegradable* and *non-biodegradable* on the right side of the board. Now, put holes with brass fasteners next to each of the pictures and also the words *biodegradable* and *non-biodegradable*. A very small sample appears in figure 3.2 showing how to set up the Electro-Board.

Make your connections of aluminum foil covered with masking tape on the back of the board, going from one brass fastener to the corresponding correct answer. Then, using the continuity tester, check to see, when turning the board over to the picture side, if you have made a correct match identifying what items are and are not biodegradable for a safe environment. The continuity tester lights up for right answers. If it doesn't, then try again till you've made the correct match.

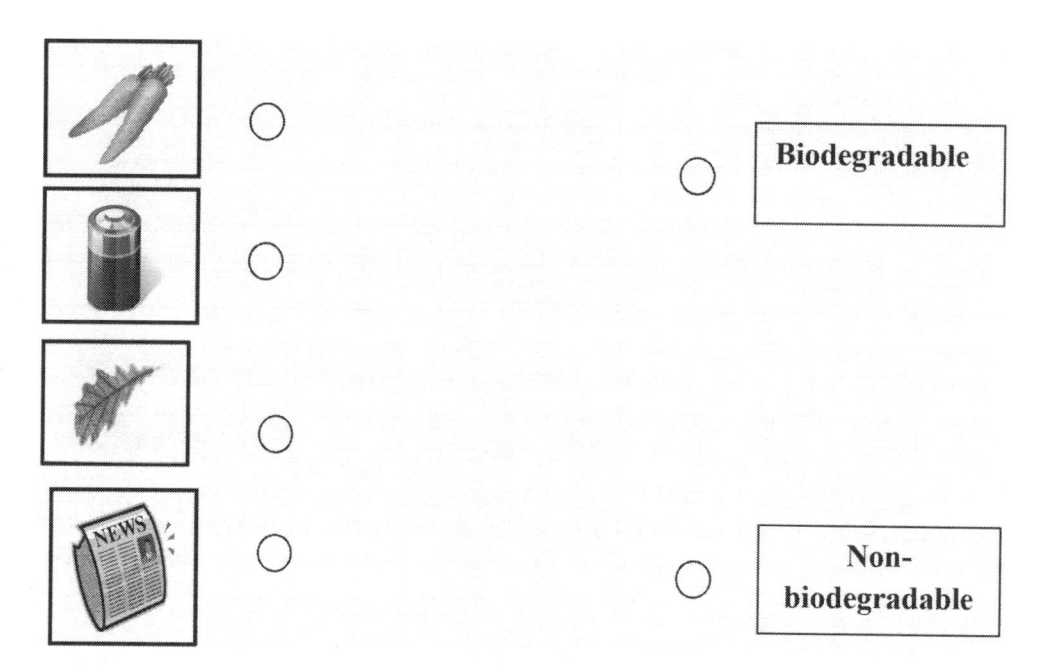

Figure 3.2. Sample Electro-board on Biodegradable and Non-biodegradable Items

3
RECYCLING CLOTHES DRYER LINT
Louis Laupheimer

Have you ever wondered what becomes of clothes dryer lint after it is removed from the dryer? Most of the time, it's just thrown in the trash and since it is biodegradable one probably doesn't give it much thought. When we were studying sustainability and recycling I got to thinking about what could be done with clothes dryer lint if I collected enough if it. Here are directions for making a bowl from clothes dryer lint and scraps of colored paper. (When you're done with this activity think of other shapes you could make and try it using the steps below.)

Materials: A blender, dryer lint, colored paper, and water.

Directions:

1. Collect a substantial amount of lint from your dryer (several cups of it).
2. Collect scraps of colored paper in whatever colors you would like; could have a combination of colors or just go for one color in particular.
3. Put the lint and the colored paper scraps in a blender and add about a half cup of water or maybe a little less. Blend to make a slur, which is a paste-like substance.
4. Take the slur out of the blender and have a small bowl upside down nearby. Press the slur onto the outside of the bowl.
5. Let the slur dry overnight or twenty-four hours.
6. The slur, now dried, should easily pull off the bowl. Remove the slur from the bowl and you've got a new bowl.
7. Now mix glue and water together and paint the bowl to make it shiny when it dries. Or a product called Modge Podge, available at art supply stores, could be used to create this shiny surface. Whichever works best for you, paint the bowl inside and out.
8. Now you can personalize the bowl if you would like and paint a design on the new bowl, or just leave it as it is and use it for storage of paper clips, crayons, stamps, artificial flowers, or other non-food items.

Caution: The new bowl is made of recycled materials, but cannot have liquid substances in it or food items that you would eat from this bowl.

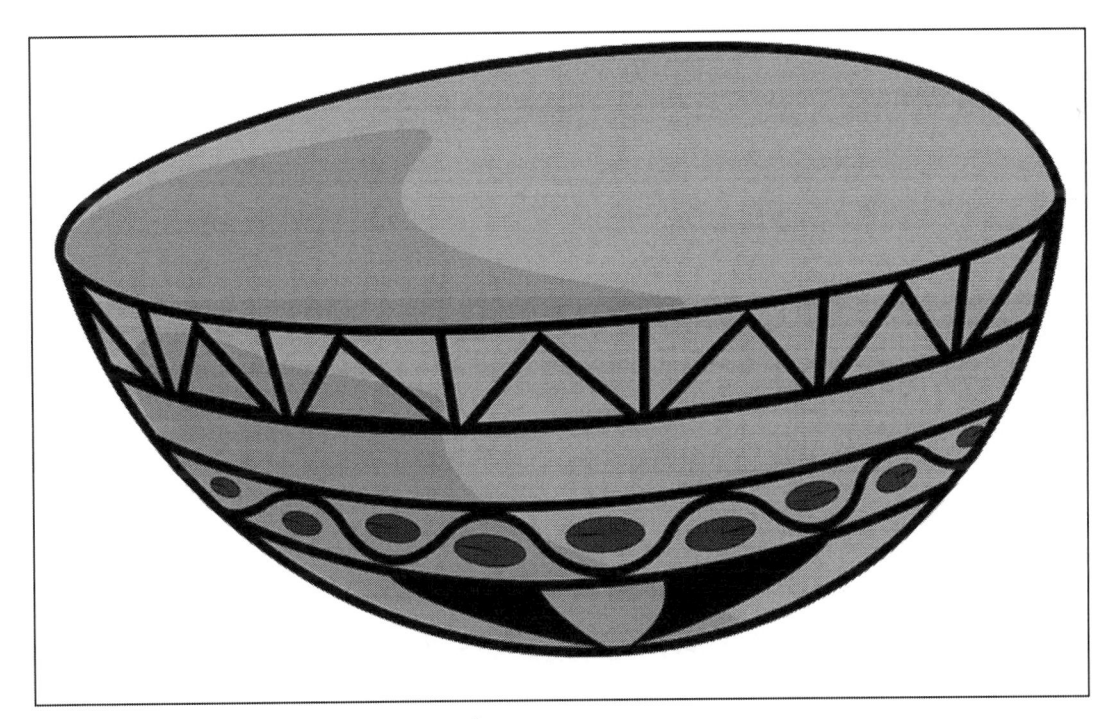

Figure 3.3. Recycling Clothes-dryer Lint Bowl

4
THE WHEEL OF ADJECTIVES
Kuljit Kaur and Xiomara Martinez

For this activity, you will look for adjectives in sentences. Create a posterboard circle as in photo 3.1. Get 12 clothespins to put on the circle. Please read the directions carefully before beginning this activity. Most importantly, enjoy pinning on those adjectives!

1. Write sentences for the Adjective Wheel.
2. Glue the sentences to the Wheel (see Photo 3.1).
3. Put the adjective that is defined on the wheel on paper and then cut it out and paste to a clothespin.
4. Clip the adjective to the sentence. Make sure all the clothespin adjectives are attached to the wheel by the sentence that has its definition.
5. Now, mix up the adjective clothespins, so each one is not with its correct definition. Hand your Adjective Wheel to a classmate and see if that person can make the correct match.
6. In order to let that person self-correct, number the clothespins sequentially on the back of it. Number each sentence with the matching number. A person may check to see if he/she answered correctly by checking to see if the clothespin number matches the sentence number. Remember: adjectives describe nouns.

Photo 3.1. Wheel of Adjectives

5
A CITY OF SHAPES: GEOMETRY AND GEOGRAPHY
Louis Laupheimer (2010)

This activity involves making a city or a neighborhood geographical area using geometrical shapes. The geographical area you use is your decision, but you'll need basic shapes to compete the illustration. For the city you'll need mostly rectangles and squares with maybe a few triangles. For the neighborhood scene you may need pictures of trees and grass shapes from clip art pictures or whatever you choose to draw into the picture, such as houses. Use your imagination and have fun with this City of Shapes activity.

Materials: Colored paper, white or light-color 8½ x 11 cardstock paper, colored pencils or crayons, computer-generated clip art. The cardstock paper is where you put your construction or drawing.

Directions:

1. Look up on a computer or in a book that has pictures the arrangement of a city or neighborhood. Actually, for your own neighborhood, you can look outside.
2. Based on your observations, draw a city of your own, but you may only use shapes. (For example: a building would be a vertical rectangle with vertical rectangles in it for windows).
3. As you draw or construct your chosen geographical area shapes using the "Insert Shapes" icon on your computer, list on a separate piece of paper all the shapes you used and how many times each one was used in the picture you made.
4. Also, as you go along write why you put things where they are and where or why you think this idea originated. This way you'll have a reference point for future constructions. Make sure to name your city and/or parts of it.

To get you started, some shapes appear in figures 3.4 and 3.5. You may cut these out on color construction paper and choose to use them for your picture(s).

Figure 3.4. City Shapes

Figure 3.5.   Neighborhood and City Shapes

Playing-the-Pages Activities   45

6
ECOSYSTEMS: TASK CARDS OR PIC-A-DOT
Jessica Hurley and M. Schiering

This is a "your choice" interactive instructional resource. You may use the following information to create Task Cards, Electro-Board, Wrap-Around, Pic-A-Dot, or some other type of board or floor game. The information is provided for definitions of ecosystem terms. You can create an illustration, use magazine pictures, or download Internet clip art for illustrations of the defined words. Let's see your creativity!

Ecosystem terms and definitions:

1. Population: A group of the same kind of living things in a community.
2. Community: All the plants and animals that live and interact with each other in a place.
3. Habitat: The special place in a community in which a plant or animal lives.
4. Niche: The role that each living thing plays in a habitat.
5. Environment: Everything that surrounds and affects a living thing.
6. Ecology: The study of how living things and nonliving things affect each other.
7. Ecosystem: A group of living and nonliving things and their environment. This includes the interaction between them.
8. Ecologist: A scientist who observes and then studies the impact of living and nonliving things on one another.
9. Succession: The series of changes in the communities of an ecosystem.
10. Pioneer Stage of Succession: When all things are new in a community.
11. Climax Stage of Succession: When a community is thick with plants and animals.
12. To keep our planet green we need to recycle, reuse, or renew materials.

Sample Task Card

Climax stage of Succession: When a community is thick with plants and animals.

Figure 3.6. Ecosystem Task Card

Sample Pic-A- Dot

A "habitat" is the _____ place in a community where a plant or animal lives.

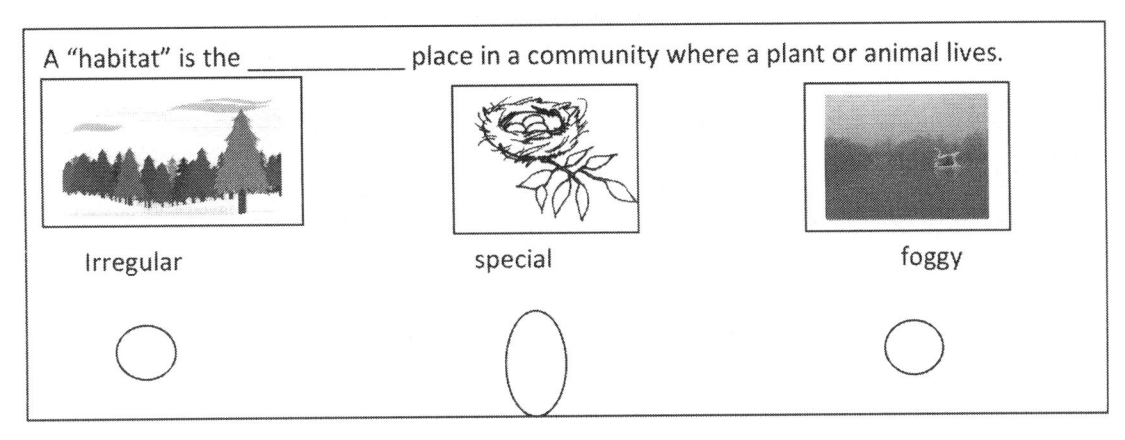

Irregular   special   foggy

Figure 3.7. Sample Pic-A-Dot Card for Ecosystems

Sample Task Card

Ecologist: A scientist who observes and then studies the impact of living and non-living things on one another.

Figure 3.8. Sample Task Card for Ecosystem

Playing-the-Pages Activities 47

7
SAILBOAT with GEOMETRICAL SHAPE
Christina Speirs

Directions: To make a sailboat from geometrical shapes you'll discover that only six of these shapes are needed. Follow the six steps to create this figure. Then, make a few more on your own and create a scene of sailboats on the water.

- Step 1: Find the *long* rectangle, cut it out, color it brown, and place it in the center of a sheet of construction paper. It should be in the vertical position. You may glue it down or Velcro it in that position;
- Step 2: Find the large right triangle, cut it out, color it yellow, and now place it to the left side of the vertical rectangle. Again, you may glue it in position or use Velcro to hold it in place;
- Step 3: Find the smaller right triangle, cut it out, color it purple, and place it to the right side of the vertical rectangle. Remember to glue or Velcro it in place;
- Step 4: Find the double-lined rectangle, color it black and cut it out, then place it, horizontally, at the bottom of that long vertical rectangle you colored brown;
- Step 5: Find the square, color it black, cut it out, and place to the left of the double-lined rectangle from Step 4;
- Step 6: Last, but not least, find the small triangle with the circle in it. Cut it out and, before placing it to the right of the black double-lined rectangle, color the circles one color and the triangle a contrasting color of your own choosing. See the next page for shapes and the one after that for how these geometrical shapes, when put together, form a sailboat.

Six Geometrical Shapes

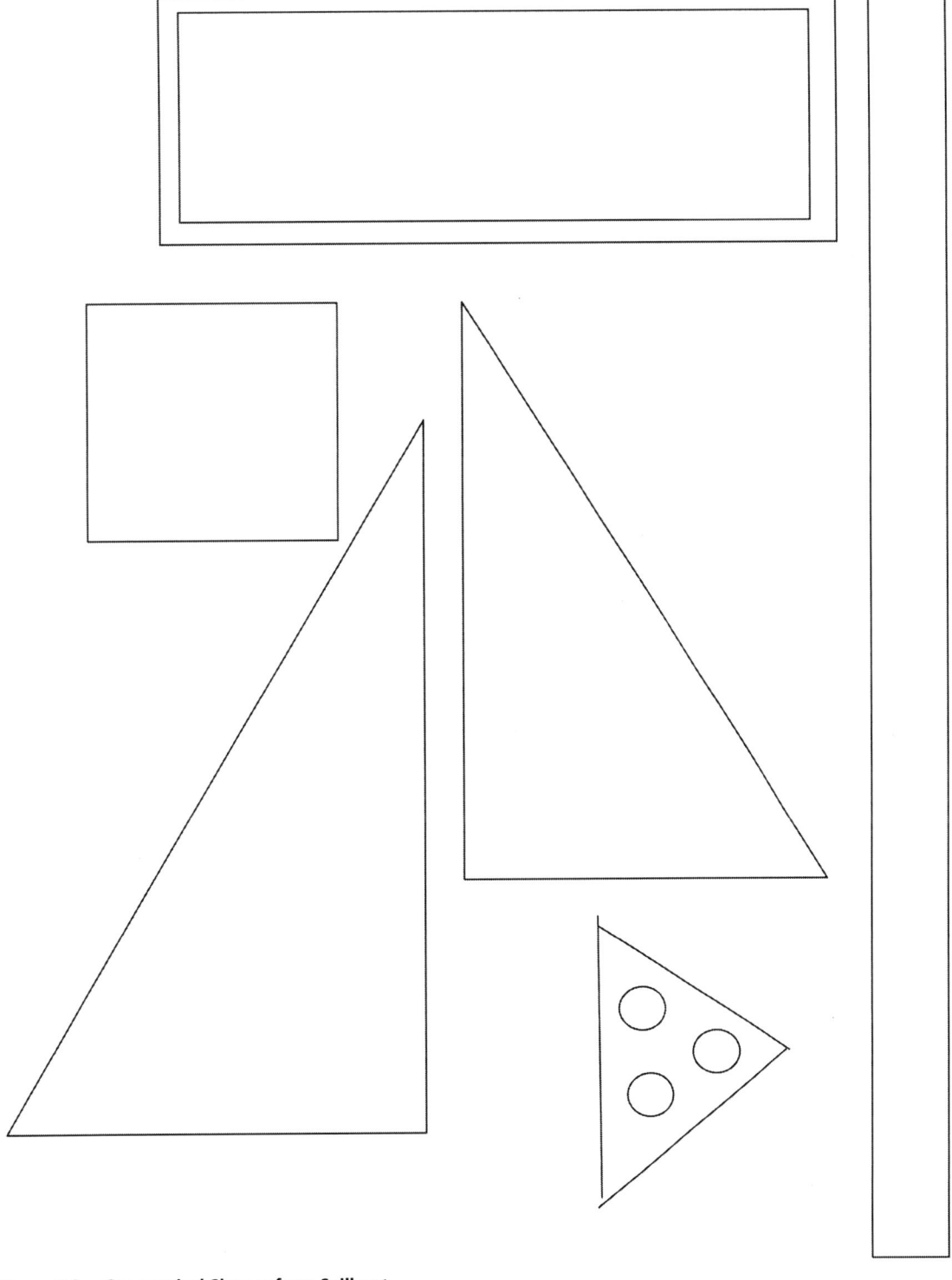

Figure 3.9. Geometrical Shapes for a Sailboat

Let's Make a Sailboat

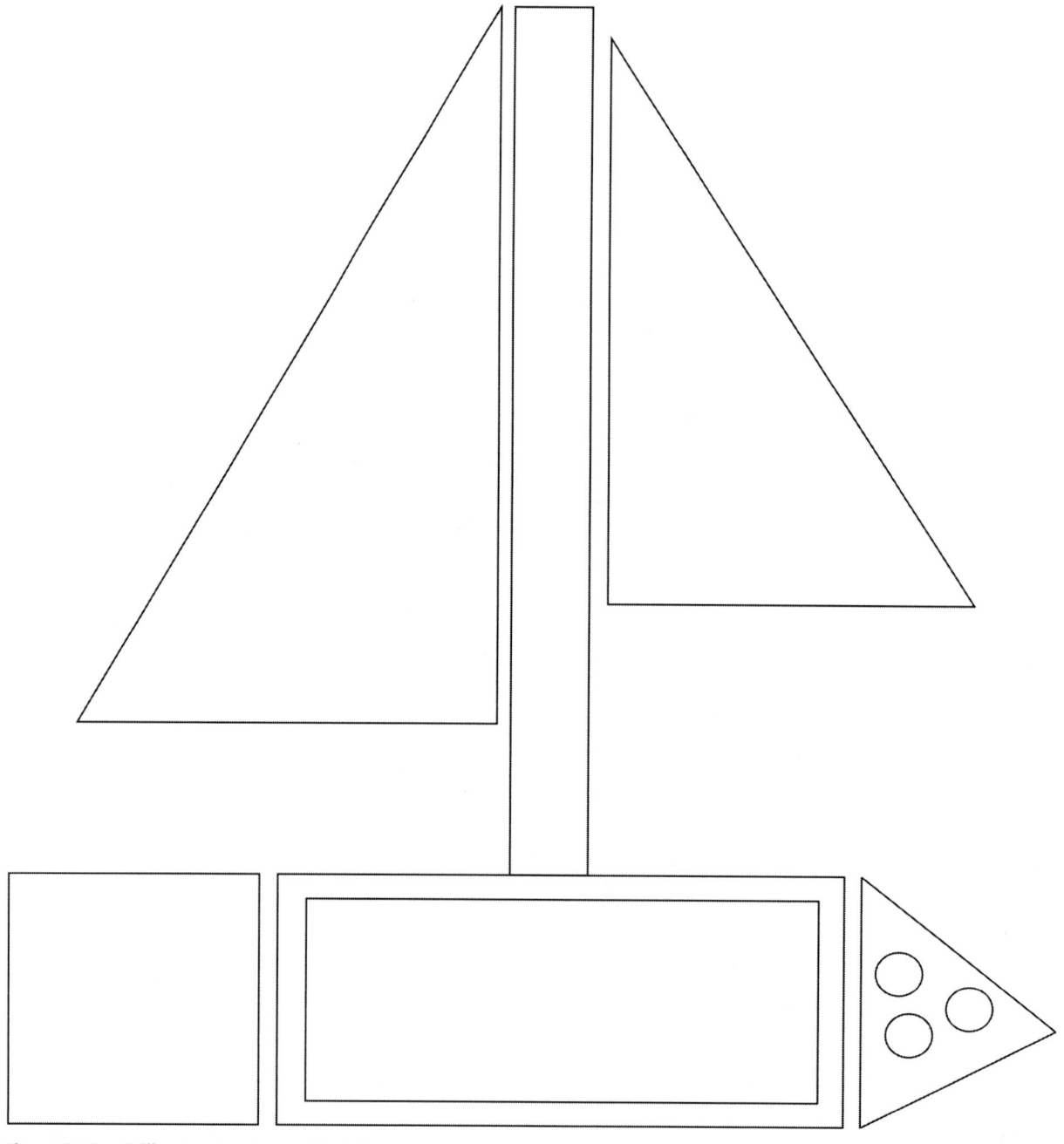

Figure 3.10. Sailboat using Geometrical Shapes

8
MAKING COMPOUND WORDS
Monika Mondesir

Directions: There are word parts you can put together to make a whole new word. This new word is called a "compound word." See the words below and using 5 × 8 index cards write the compound word. Example: air + port = airport. You should have twenty-three compound words in all when you're finished. Be sharp and see which two words are used more than once.

team bull end mate cheese sand rain dog box walk work board in life melon storm forest disciplinary session fisher burger complete rubber school boat tail made side news week cake time mom inter star play day man paper sharp house and sky house black water super store thunder grand market book sail fish pony week scraper shooter

9
DECISION MAKING: FINDING THE BEST SOLUTION
Amy Guerrara O'Hara

At the outset, the purpose of this type of graphic organizer is to recognize the steps taken to make a decision in a piece of literature or personal circumstance. The problem and solution are related to those instances. The use of critical thinking is evident. Further analysis of the decision-making process is heightened when analyzing *why* a particular decision was formulated. Children benefit from seeing this process's scope and sequence by examining their own thinking and feelings, as they prepare to make decisions. Applied comprehension is evident with cognitive awareness leading to self-actualization, the highest level of metacognition.

This activity can be done on a computer, or make this activity interactive, it is suggested that the graphic organizer be done on a foam-core board as an attachment to the IBR. Using the book *Pippi Longstocking* by Astrid Lindgren, teacher Amy Guerrara O'Hara offers you the opportunity to see how this decision making is applied in graphic-organizer format (figure 3.11a) regarding whether lead character, Pipi, should go to school or not. The graphic organizer is done on 8.5 × 11 paper. The interaction is filling in the sections on the paper by first printing what is to be in the section, then cutting it out and pasting it in the proper place. Remember there should be at least three Choices, three Possible Positive Outcomes and three Possible Negative Outcomes before there's a Final Decision, which is reflected in the possible outcomes you wrote.

As you can see, figure 3.11b is a template for you to use to make your own Decision-Making Graphic Organizer. Now, you can select a situation from the present or past that you think requires or required, respectively, a decision. Or, like the Pippi graphic organizer, you can select a book's character and make up a problem based on the context of the story. Pick your problem and fill in each section. Decorate the board or paper, if possible, to align with the theme of the board's topic. When you're done, share this project-based work with someone.

Working with a friend, talk *with* one another about a world situation or a school one that is of concern. This could be about making sound relationships, bullying in school, harassment, class schedule, making friends, ways for passing tests, realizing main ideas in a story, whether to take driving lessons, where to purchase a house or apartment. You know best the issues that have an impact on your life.

Now, still working with a partner, state the problem and then think of three possible solutions to that problem. These will be called, Choices. This is followed by you recording three Possible Negative and then three Possible Positive outcomes for each of the Choices you've made. Taking this information, make a Final Decision and use what's in the various Positive and Negative sections to state how your collaboration resulted in that final solution. Place this material on the graphic organizer like the one seen in figure 3.11b. Then, present your decision-making process to the class, parents, and/or friends. See what their reaction is and record any suggestions they may have about your decision.

Photo 3.2 is provided on an upcoming page. This Decision-Making Graphic Organizer was one done on foam core board by Joanna Gianesses (2015, Fall). Her "Problem" addressed selecting a graduate school to attend, or not doing that. Her "Choices" were to remain at her bachelor's degree college and specialize in speech-language pathology, or go to Molloy College and get her master's in childhood education, or not go to graduate school at all.

Two of Joanna's positives for the first choice focused on not transferring schools and being in a specialty area getting a higher-paying job with a degree in speech pathology. The possible negatives addressed the competitiveness in the field, and then not having a classroom belonging to only her. The two remaining "Choices" were influenced by having her own classroom, which was a huge plus, and the lower salary being one negative. The idea of not going to graduate school meant saving money, but not being able to support a family or being bored with staying home.

The Final Decision incorporated possible positive and negatives from each of these sections under the "Choices." Ultimately, Joanna selected to go to Molloy College for her master's in childhood education. She realized she truly wanted to have her own classroom, and a lower salary for not being in a specialty area wasn't all that important to her.

Decision Making Graphic Organizer

The problem/issue: Should Pippi go to school?

First choice:	Second choice:	Another idea:
Yes, Pippi should go to school.	Pippi stays home at Villa Villekulla	Pippi travels to find Papa

Possible negative outcomes:
- Missing Mr. Nilsson,
- Missing horse,
- Will have to follow school rules.

Possible negative outcomes:
- Loneliness
- Won't learn math
- Won't learn other subjects like science, language arts, or spelling

Possible negative outcomes:
- Could get lost,
- Tommy will be missed,
- Annika will be missed.

Possible positive outcomes:
- Will learn a lot,
- Will be with her friends Tommy and Annika,
- Will be smarter.

Possible positive outcomes:
- Hang out with Mr. Nilsson,
- Hang out with horse,
- Clean things.

Possible positive outcomes:
- Learn about other countries,
- Could find Papa,
- Could become a Cannibal Princess.

Final decision with an explanation of how you came to this decision:

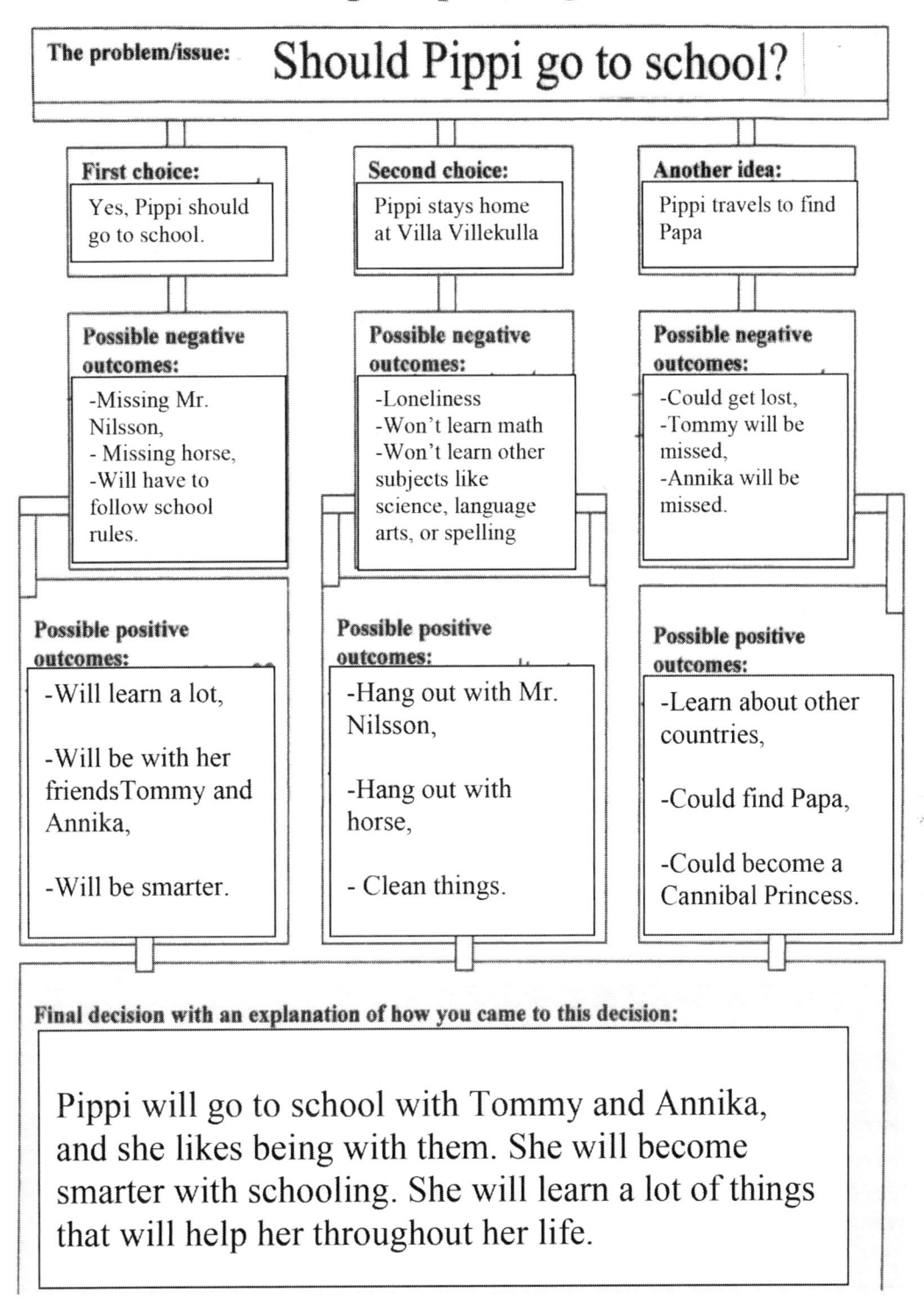

Pippi will go to school with Tommy and Annika, and she likes being with them. She will become smarter with schooling. She will learn a lot of things that will help her throughout her life.

Figure 3.11a. Decision-making Graphic Organizer from Pippi Longstockings

Decision Making Graphic Organizer

Problem:

- **Choice #1**
  - Three Possible Positive Outcomes:
  - Three Possible Negative Outcomes:
- **Choice #2**
  - Three Possible Positive Outcomes:
  - Three Possible Negative Outcomes:
- **Another Idea**
  - Three Possible Positive Outcomes:
  - Three Possible Negative Outcomes:

Final Decision and Why I made this Choice:

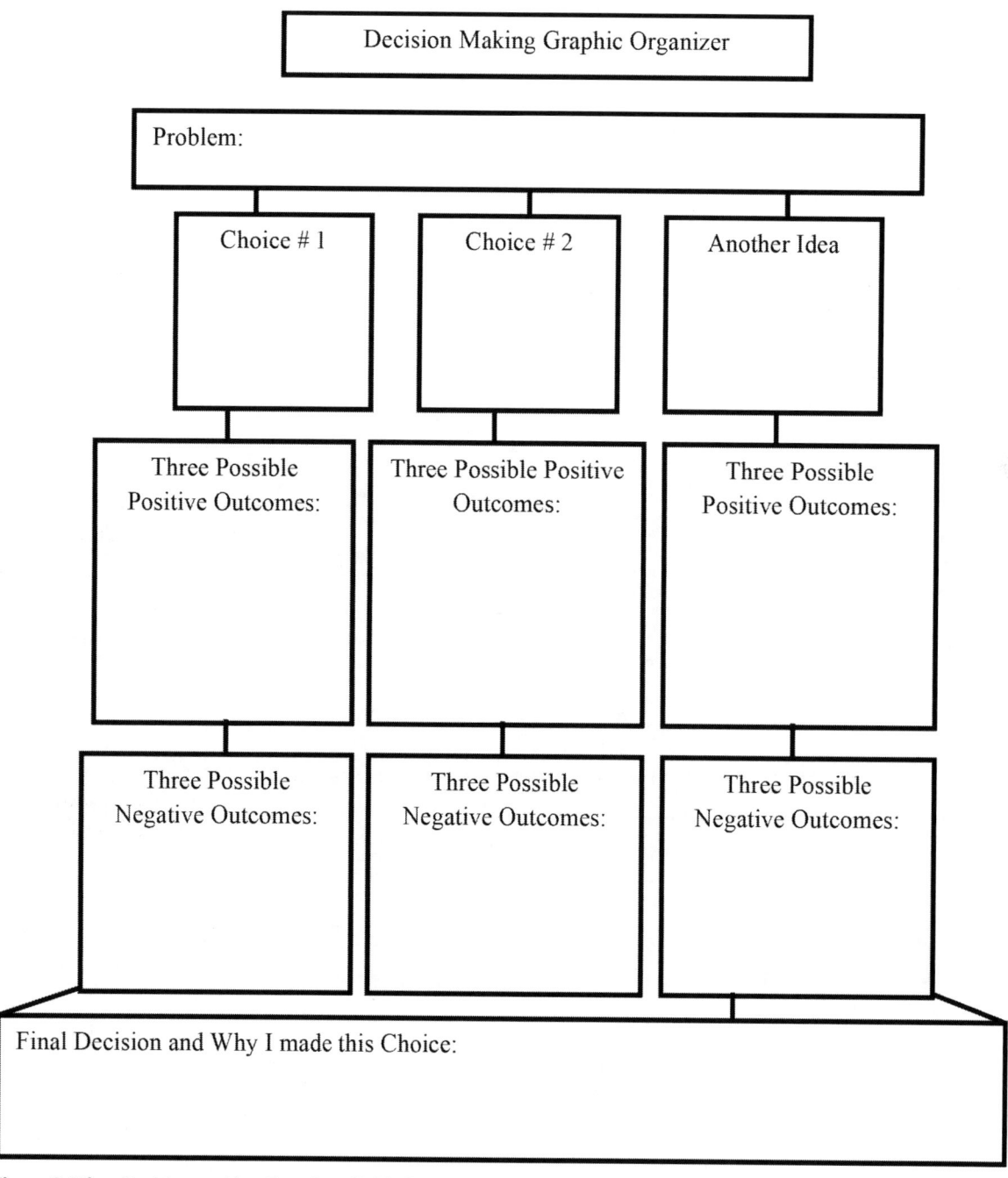

Figure 3.11b.   Decision-making Template (Schiering, 2001)

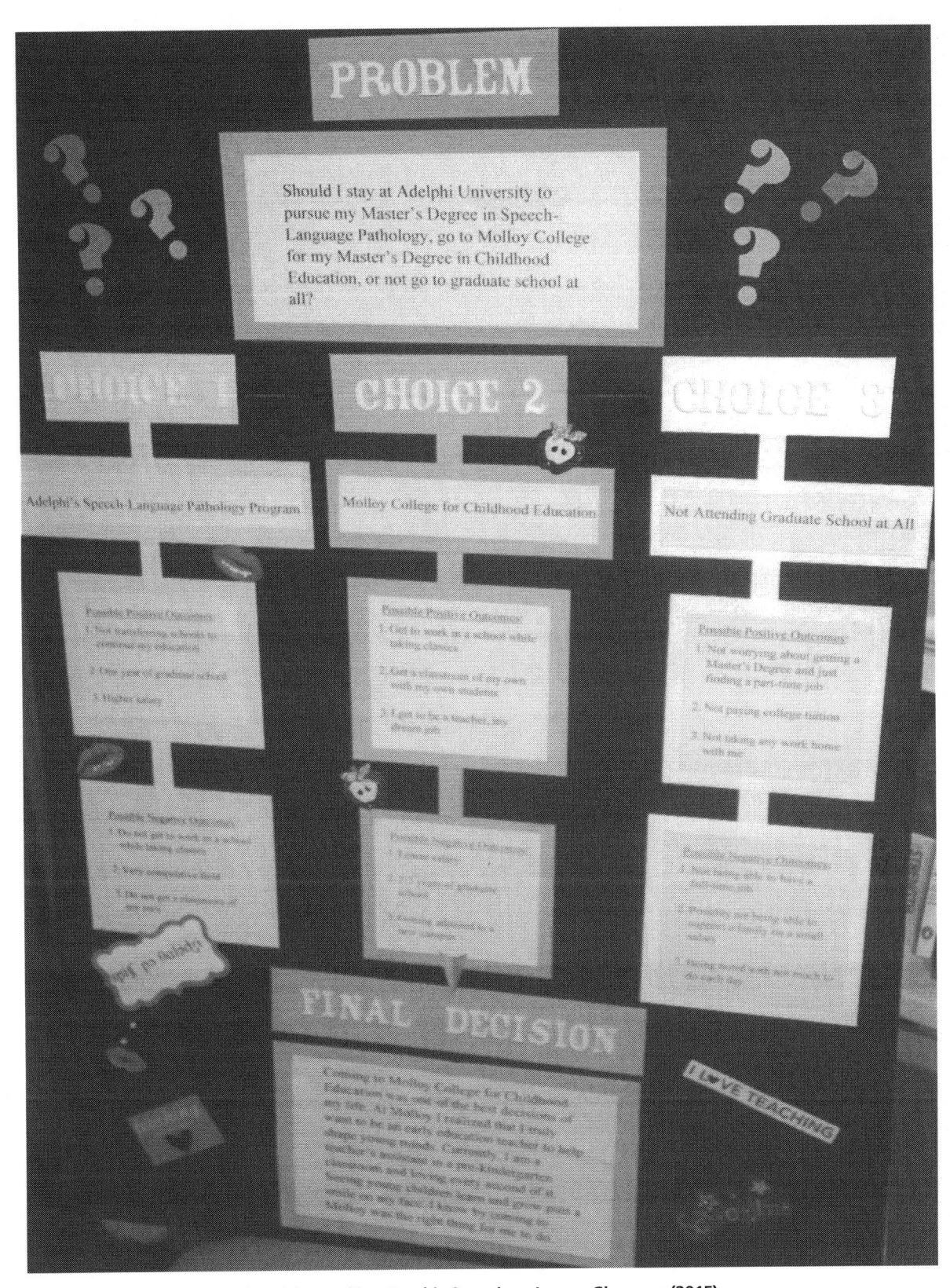

Photo 3.2. Foam-core Board Decision-making Graphic Organizer, Joanna Gianesses (2015)

10
MATH FLOOR OR WALL GAME
M. Schiering

This activity is referred to as a floor game (Schiering, 2011). That's because a shower curtain liner is used, and it is placed on the floor. Or, it's a wall game when the shower curtain liner is taped to the wall and a beanbag is thrown at the answer.

Math floor game: If used as a floor game, as illustrated in figure 3.12, the players remove their shoes to step on the answers to questions represented by shapes with different numbers on each shape on the liner. These shapes are drawn using a black permanent-ink magic marker.

A series of equation question cards are made with the answer on the reverse side. Two to four persons may play this game. When a shape is mentioned, the player needs to step on that shape. A correct answer to the question provides the move to the correct shape, saying the answer and the shape, if applicable. But, what if the answer is equal to more than one shape's number? Let's say the answer is 31, and you only have shapes with numbers one (1) through ten (10). Then, an example of what to do would be that the player steps three times on the number 10 and steps one time on the shape with the number 1 to signify knowing the answer. A person would say 31 and/or three triangles and one square. (The design of the shower curtain should be attractive and inviting.)

Math wall game: This game may also be used as a wall game with a beanbag used for tossing at the shapes and questions addressed in accordance with the numbered space. The game progresses just as it did with the floor game. If a "throw" is not on target, or the question can't be answered, then the player loses his/her turn and the next player goes.

Reciprocal Thinking Phases skills: For this activity these involve *recognizing* the rules of the game, *classifying* shapes, and the *organization* of these. *Generalizing* is experienced with the types of questions being in the math discipline and *problem solving* required through *decision making* to provide answers. One must be an *active listener* as the questions are posed orally. *Tolerating* using a beanbag toss for the wall game may be an issue. *Recalling* addition and subtraction components in math, as well as *reflecting* on answers and *recognizing* the shapes on the game is evidenced when *self-actuating* occurs by moving from one shape to the next.

Five sample math floor or wall game questions:

1. What is the sum of the square and the oval (1 + 6)?
2. What is the sum of the circle, oval, and triangle times the rectangle (5 + 6 + 10 x 2)?
3. What is the sum of the circle and the triangle minus the crescent shape (5 + 10 – 11)?
4. What is the sum of the triangle, diamond, and star, minus the square (10 + 11 + 7 – 4)?
5. What is sum of the cylinder times the oval (3 × 6)?

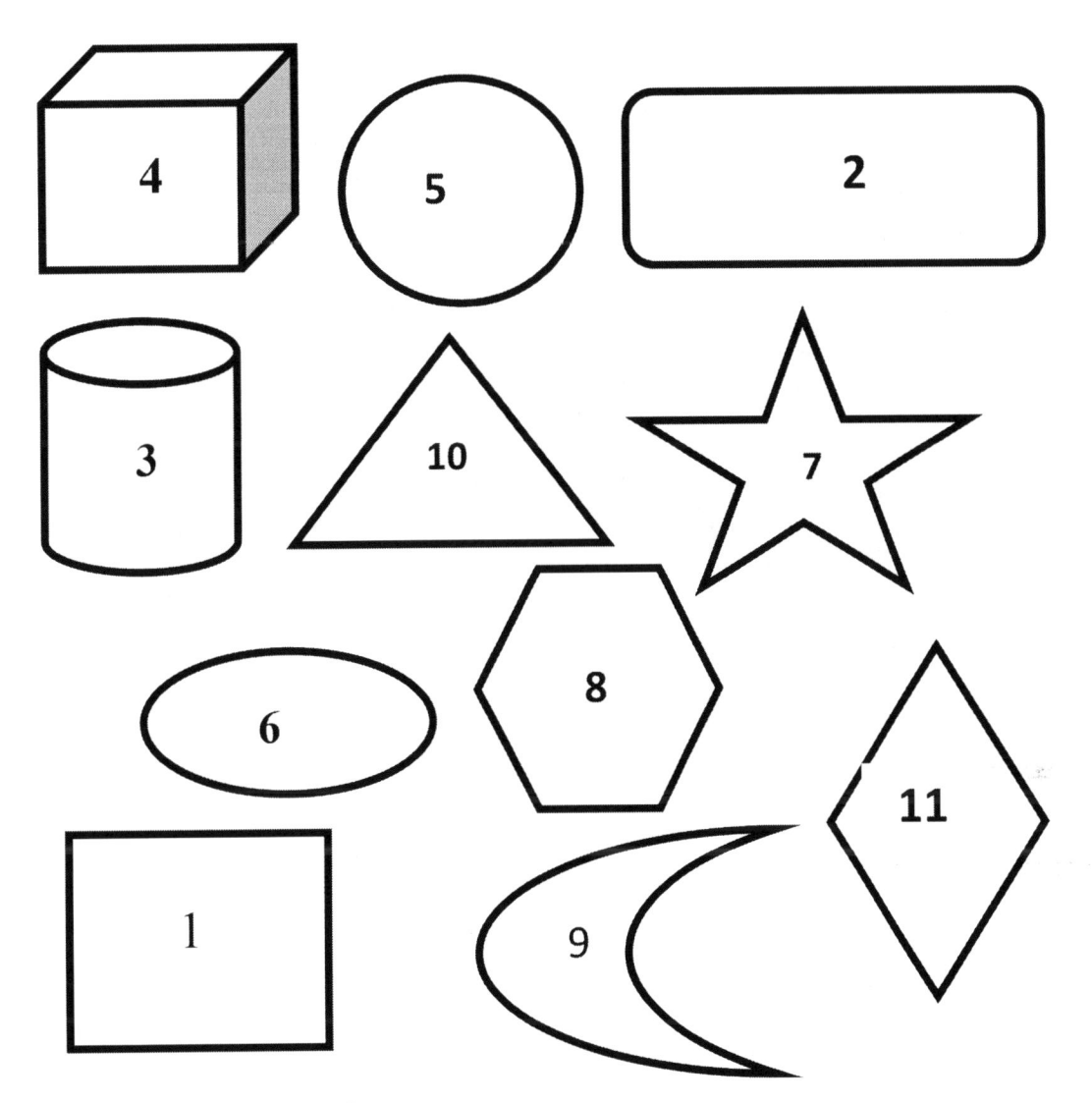

Figure 3.12. Math Floor or Wall Game

Playing-the-Pages Activities

11
SEASONS ELECTRO-BOARD
Danielle Voltmer and Dana Defliese

Directions: Look at figure 3.13. On the reverse side make the connections with aluminum foil going from one of the front-side symbols to the matching seasonal word, which means covering the brass fastener at each end. Put masking tape over the foil that connects the brass fasteners to their correct seasonal word. Then, use a piece of paper to cover the answers and go to the front side of the Electro-Board. Use the continuity tester to match the seasonal words with the correct season. (The Electro-Board is explained in section 2, photos 2.5 and 2.6).

To make this activity, cut and then paste figure 3.13 on cardstock paper and follow the directions above.

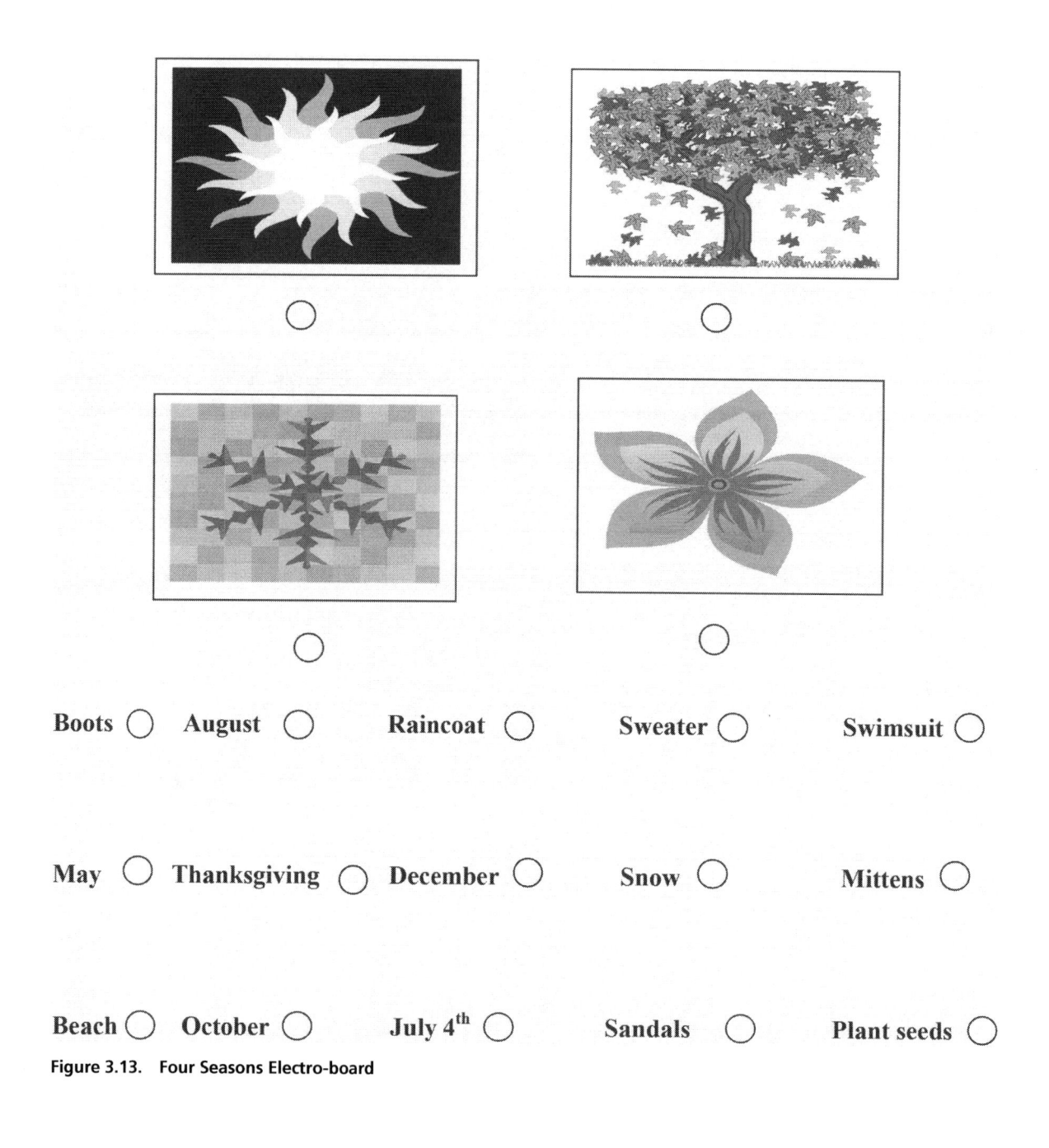

Boots ○ **August** ○ **Raincoat** ○ **Sweater** ○ **Swimsuit** ○

May ○ **Thanksgiving** ○ **December** ○ **Snow** ○ **Mittens** ○

Beach ○ **October** ○ **July 4th** ○ **Sandals** ○ **Plant seeds** ○

Figure 3.13. Four Seasons Electro-board

12
WEATHER WHEEL
Danielle Voltmer and Dana Defliese

This activity has you making a Weather Wheel of the four seasons: fall, winter, spring, and summer. It's time to get creative using these materials: crayons or markers, scissors, oak tag or poster paper, and glue.

Directions: See photo 3.3

1. Draw one big circle, and then another medium-sized circle on the large paper.
2. Cut out both circles.
3. Cut a large wedge out of the medium sized circle.
4. Place the second circle on top of the first circle. Poke a hole through the center of each circle and attach with a brass fastener.
5. Label the circle on top "Four Seasons."
6. On the big circle label the twelve months around the edges.
7. Cut a wedge out of that top circle to match the names of the months in a particular season, as shown on photo 3.3.
8. Label what season goes with the months directly under those months and then draw some items associated with that season under the season's name.
9. Spin or move the top Wheel to reveal a particular season.

Photograph 3.3 is of the Weather Wheel. Have a look and make your own Weather Wheel to share with others for learning about the months in each season and things associated with that season.

Reciprocal Thinking Phases skills: Recognizing, realizing, classifying the four seasons is done when they are named on the larger circle's rim. *Recalling* and *initial + advanced decision making* and *problem solving*, as well as *sequencing* and *inventing* are done when the pictures to represent each month are made. *Communicating* happens when the Weather Wheel is moved from one season to the next and *self-actuating* occurs then as well.

Photo 3.3. Four Seasons Weather Wheel

Playing-the-Pages Activities

13
NAME THAT U.S.A. STATE and ITS CAPITAL
Nicole DiBlasio

On this page and the next are the names of the fifty U.S. states and each one's capital. One way to learn them is to create Flip-Chute cards and use them until they're easily recalled.

Directions: Make fifty Flip-Chute cards.

1. Using cardstock paper or oak tag paper, sometimes called poster board, measure the paper to be 2½ inches wide by 2 inches high.
2. Notch the upper-right corner.
3. Trace that Flip-Chute card forty-nine times.
4. On the upper-right side of each notched card put the name of one of the United States of America.
5. Now, turn the card *upside-down* and place the name of that state's capital. When you do this, *the notch will be in the bottom right corner.*
6. Cut out the fifty Flip-Chute cards. Put a state name on one side and the capital on the other side.
7. Insert one card at a time into the top chute of the Flip-Chute and be sure when you insert it that the notch is in the upper-right corner with the name of the state facing you. Of course, for this activity you could do the capital first with inserting the card in the top slot where the notch is in the bottom right corner of the card. The names of the states are written for you, alphabetically and numbered, on the following page in large font. The names of each state's capital city are provided on the page after that. It's done in the order of the states. See figures 3.14 and 3.15.

U.S.A. STATES

1. Alabama
2. Alaska
3. Arizona
4. Arkansas
5. California
6. Colorado
7. Connecticut
8. Delaware
9. Florida
10. Georgia
11. Hawaii
12. Idaho
13. Illinois
14. Indiana
15. Iowa
16. Kansas
17. Kentucky
18. Louisiana
19. New Hampshire
20. New Jersey
21. New Mexico
22. New York
23. North Carolina
24. North Dakota
25. Ohio
26. Oklahoma
27. Oregon
28. Maine
29. Maryland
30. Massachusetts
31. Michigan
32. Minnesota
33. Mississippi
34. Missouri
35. Montana
36. Nebraska
37. Nevada
38. Pennsylvania
39. Rhode Island
40. South Carolina
41. South Dakota
42. Tennessee
43. Texas
44. Utah
45. Vermont
46. Virginia
47. Washington
48. West Virginia
49. Wisconsin
50. Wyoming

Figure 3.14. Names of States

NAMES OF STATE CAPITALS

Montgomery; Juneau; Phoenix; Little Rock; Sacramento; Denver; Hartford; Dover; Tallahassee; Atlanta; Honolulu; Boise; Springfield; Indianapolis; Des Moines; Topeka; Frankfort; Baton Rouge; Augusta; Annapolis; Boston; Lansing; St. Paul; Jackson; Jefferson City; Helena; Lincoln; Carson City; Concord; Trenton; Santa Fe; Albany; Raleigh; Bismarck; Columbus; Oklahoma City; Salem; Harrisburg; Providence; Columbia; Pierre; Nashville; Austin; Salt Lake City; Montpelier; Richmond; Olympia; Charleston; Madison; Cheyenne

Figure 3.15. Names of Capitals of U.S.A. 50 States

14
PUPPETRY THEATER
Lisa Connor and Dana Gerbino

About these pages: Two teacher candidates, as named above, chose for their IBRs (2013) on *James and the Giant Peach* by Roald Dahl to address puppet shows. Puppetry plays require acting, setting, dialogue, making puppets and a stage, synthesizing material, and having a good time as portions of the story are recalled for audience enjoyment. Role play/puppet play brings collaboration to the classroom setting.

Directions for puppets: Select characters from your book to be part of a puppet show. Lisa and Dana used the Internet to get paper puppets of their book's characters. You may look online for character cutouts or simply make/draw your own. Then again, if there are animals in the story, you may have stuffed ones to use as puppets. If the puppet is a paper cutout, then color these and place them with glue or Velcro on a tongue depressor or drinking-straw.

Directions for Puppet Theater: Obtain a Tri-fold Board. Lay it down on the floor with plastic sheeting under it. Draw a rectangular shape that will be cutout to form an opening on the board. This is done in the center section, as shown in figure 3.16. Stand the board up and place either construction paper on the sides of the opening or some fabric to look like these are curtains. Put the Tri-fold Board Theater on a desk top or table. Stand behind the opening, hiding yourself from view with your puppets, which are made from paper and placed on tongue depressors or some sort of stick, doing the role play.

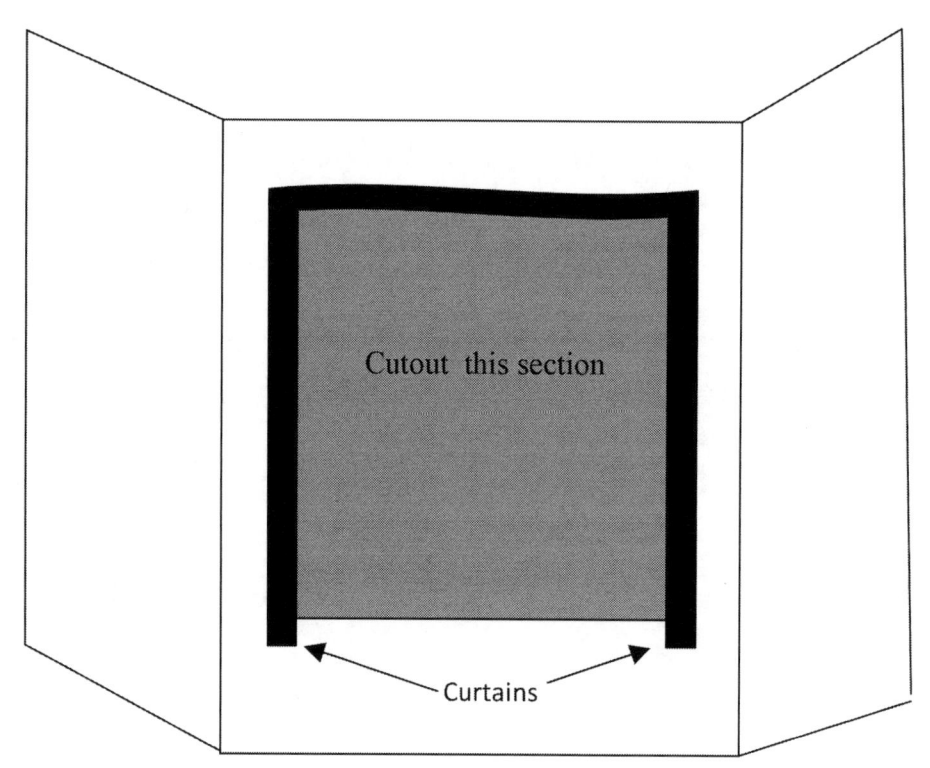

Figure 3.16. Puppet Theater

15
ROLE-PLAY THEATER
Six International Traits of Good Character
M. S. Schiering

Perhaps you'd like to do a role-play theater. In such a case you'd get together with a group of friends, dress in appropriate costumes for the story you'll portray, and act out a scene from the book you've read or scenario selected. This might be acting out a situation that is a common social reality in your school or neighborhood. Several such topics/scenarios that relate to character development and problem solving are presented below.

Remember, the six traits of a person of good character are: respectful, caring, fair, tolerant, responsible, and trustworthy. You are addressing a role-play response in these scenarios that makes it clear you are a person of good character. Also, decide if your role play will be scripted or not as you collaborate with the other actors in your scenario performance. Finally, realize a role play requires animation and gesturing, as well as movement from one place to another as you emphasize your reasoning by answering the scenario problem and/or question. If you choose to do so, once the role play has been completed, ask the viewers to recommend what they might have done in a similar situation.

Scenario 1. There's going to be a birthday party that everyone says will "rock." Looking at the guest list you made, it's obvious that two people have been omitted. The reason you omitted them is because you're concerned that other people in the class don't like them. Your close friend notices the list, and she likes those omitted persons. Role-play your conversation, with your friend challenging you for not inviting those two persons. (The role play needs a solution to the problem.)

Scenario 2. You are standing alone in front of the class about to give a presentation. You are silent for an extended period of time. Suddenly, one of your classmates yells out, "Hey, what's wrong with you?" How do you respond? Should there be others in the role play, and if so what should those persons say?

Scenario 3. It's raining and the class was scheduled to go on a walk around the school grounds. The teacher says that the class can't go because of the bad weather. What do you think is the best way to find an alternative so the class won't be so disappointed? How do you problem-solve when it's clear the walk-about has to be canceled?

Scenario 4. Alex and Gary are going fishing and only one of them has the proper equipment for this activity. What are ways they can enjoy this event without one person feeling left out of the going fishing experience?

Scenario 5. There are three friends at a baseball game and one person has popcorn. You want some of this tasty treat. You reach out and take the popcorn from the person who is holding it in his or her hand. A moment later you think this may have not been the right thing to do. What is the best way to have some popcorn without just taking it from the person holding the box of it?

16
ROLE-PLAY THEATER: HIGH SCHOOL LEVEL
Donna Ferrentello: Croton, New York

While in my senior year of high school, my English teacher asked us to do an "author paper." An author paper is a review of one selected novel or work by the author and relating some of the author's biography with this particular work. I chose Carson McCullers, who was a Southern writer and author of *The Heart Is a Lonely Hunter*.

When our papers were completed, our teacher selected a day that would be our presentation day of our author experience. Instead of having us read our paper or speak about our author in a formal presentation to the class, she asked us to role-play our author in a unique experience. She organized our desks in a number of stations. Each student/author would sit at a different station that had our author's name on a sign. Our teacher provided coffee, tea, juices, and refreshments for the class. Also, she had sent out invitations to the principal, vice-principals, other staff and faculty to attend our "Author Tea" that day.

When people came into the class, they could freely choose which author to visit. They had been instructed to ask us questions such as: Where did you grow up? What influenced your writing of this novel? What is the theme of the novel? Can you tell me something about the plot or characters in it? What is a favorite event or passage from your book? The visitor would then move from table to table interviewing the various authors present.

17
CUTOUT VELCRO STORY MAP
Cathryn Maloney

The story elements are the focus of this workbook page. These include the characters, setting, mood, events, problem, and solution of the story. When you identify these you are dealing with recognizing the main idea, as well as details of the story being addressed.

Directions:

1. Observe the Story Map Elements in figure 3.17.
2. Cut out each section and enlarge it, as you place these on a foam core board.
3. Fill in each section and include the following:
   a. Characters: The name of that person, animal, or object and either a personality trait or relationship to other characters in the story;
   b. Setting: The place the story occurred and if possible the time in which the story took place—years ago, present time, future, or in the moment;
   c. Mood: Feelings expressed in the story;
   d. Events: At least five things that happened sequentially should be provided;
   e. Problem: What situation the main character(s) faced is given;
   f. Solution: The decision that was made by the characters to solve the problem.

The Lion and the Mouse: An Aesop Fable

Once when a Lion was asleep a little Mouse began running up and down upon him; this soon wakened the Lion, who placed his huge paw upon him, and opened his big jaws to swallow him. "Pardon, O King," cried the little Mouse; "forgive me this time, I shall never forget it; who knows but what I may be able to do you a turn some of these days?" The Lion was so tickled at the idea of the Mouse being able to help him that he lifted up his paw and let him go. Sometime after the Lion was caught in a trap, and the hunters who desired to carry him alive to the King, tied him to a tree while they went in search of a wagon to carry him on. Just then the little Mouse happened to pass by, and seeing the sad situation, in which the Lion was, went up to him and soon gnawed away the ropes that bound the King of the Beasts. "Was I not right?" said the little Mouse.

Moral of Aesop's Fable: Little friends may prove great friends.

Your Name_____

Characters

Setting

The Lion and the Mouse

By: Aesop

Events

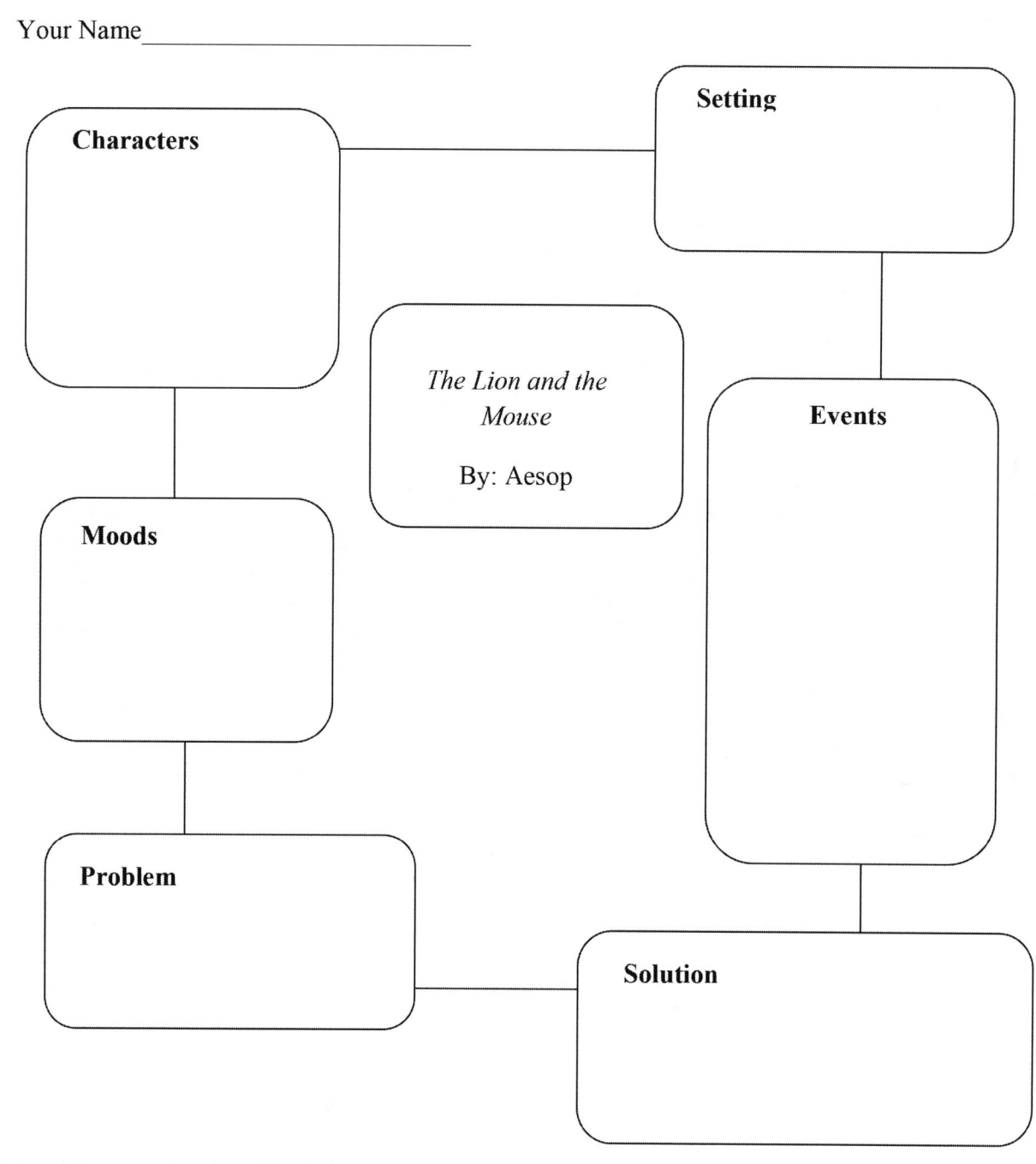

Moods

Problem

Solution

Figure 3.17. Story Map Graphic Organizer

18
MATHEMATIC FLASHCARDS
Meghan Sullivan

Materials: Deck of playing cards, construction paper or cardstock paper, markers, scissors, glue or glue stick

Directions: Trace the outline of a playing card onto the paper of your choice. Then, cut out the card shape and glue it to the side of the playing card without the number on it. Write an equation that has the answer on the back of the card where the number and hearts, diamonds, spades, or clubs appear. Repeat this for as many flashcards you'd like, but at least twenty.

Look at the equation, give an answer to it if playing with a partner or, if alone, do this mentally. Turn the card over and whatever the face value of the playing card is, then that is the answer. Jacks = 20, Queens = 30, Kings = 40, Aces = 1. Examples of this are done with text boxes with numbers and/or words in figure 3.18.

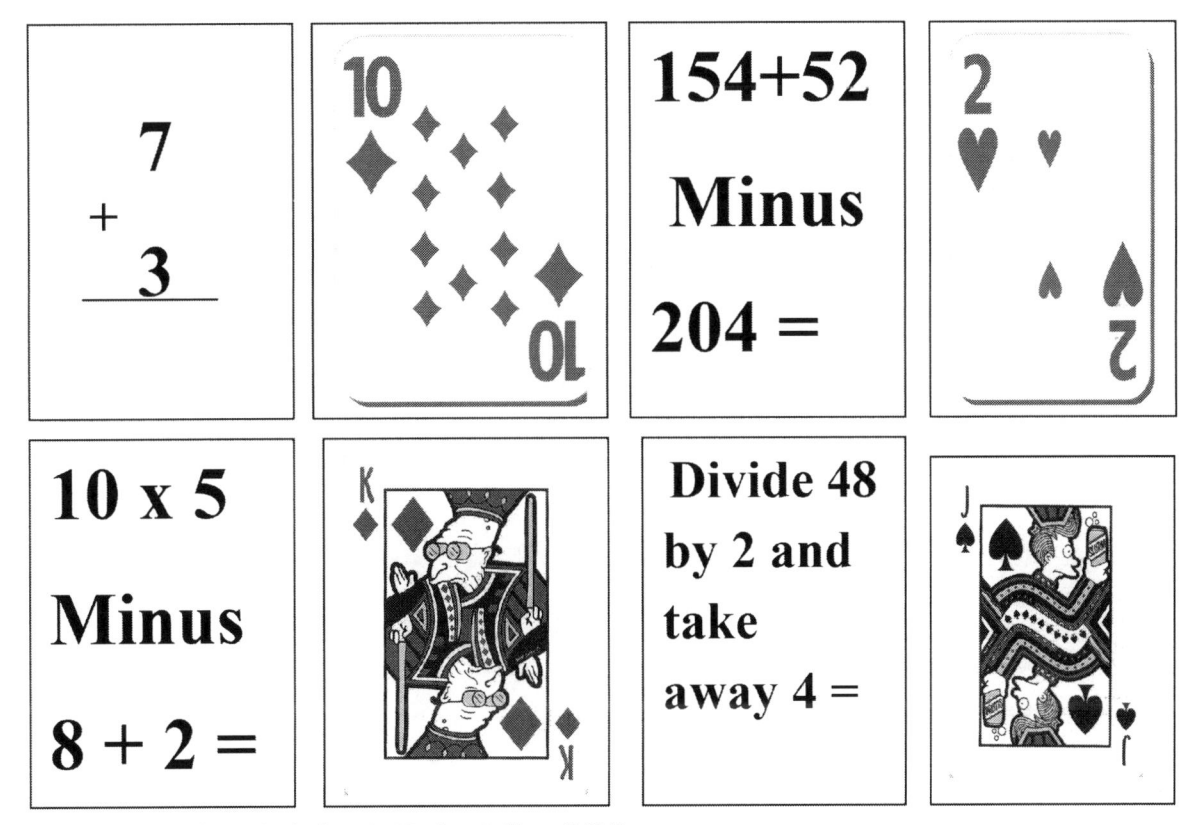

Figure 3.18. Mathematic Flashcards, Meghan Sullivan (2014)

19
NECKLACE SEQUENCE-OF-EVENTS
Danielle Tomlin and Kaitlyn Gaynor

Materials: Different color cardstock paper or index cards, computer paper, yarn in different colors, a one-hole hole puncher, a list of your daily events or book of your choosing.

Directions: You are going to be making necklace sequence-of-story-events cards and/or necklace sequence-of-your-daily-events cards. This is a two-group or whole-class interactive experience.

1. Cut out fifteen 7 × 2½ inch strips of cardstock paper.
2. Record on notebook paper a list of fifteen events from a typical day in your life. (You could use a special event and break it into ten to fifteen segments. Or you may select a book you read and choose the same number of events from that. List these in sequential order.)
3. Using a computer and large font, type these events with the length of the sentence at 6 inches, leaving 1 inch of space above and below each sentence and print them out.
4. Cut out the printed sentences with a measurement of 6 × 2 inches.
5. Punch a hole in each upper-left and upper-right corner of the cardstock strips; that's where the yarn will go.
6. Loop the yarn through each hole and tie so the figure forms a necklace.
7. Paste the sentence strips that have the events on them onto one side of the 7 × 2 inch cardstock paper and put the order of that event on the backside (1, 2, 3, . . . 15). See below for how this will look.
8. The final step is to place the sentence sequence-of-events-necklaces around classmates' necks, designate a person to read the events and arrange the wearers in sequential order. Check the back of the cards to see if you were correct.

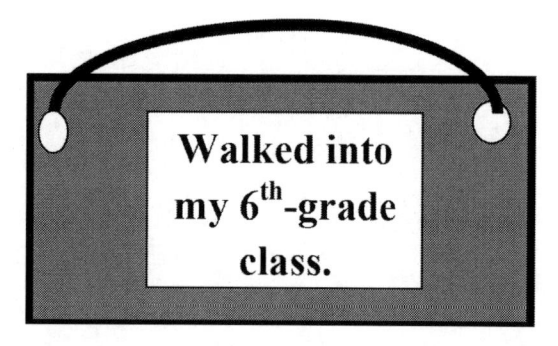

Figure 3.19. Necklace Sequence of Events

20
THE METAMORPHASIS OF A BUTTERFLY
Lauren Spotkov

Metamorphosis is a process that some insects go through before becoming an adult. The process of metamorphosis includes the following four stages:

- Egg: A tiny object that the caterpillar hatches from. The egg is laid on a leaf near the mother butterfly.
- Larva: Another name for the caterpillar once it hatches. The caterpillar's job during this stage is to eat and grow.
- Pupa: Also known as the chrysalis, the pupa is the caterpillar's transformation stage into a butterfly.
- Adult: The last stage of metamorphosis, when the chrysalis cracks, and the butterfly emerges.

Materials: Construction paper, scissors, glue, crayons or markers
Construction Directions:

1. Color in each stage of metamorphosis.
2. Cut out each stage of metamorphosis.
3. Match the pictures of the different stages of metamorphosis in the order in which the stage occurs on each butterfly wing section (Example: The wing labeled #1 will match up with the first stage of metamorphosis, which is the Egg stage).
4. Glue the correct pictures on their corresponding wing-sections.
5. Color in the rest of the butterfly.
6. Cut out the template of the butterfly.
7. Glue the original template onto a piece of construction paper.

Figure 3.20. Butterfly Template

Playing-the-Pages Activities

Pupa:

Egg:

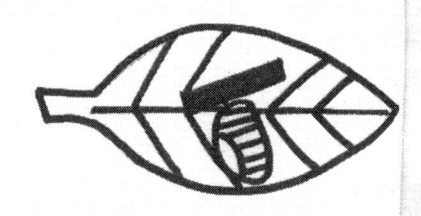

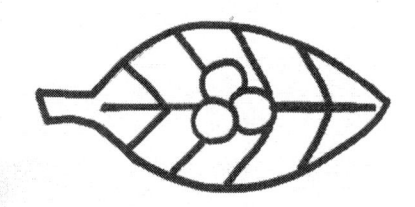

Adult:

Larva:

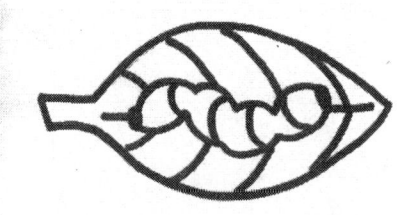

Answer Key:

1. Egg
2. Larva
3. Pupa
4. Adult

Figure 3.21. Stages of a Butterfly Life Cycle

21
LITERARY ELEMENTS for THEME-BASED STORY MAP
Lauren Spotkov

Bubbles, the smiling fish was always happily swimming along in the ocean, but he swam slower than his friends because he had an injured fin. Bubbles always loved going to the Under-the-Sea Academy because he was the smartest fish in his class, and he loved learning about the ocean. One day when Bubbles was playing with his friends, he heard whispers coming from behind the coral reef.

Bubbles swam up to the reef, but as soon as he did, the whispers faded. He then turned around to see two of the biggest, toughest fish in his class talking to his friends about how he was different and not as cool as they were, because of the way he swam. Bubbles's friends stood up for him, but they wondered how Bubbles could be so happy.

Bubbles's friends froze when they saw him and did not say a word because they did not know why Bubbles was so content. Bubbles then swam back to his friends, and they all asked him why he was always so happy. "I am smart, and I like to swim. I don't mind if I swim slower than other fish. Not everyone has to like me, as long as I like myself," said Bubbles. All the fish then began to realize that all of their qualities made them the unique fish that they are.

Story Elements:

- Setting: Where the story takes place.
- Characters: Someone the story revolves around.
- Mood: a state of mind or feeling in the story.
- Events: important things that happen throughout a story.
- Problem/Conflict: Something that the main character has to overcome.
- Solution: How the problem is solved.
- Message: A lesson that can be learned from the story.

Materials: Construction paper, scissors, glue, crayons/markers, and fish template

Construction Directions:

1. Cut out the template of the fish.
2. Glue the template onto a piece of construction paper.
3. Cut out five scales for the fish by using the provided template.
4. Color each scale a different color using crayons or markers.
5. Glue the left-hand corner of each scale onto the template.
6. Identify the literary elements: the setting, the characters, the mood, the events, the problem/conflict, the solution,
7. Lift up each scale and write an example of that literary element in the story.

Figure 3.22. Fish Cutout of Story Map Design

Figure 3.23. Fish Template Story Map

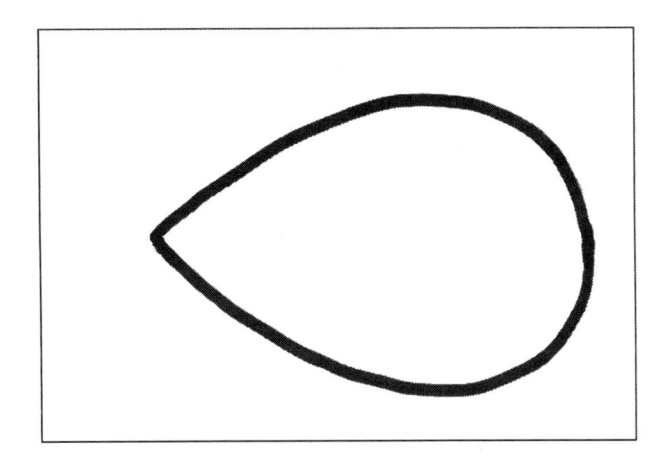

Figure 3.24. Fish Fin for Story Map Element

Suggestion: When you want to write a story think of the literary elements of character, setting, mood, events, problem, and solution. Place these on paper and fill in each section to develop the main components of your story. Be sure to select a topic you like and have action events to create interest in your story. Then, after this is completed, write your story, as all elements will be addressed through your sequencing and organization.

22
PORTRAIT OF ADJECTIVES
Lucia Sapienza

Materials and Directions: In the center of a 5 × 7 or 8 × 10 inch paper-drawn picture frame, draw a self-portrait. When you are finished, along the frame and using a text box, write an adjective about yourself to put in there. If you'd like, use your computer again to make each descriptive word three-dimensional. See figure 3.25. And remember, while you are being creative, to put the word "creative" in the frame.

Figure 3.25. Adjective Portrait

23
MATCH THAT WORD
Cathryn Maloney

Directions: Match the word on the left with the correct definition on the right. Write the letter on the blank line. Then, make this activity into an Electro-Board or Wrap-Around for others to play. (See section 2 for these interactive instructional resource templates and directions.)

Word
___1. Pupils
___2. Gullible
___3. Languish
___4. Triumph
___5. Salutation
___6. Humble
___7. Oblige
___8. Hallowed
___9. Radiant

Definition
A. To waste away or be neglected
B. A greeting showing respect or affection
C. Modest and not proud
D. A person who is taught by another
E. Sacred or holy
F. Believing anything anyone says
G. A great victory, success, or achievement
H. Bright and shining
I. Make someone legally bound to do something

24
PASTA SKELETAL DESIGN
Alyssha Miro

Materials: Different pasta shapes, picture of a human skeleton, black paper, and white pencil for labeling.

Directions: Using a body parts–labeled picture of a human skeletal system and different shapes of pasta, arrange the pasta to match the bones in the human body so you are making your own skeleton. Do this on black construction paper. Then, label the major bones using your white pencil. Be sure to include skull, leg, arm, fingers, etcetera. See photo 3.4 to serve as a guide for this construction. When we're done with the illustrations of the skeletal system, we'll create a hall display of your work. See photo 3.5, which illustrates the hall display.

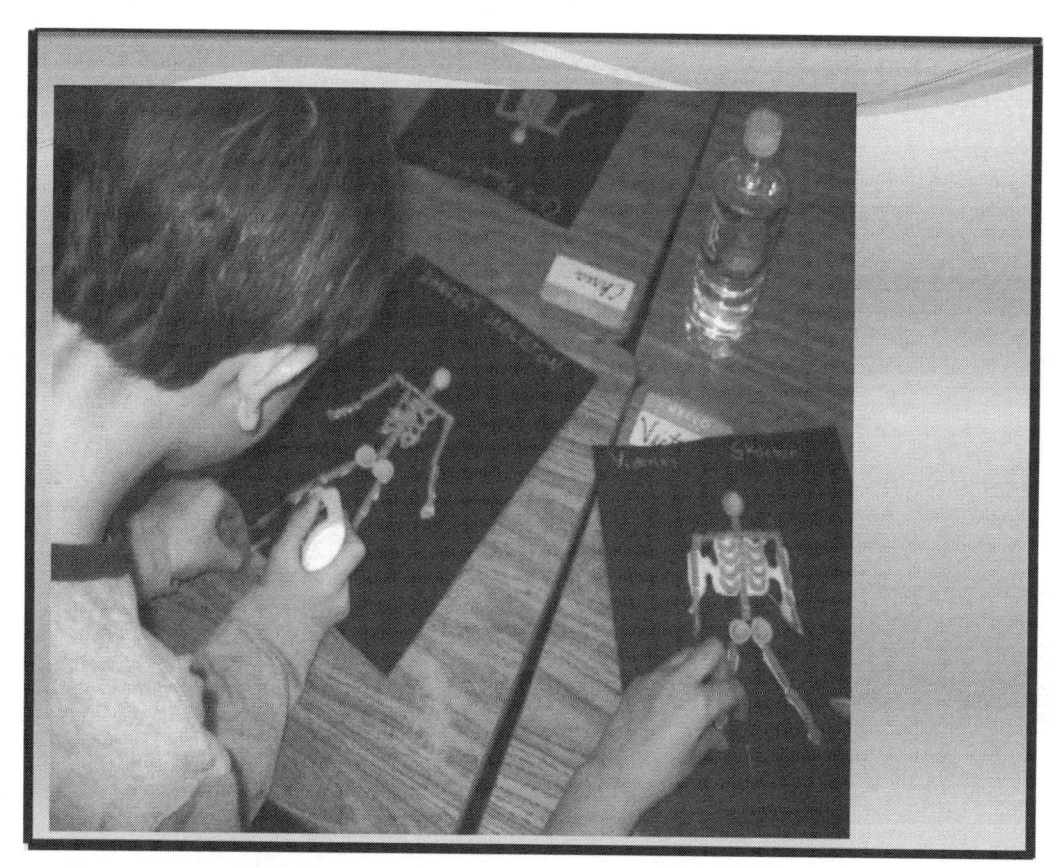

Photo 3.4. Pasta Skeletal Designs

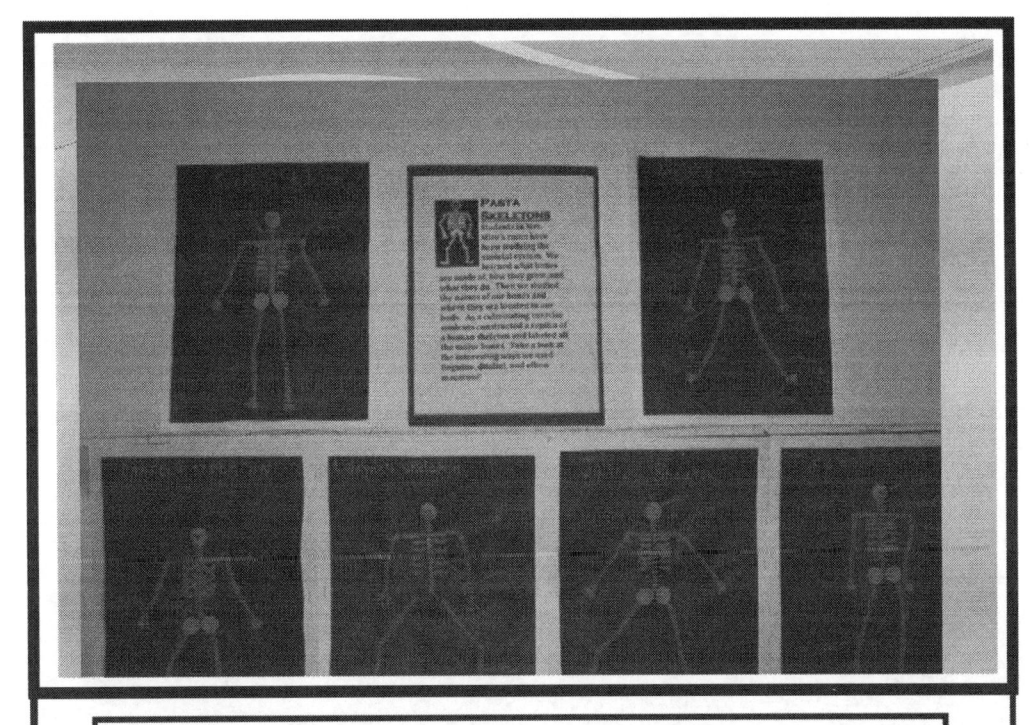

Hall Display of Skeleton system by Mrs. Miro's 4th Graders

Photo 3.5. Wall Display of Pasta Skeletal Designs

Playing-the-Pages Activities 77

25
PHASES of THE MOON
Alyssha Miro

Materials: White cream-filled cookies with a dark-color exterior, computer, and paper.

Directions: Using information from a science textbook or online, find illustrations of the moon phases. At a minimum have the three phases of a full, half, and quarter moon. Then, scoop off the cream part of the cookie to match the moon shapes. See photo 3.6 for an example of this activity.

Photo 3.6. Phases of the Moon

26
CREATING A CONSTELLATION AND CREATIVE WRITING
Jolie Schiering

Materials: One black and one white sheet of construction paper, masking tape, scissors, pencil, and one-hole hole puncher.

Directions: Taking a piece of black construction paper, create a shape on it by drawing with a pencil. Then punch holes along the lines you drew using a hole-puncher, or your pencil's point.

This will be your new constellation, which becomes visible when you put a piece of white construction paper behind the black one. Tape the sides of the white and black paper together. Using your fabulous imagination, think of a story about how your constellation came into the night sky. Write this on notebook paper and tape the writing to the constellation. Hang up your work and share it with someone. A sample constellation and creative writing story appear below. (If you are doing this on a computer you may go to Insert, click on the Shapes button, and choose the star; put these on a filled-in black text box, as seen below. If you do that, then you won't need the white paper.)

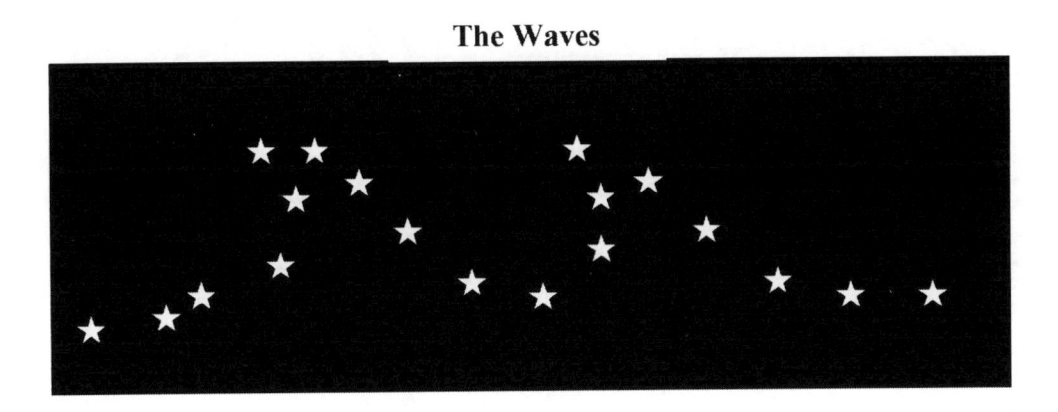

The Waves

A thousand years ago there were two friends who played at the seashore every day. As adults they became fishermen. One day when returning home from fishing, a storm hit and their boat was swept into the sky. It made an impression on all the stars around it before it went back to the earth's ocean and the fishermen were safely home. Ever since then, looking in the night sky, one can see the waves they experienced the day of the storm.

Figure 3.26. Constellation of the Waves

27
CHARACTER MAP
Amy Guerrara O'Hara

Materials: Notebook/lined paper, a story about you, or events from the life of a character in a story you've read, Character Map graphic organizer.

Directions: Create the form shown in figure 3.27a on unlined paper. Select four personality traits of the character you've chosen from a book, or yourself, and then four incidents that support that personality trait. Add border-pictures or decoration for the boxes to make your work especially attractive.

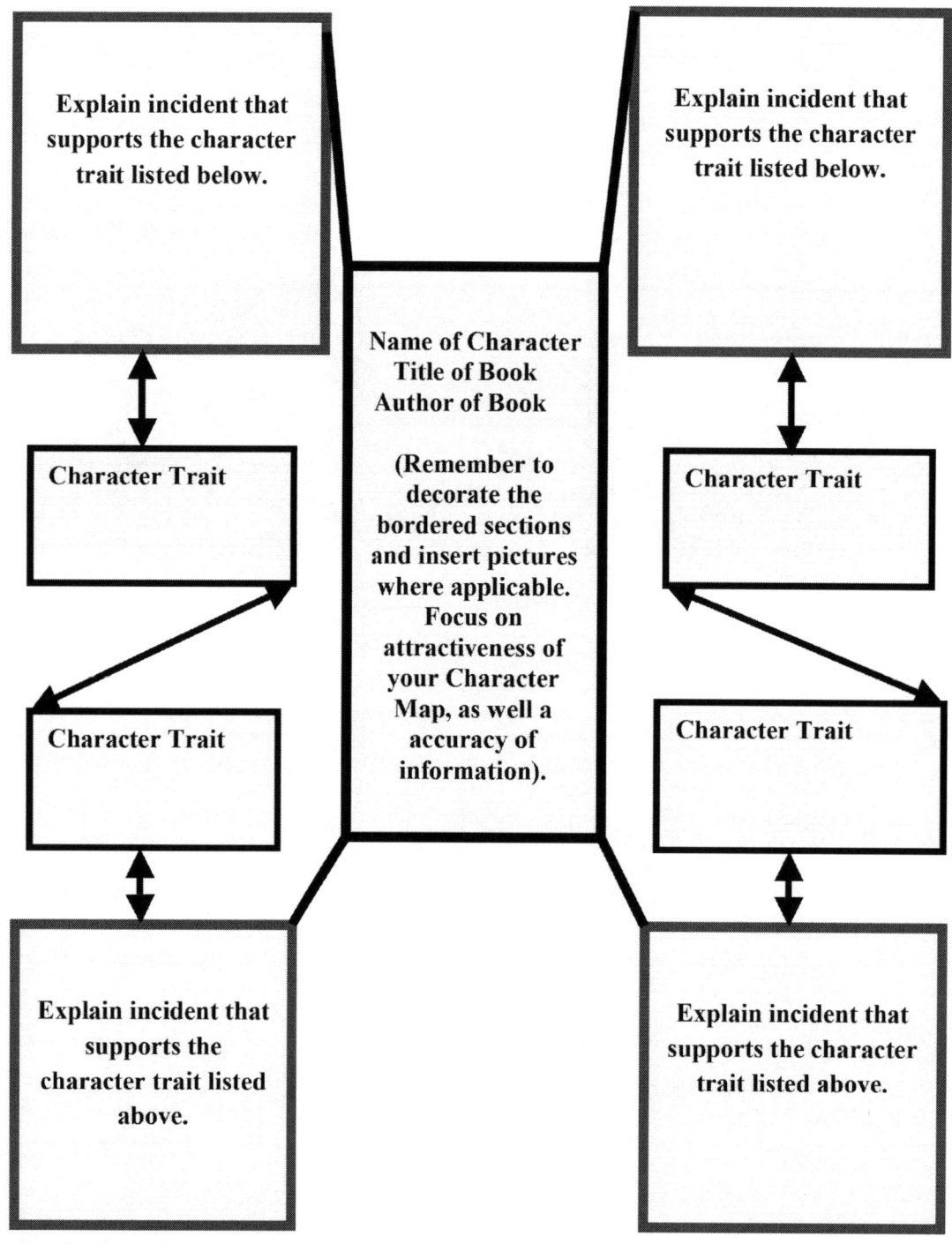

Explain incident that supports the character trait listed below.		Explain incident that supports the character trait listed below.
↕	Name of Character Title of Book Author of Book (Remember to decorate the bordered sections and insert pictures where applicable. Focus on attractiveness of your Character Map, as well a accuracy of information).	↕
Character Trait		Character Trait
Character Trait		Character Trait
↕		↕
Explain incident that supports the character trait listed above.		Explain incident that supports the character trait listed above.

Figure 3.27a.   A: Character Map

28
WRAP YOUR MIND AROUND THIS TIMELINE
Keri Korwan and Jaclyn Shea

Materials: Worksheet with the events and dates from the book *Number the Stars* by Lois Lowry, glue, scissors, cardstock paper, one-hole hole-punch, long piece of yarn, and pencil.

Directions:

1. To create a Wrap-Around Weave Timeline, glue the events to the left side of a piece of cardstock paper and the dates to the right side. It is important to not glue the event and matching date across from each other, so remember to mix them up! Make sure to leave enough room between each event and each date so that all of them can fit on one piece of cardstock paper.
2. After this is done, use a hole-punch to create six circles along both the left and right edges of the cardstock paper. Or, as shown in figure 3.27b, these holes appear directly centered *under* the event and the date.
3. In the top left corner of the cardstock paper, punch one more hole. Make sure it is a complete circle.
4. Using a long piece of yarn, tie a knot through the upper top circle. Put the yarn through the hole at the date that it occurred. Pull it around the back to the next event and continue weaving. Make sure to weave the yarn until all dates are matched with the events or vice versa.
5. When this is completed, use a pencil to trace the pattern made by the yarn on the back of the cardstock paper. This is important, as you will need the yarn to line up with this pattern to make sure that you correctly matched the dates and events.
6. If you don't know the answers when you make this Wrap-Around Weave, then check an encyclopedia or the Internet about "historical dates."

Figure 3.2b. Wrap-around Timeline Weave

Event	Date
Allies invade Normandy, France	March 1933
Denmark falls without a fight, sinking its own navy in Copenhagen Harbor	September 1939
Germany surrenders to Allies	April 1940
The United Kingdom (UK) and France declare war on Germany	December 1941
Japanese Imperial Fleet bombs U.S.A. Pacific Fleet in Pearl Harbor	June 1944
The Third Reich is formed in Germany	May 1945

29
SANDWICH BOARD GUESS WHAT OR GUESS WHO
Dr. Angela Sullivan

Materials and Directions: You'll need duct tape, poster board, crayons and/or markers for drawing, scissors, and Internet pictures. You'll be creating a Sandwich Board for this activity and wearing it over your shoulders. On the back side you'll describe an event, which may be selected from those samples given in figure 3.29. On the other side you are to get a picture off the Internet or draw one that shows what's described on the other side. The object of this activity is to have several people making the Sandwich Boards and then exchange them. Someone describes what's written on the back side of the sandwich board and you guess what you represent. See figure 3.28 for how these Sandwich Boards look and figure 3.29 for one idea about what to put on them.

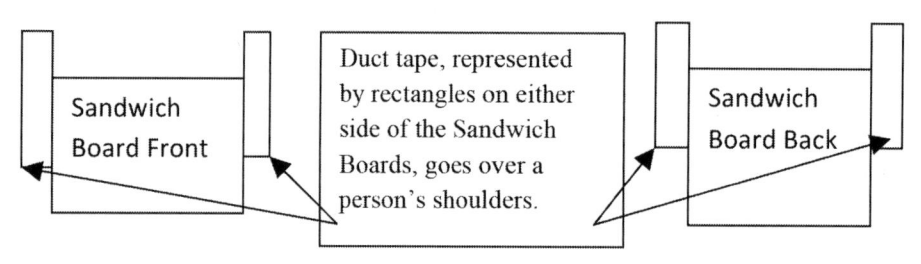

Figure 3.28. Sandwich Boards

The Sandwich Board is worn over one's shoulders. The views in figure 3.28 show the poster board attached to the duct tape in the front and back. See figure 3.29 for information that may go on the front and back of the poster board. These are just suggestions and you might want to make your own with story characters and quotations or a geographical location and name of a state or country. Remember that on the front of the Sandwich Board there needs to be some type of illustration.

Front of Poster-board   *Back of Poster-board*

Type of Cloud   **Description of cloud**

Type of Cloud	Description of cloud
Cirrus	High-level cloud that's Wispy, light, feathery and Signifies fair weather
Nimbus	Low level clouds that are dark grey and signify a storm is coming.
Tornado	Funnel shaped clouds that touch the ground with high-speed winds.

Figure 3.29. Sandwich Board Pictures and Definitions

Playing-the-Pages Activities   83

30
FLIP-CHUTE VOCABULARY MATCH
Keri Korwan and Jaclyn Shea

Directions: Using unlined index cards this activity requires making Flip-Chute cards. Remember to notch the upper-right corner of the 2 × 2½ inch cards. Then, look at the list of words and definitions below. On the side of the card with the notch in the upper-right corner put the word, and then turn the card *upside down* so the notch now appears in the lower-right corner. This is where you write the provided definition. (If you don't have a Flip-Chute then, go to section 2 of this book and follow the directions for making this interactive instructional resource.)

Twenty-one words and definitions:

1. Lanky: tall, thin, and bony
2. Sneering: contorting the face in a way that shows scorn
3. Obstinate: firmly sticking to one's purpose or opinion
4. Impassive: without emotion, calm
5. Suitable: appropriate, fitting, becoming
6. Trousseau: an outfit of clothing for a bride
7. Dawdle: to waste time, move slowly
8. Haughty: proud, snobbish, and arrogant
9. Holster: a sheath-like carrying case for a firearm
10. Suspicious: tending to excite or suspicion
11. Seldom: on only a few occasions; rarely
12. Timid: lacking in courage, or bravery; shy
13. Poised: composed, dignified, and self-assured
14. Surge: a strong, wavelike, rush, or sweep
15. Rummaging: searching thoroughly or actively through
16. Gnarled: bent; twisted
17. Don: to put on or dress in
18. Brusque: abrupt in manner; blunt; rough
19. Insolent: boldly rude or disrespectful
20. Implore: to beg urgently as for aid or mercy
21. Hasty: speedy; quick; hurried

More Flip-Chute ideas: Begin with the side that has the notch on upper-right corner (urc), and then turn the card upside down, which is the side where the notch is in lower-right corner (lrc) position for writing the response/answer.

1. *Who said that?* Take quotes from a book you read. Put a character's quotation on the urc side and on the lrc place the name of the character.
2. *Math magic!* On the "urc" side put an equation for addition, subtraction, multiplication, or division and on the "lrc" put the answer to that equation. Or, you may want to do a word problem on one side and the solution to it on the other. The word problem may call for one or more math functions to be done.

Other ideas: Or, you may want to have a state's name and its abbreviation on the flip side. Another idea for this educational game is to address consonant blends. On one side have a picture of a clown and the other side the word *cl*own with the first two letters or consonant blends *italicized*. Some pictures, words, and italic consonant blends are: (a) picture of a brown circle and *br*own, (b) picture of a sled with *sl*ed on the flip side, (c) picture of a flower and *fl*ower on the other side, (d) picture of a crayon and *cr*ayon on the other side, (e) picture of a glass of water on one side and the word *gl*ass on the other side, (f) picture of someone pushing a baby carriage and on the flip side the word pu*sh*.

Suggestion: Any of the above mentioned Flip-Chute activities could be converted to Task Cards or an Electro-Board. See the next activity as an example.

31
ELECTRO-BOARD MAP!
Danielle Rosenberg and Jaqueline Garay-Cruz

This Electro-Board game allows students to match names of locations to their location on a map in a fun, unique way. A teacher can make an Electro-Board for their students to test their knowledge of locations and the names of these places. These can be the size of a bulletin board or a piece of poster board or notebook paper size. Students can make them as part of a project or assignment.

Materials: cardstock or construction paper, thumbtacks, aluminum foil, masking tape, glue, marker, continuity tester

Directions:

1. Find one or two large, clear pictures of a map of the location you are focusing on. Select five to ten places you would like students to locate. Be sure to select locations that are not too close to each other to avoid confusion.
2. Write the names of the locations in one section of the paper (such as the bottom or to one side) and push a thumbtack next to each written location. Label each location on the back of the paper as well.
3. After gluing the maps onto cardstock or construction paper, push thumbtacks through the spots on the map of the locations that you would like students to locate. After pushing each thumbtack through, be sure to label each location with numbers or letters on the back of the paper.
4. On the back of the piece of cardstock or construction paper, connect the thumbtacks of the matching locations with aluminum foil. Be sure to cover the entire thumbtack. Use masking tape to completely cover the aluminum foil.
5. Use the continuity tester to test each location on the front side to be sure they are matched up correctly. Glue or tape a piece of paper over the back of the cardstock or construction paper so that there's no revealing of the answers to this activity.

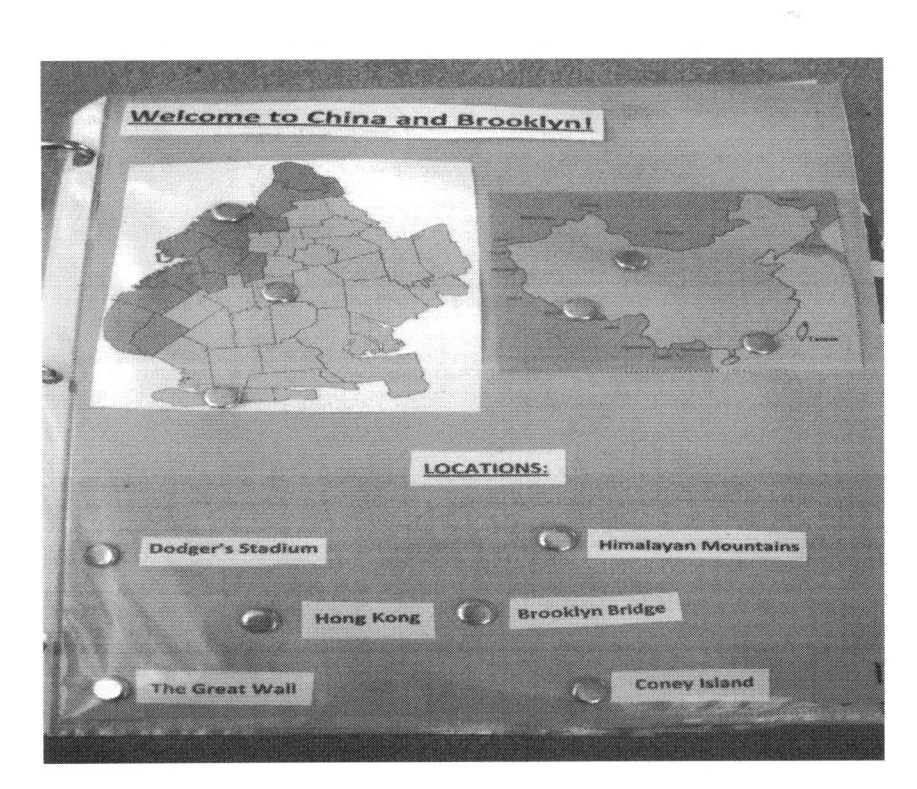

Photo 3.7. Electro-board Geographical Locations: China and Brooklyn, NY

32
THREE-DIMENSIONAL GEO-BOARD WORD SEARCH
Seth Schiering

Materials: You'll need a 12 × 12 or 18 × 24 inch wooden board, pushpins or nails with hammer, rubber bands, hole-puncher, and some cardstock paper.

Directions: Place pushpins in the wood at equal intervals or hammer in nails. See figure 3.30 for spacing of the pins or nails. Put the cardstock paper over the pins or nail-heads. This is called an overlay. Then, put the letters "above" each pin or nail. Be sure to select letters that you know will either vertically, horizontally, diagonally or backwards make words. Place rubber bands around those push pins or nails to show the words on the Word Search.

Another idea: Use the Geo-board without the overlay and use the rubber bands to make shapes such as rectangles, squares, or triangles. See how many geometrical shapes you can make and how many times you make them (Croft and Hess, 1980.

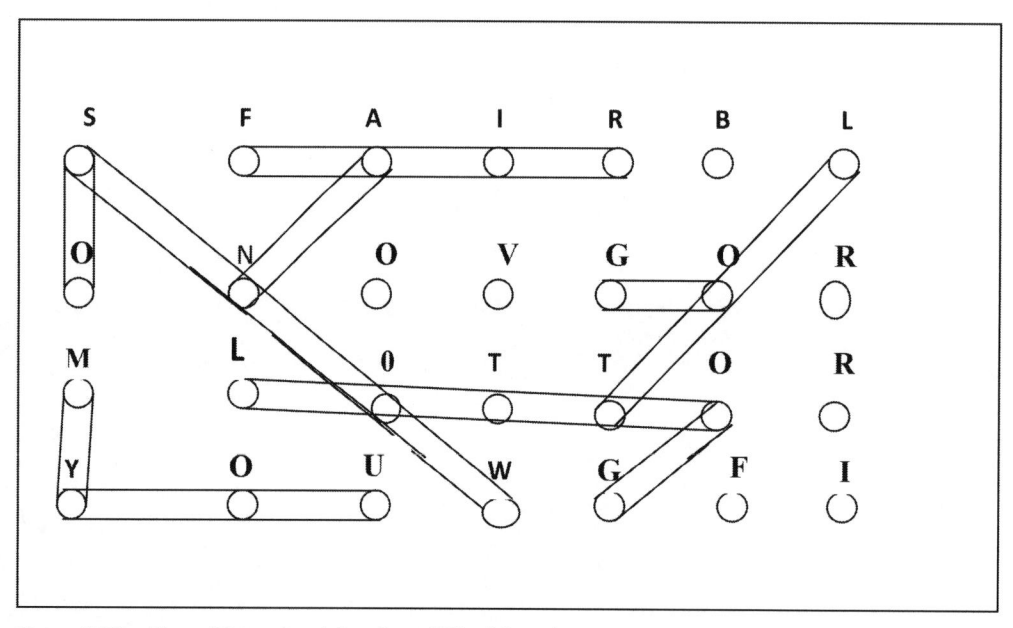

Figure 3.30. Three Dimensional Geo-board Word Search

33
CIRCLE OF KNOWLEDGE
M. S. Schiering

Materials and Directions: Notebook paper, Smart Board, tally sheet, good attitude! This game requires you being in a partnership or small group of three to six persons. The subject area is science and the topic is ecosystems and sustainability. The object is to list, in your groups, in three minutes, all the words related to the topic that you can recall. Choose one group member to be the recorder.

As you go around the room each group states one of the words on their list. A point is given for each item. However, if your group hasn't gone yet and one of the words you have is mentioned, then there is "no point given." The Smart Board (or other board) serves as a tally sheet, and the team with the most points wins. Some words that may be used are: ecologist, biodegradable, rock, lake, succession, trees, recycle, reuse, forest, swamp, pond, hills, plateaus, mountains, and so on.

The Circle of Knowledge may be used with other topics (Circle of Knowledge from Dunn, 1992).

Figure 3.31. Circle of Knowledge

34
NOUNS, VERBS, ADJECTIVES FLOOR GAME: EDU
Kirstin Rochford: Integrated ELA and Reading

Materials: You'll need an 8 × 11 piece of construction paper, thirty 5 × 8 index cards, dark-color magic marker, one shower curtain liner, open area on a floor.

Directions: On ten index cards write a noun: person, place, thing, or idea. On ten index cards write an action verb, which is a word that shows movement, and on the remaining ten cards write adjectives, which are descriptive words. On the back of each card write the part of speech that's on the front of the card. Shuffle the cards.

On the construction paper write the words *Noun, Verb,* and *Adjective,* respectively. Cut these out and put them at the top of the shower curtain liner. Next, draw vertical lines between these from the top of the shower curtain liner to the bottom of it to make columns. Hand the cards to one person, but not more than two persons.

The game player puts the index card in the correct column without looking at the back of the card. This game is self-corrective, as turning over the cards after they've been placed in the column titled *Noun, Verb,* or *Adjective,* the correct part of speech will be revealed. See figure 3.32 for an abbreviated example. Using articles, conjunctions, and/or preposition cards, which you make, see how many nouns, verbs and adjectives you can use to make sentences. (Example from Floor Game: The sister ran to the purple house.)

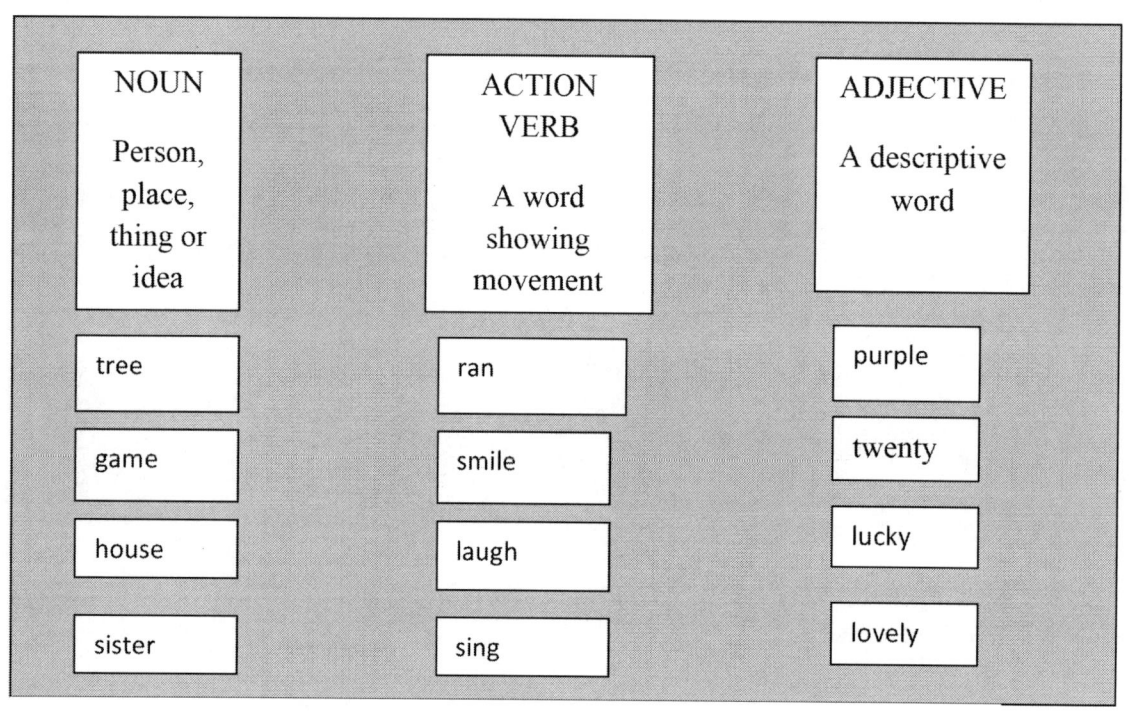

NOUN Person, place, thing or idea	ACTION VERB A word showing movement	ADJECTIVE A descriptive word
tree	ran	purple
game	smile	twenty
house	laugh	lucky
sister	sing	lovely

Figure 3.32. Floor Game: Nouns, Verbs, and Adjectives

35
HOW'S THE WEATHER OUT THERE? TASK CARDS
Nicole Bernard, Nicole DiBlasio, and Jacqueline Gelbart

Materials: Paper folder with two pockets at the bottom, pencil, duct tape, ruler, scissors, Velcro, markers and/or crayons

Directions for Task Card Holder:

1. Open the folder with the pockets facing you (see figure 3.33).
2. Cut the folder in half along the vertical crease.
3. Use a ruler and measure 2 inches from the top of the pocket, as shown in figure 3.34.
4. Now fold the folder along the line you just drew.
5. If there is part of the folder hanging over the bottom, cut it off. The edge should be aligned with the bottom.
6. Decorate your folder to match the theme of the cards inside it.
7. Put a piece of Velcro on the top and bottom of the folder so when you close it, it sticks together.

Directions: After making a Task Card Holder (see figures 3.33 and 3.34) find the definition of the word in the Glossary on page 95. Then see figures 3.35 through 3.39, which are the Task Cards for this activity. Write the definition that goes with the picture on each card (see glossary). Next, cut out the Task Card and also along the dotted line that separates the picture side from the definition side. Now mix up the cards! See if you can remember the weather terms and match the picture to the definition. The words and definitions should match like puzzle pieces.

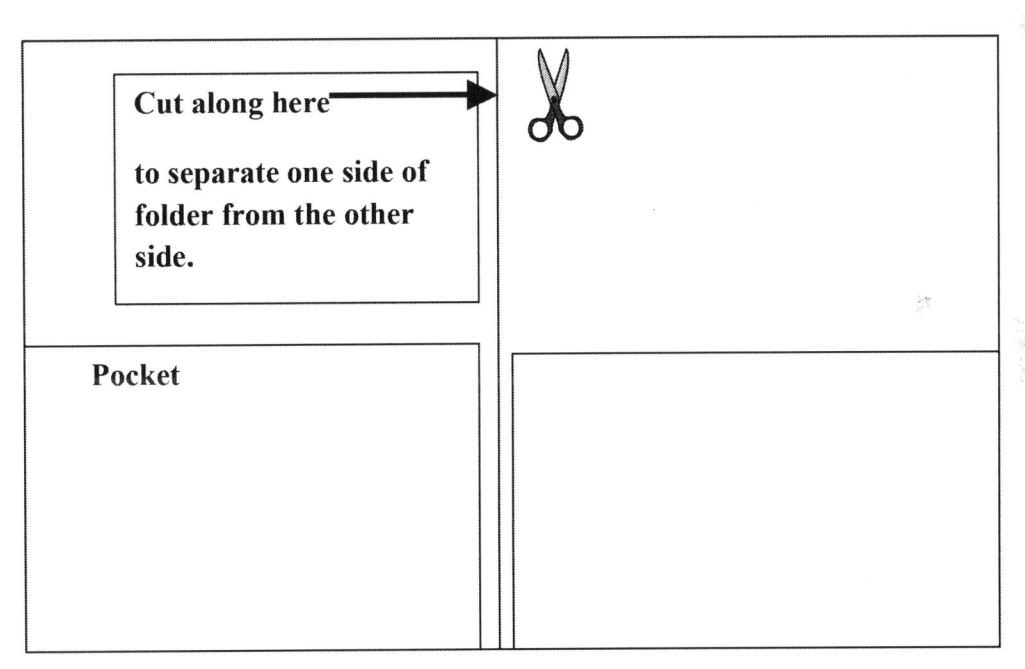

Figure 3.33. Folder

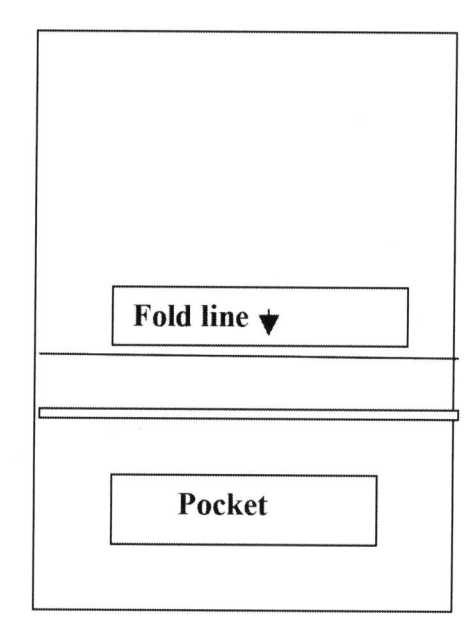

Figure 3.34. Task Card Holder Completed

Fold line ▼

Pocket

Rain

Cumulus Clouds

Condensation

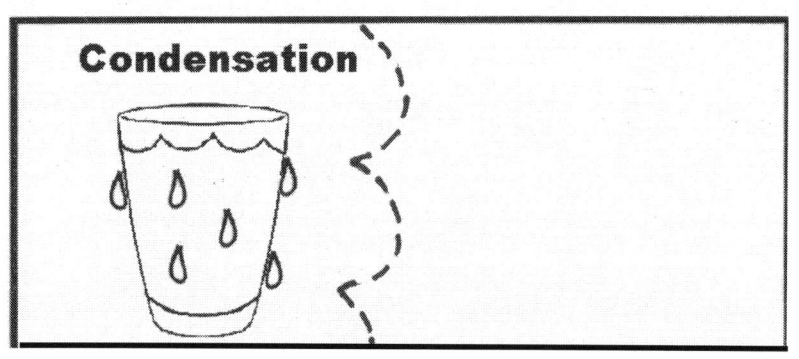

Figure 3.35. Three Weather Task Cards

90   SECTION 3

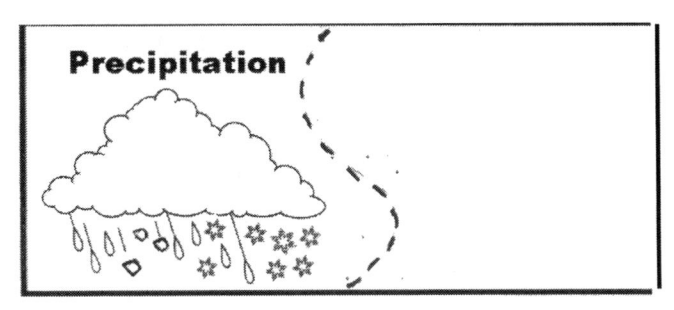

Figure 3.36. Three Weather Task Cards

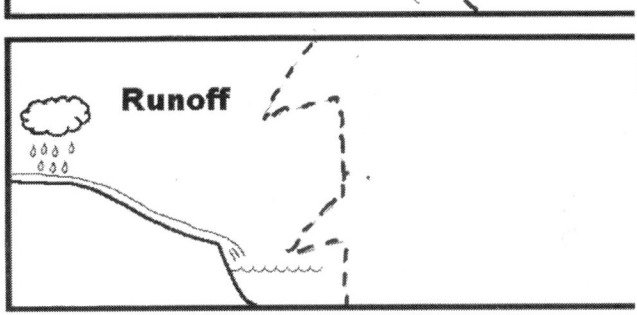

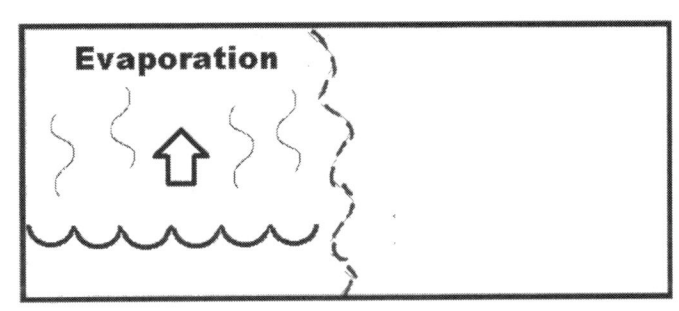

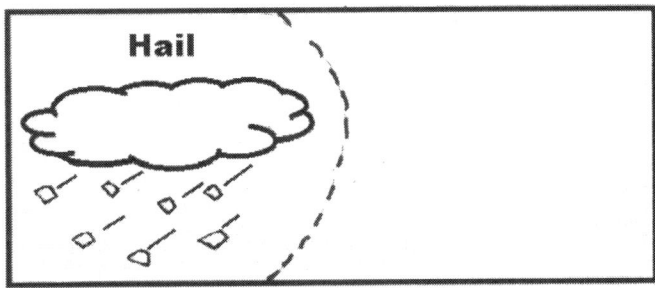

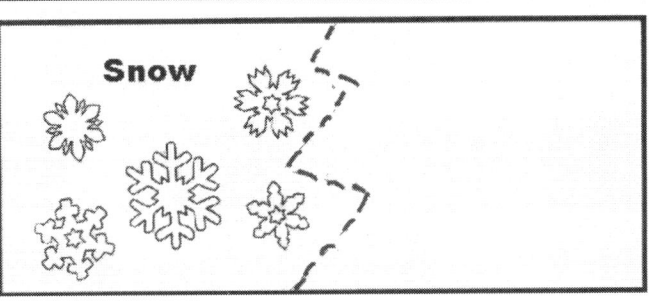

Figure 3.37. Three Weather Task Cards

Playing-the-Pages Activities 91

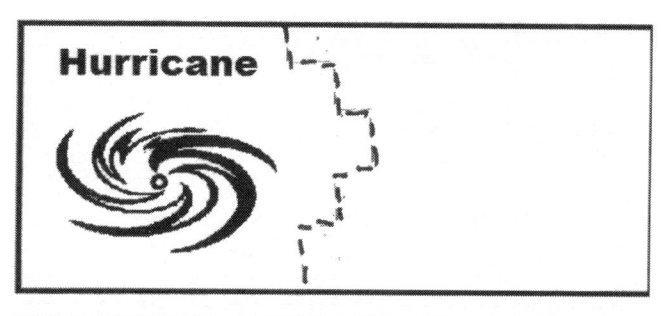

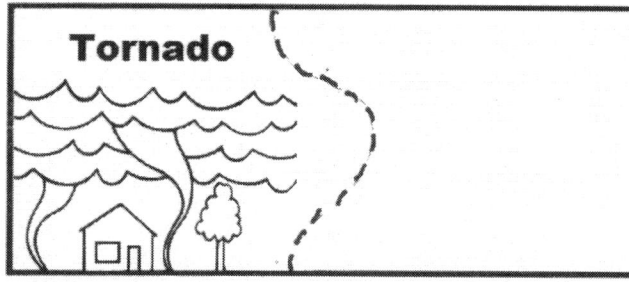

Figure 3.38. Three Weather Task Cards

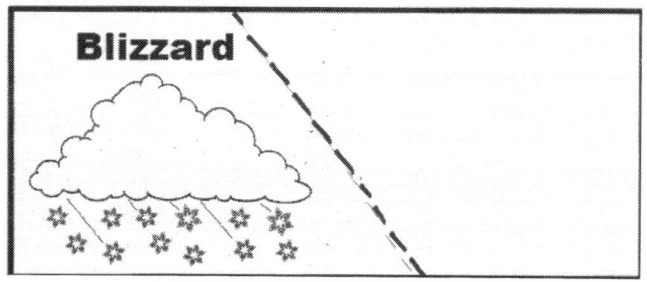

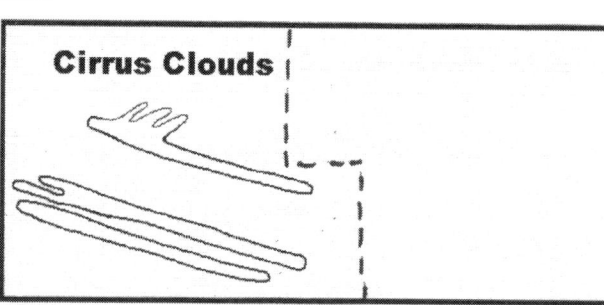

Figure 3.39. Three Weather Task Cards

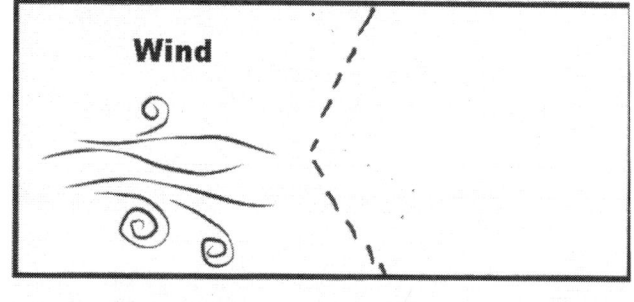

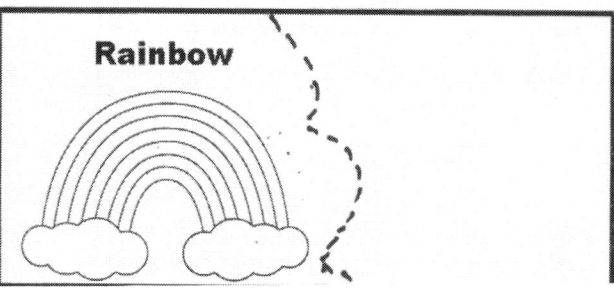

92 SECTION 3

Glossary:

Blizzard: An intense winter storm with falling and/or blowing snow
Cirrus Clouds: High-altitude clouds appearing in the form of strands or threads
Condensation: Water vapor in the air that condenses from a gas into a liquid form
Cumulus Clouds: Large, puffy, white clouds with a flat base
Evaporation: To turn from liquid into vapor
Hail: Pellets of frozen rain
Hurricane: Intense storms with swirling winds up to 150 miles per hour
Precipitation: Water released from clouds in the form of rain, freezing rain, sleet, snow, or hail
Rain: Water vapor in the atmosphere that condenses and falls from the sky to Earth
Rainbow: A colorful arc in the sky, which results from rain and sun
Runoff: Water from rain or snow that flows over the surface of the ground into streams
Snow: A frozen form of precipitation that falls as ice crystals formed into flakes
Stratus Clouds: Low-lying extended gray cloud formations with a relatively flat bottom
Tornado: A funnel cloud between 300 and 2,000 feet wide that travels at a speed of 20 to 45 miles per hour with spinning columns of air that drop down from a severe thunderstorm
Wind: Air as it moves naturally over the surface of the Earth

36
SEQUENCE OF EVENTS
Dr. Donna Ferrantello, High School English Teacher
College Literature and Writing Professor

Sometimes on rainy days, a teacher needs to have creative methods to enhance student motivation and interaction as well as to allow students to have fun. It can become tedious to always ask students to face the challenging work of learning how to write high school essays. For a high school English class, I invented a game-style exercise that gave students practice in learning the basics of good essay form and logical thought development. I called this method "Solving Essay Puzzles."

First, I selected sample age-level, well-constructed, and interesting 500- to 750-word essays on various topics. Then, I took scissors and cut up each essay paragraph by paragraph. Paragraphs for each essay were placed in individual envelopes labeled with the title of the essay. When students came into class, they were instructed to pick an envelope and lay the paragraph pieces out on their desk or table. I asked them to see these disconnected and mixed up paragraph papers as pieces of a single essay puzzle. Their task was to find the sequential and logical order for these paragraphs. The goal was to reproduce the original essay form by connecting all paragraph pieces together. When they completed the possible order of the paragraphs, I gave each student a full copy of the original essay. Students then checked the order of their paragraphs to see if they got the correct coherent form of the essay. Students could work alone and/or also experience working with a partner for their second essay puzzle.

This game-style exercise required different skills to practice: (1) Students needed to identify the main thesis or topic of the essay and select the introductory paragraph that introduced this topic; (2) Students analyzed and identified the sequence of paragraphs by the logic of thought development. This development can be discovered by reading the content of each paragraph and finding transition sentences at the beginning and/or end of well-constructed paragraphs; (3) Students identified the conclusion paragraph that provided closure, short summary, and/or further implications of the essay topic.

My innovative class exercise in learning the elements of a coherent, well-constructed essay created an interactive and fun way to experience reading and analyzing literature by solving a puzzle. It also provided role models of well-written essays and the experience of reading about interesting topics. When the day is rainy and students are at a low ebb, take out your "essay puzzles" and let the game begin!

Another idea is to take an actual blank puzzle and write the sequence of events on the puzzle pieces going from left to right. Students put the puzzle pieces together to form the scope and sequence of the story. Or learners can write on sentence strips the sequence of events and put them on the table for a kinesthetic activity. See next page for sample.

Story: Tom and Sue were at the store to buy fresh fruit. They specifically wanted apples, because they wanted to make an apple pie. First they got the apples, then a pie crust that was ready-made. Next they went home and heated the oven, got out the mixing bowls and recipe book, followed by the ingredients for making the pie. Everything was ready when they were interrupted by the doorbell ringing.

Tom wondered who it could be, but Sue told him that she'd invited her friend Sally over to help make the pie. Tom asked, "Does that mean she gets to eat some of it?" "Of course," said Sue. Tom, Sue, and now Sally worked together to make the apple pie. When it was done they set it on the table to cool for eating later that day. But, Regor, Tom and Sue's dog, had been watching them and figured he'd get some of that pie. He snuck quietly into the kitchen where the pie was cooling on the table. "It smells wonderful," he thought. Just as he placed his front paws on the edge of the table, Sally walked into the room. "What are you doing?" she asked Regor, who got down fast and ran into the other room. Sue and Tom came in to discover that Sally had saved the day! The three of them sat down to have some pie and saved a little for Regor.

Sequence –of-Events Table Game

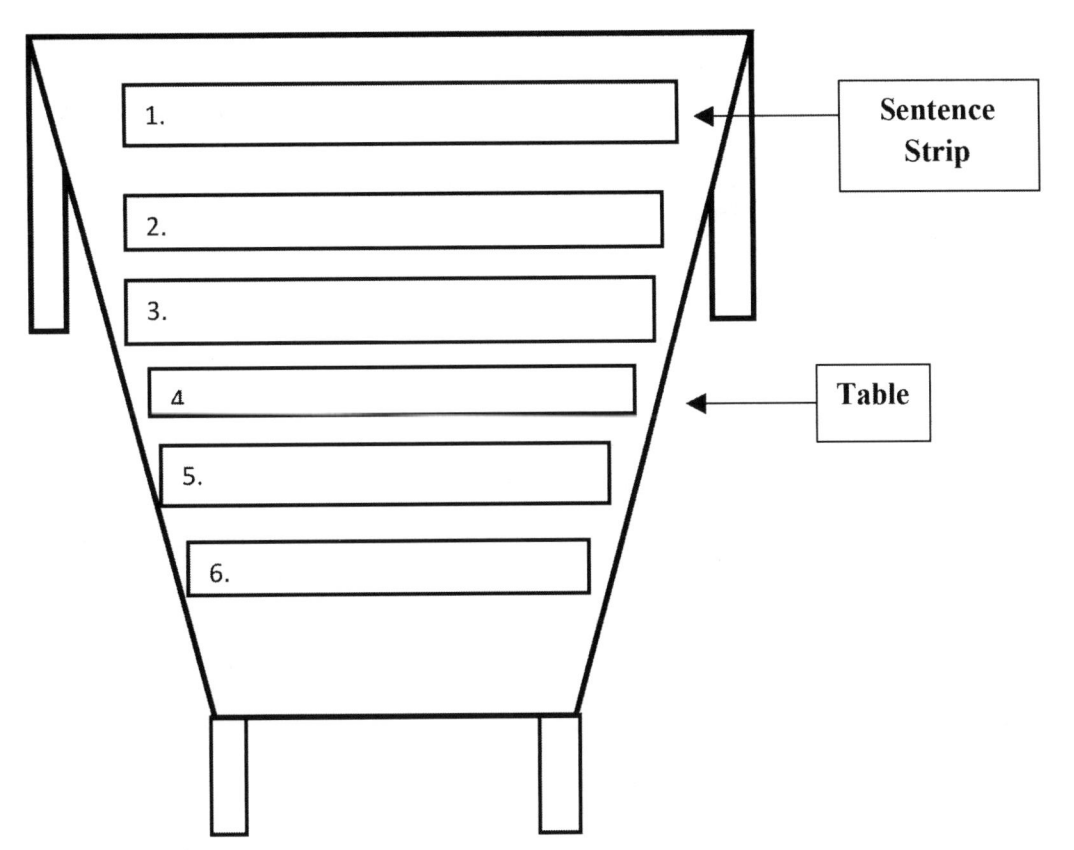

1.
2.
3.
4.
5.
6.

Sentence Strip

Table

Figure 3.40. Sequence of Events

Playing-the-Pages Activities 95

37
MATH PUZZLE
Wyatt Ressa

Directions: Take a piece of 18 × 24 poster board and divide it into a jigsaw puzzle. In each piece put a math problem and answer. Cut apart the puzzle pieces and put the puzzle together for a complete Math Puzzle game.

Photo 3.8. Puzzle Maker Wyatt Ressa

38
SPYGLASS MULTIPLICATION
Anthony Romano

Using a spyglass as a tool to aid students in their comprehension of mathematical facts is both fun and effective. The activity appeals to visual, kinesthetic, and tactile learners and is a partner activity, which promotes communication between peers in an educationally supported environment. To create your own spyglass, follow these steps

Directions for Spyglass:

1. Purchase a cardboard cylindrical tube used for shipping posters and maps, which can be found at a shipping vendor such as USPS. As an alternative you could tightly roll oak tag or use a paper towel roll.
2. Once you have your cylinder, measure it to your desired length.
3. Choose one side to be your viewing side (this is the side the students will look through).
4. Measure 4 inches from the opening and mark it with a pencil.
5. Cut vertically down, preferably with a serrated or sharp fine blade. Cut vertically, as straight as possible, about one-half but no more than three-quarters of the way through the tube. This will be where your question card goes. The students will see this card first.

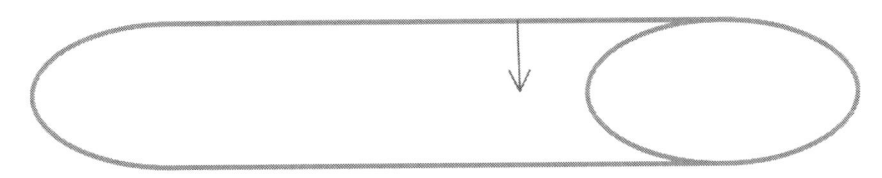

Figure 3.41. Spyglass

6. Now measure 3 to 4 inches behind that cut, farther down the cylinder, and mark that spot.
7. Cut vertically down as you did in step 5. Try to match the previous cut. This is where the answer card goes. When the students lift the first card up the card with the answer will be seen.

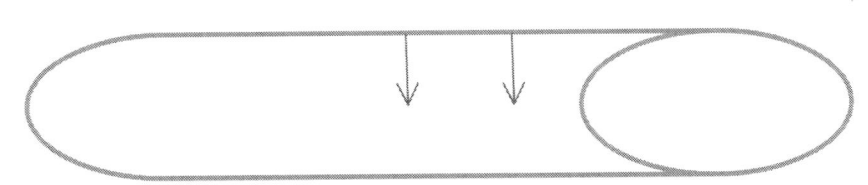

Figure 3.42. Spyglass with Inserts

The reason you are keeping the cuts close is so that you do not compromise the structure of the cylinder and so the cards are not too far from the student's eyes.

Card Construction:

1. Take two large index cards and place them into both slots on the cylinder vertically. See if your cuts match up. (Do the cards look the same or is one uneven? Make adjustments if need be.)
2. Trace on the card the curved line where the card meets the cylinder.

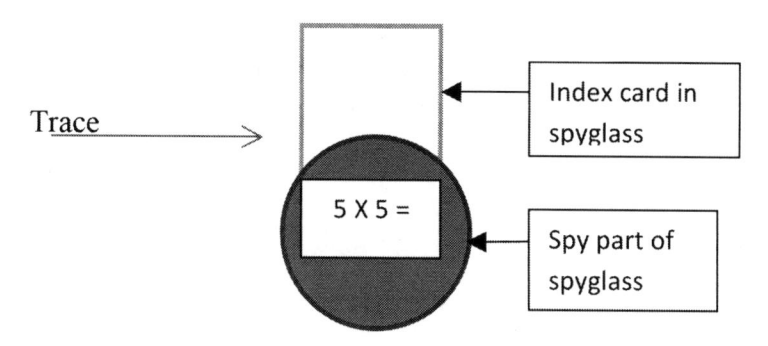

Figure 3.43. Math Card Equation

3. Below this line on the card will be what your students will see.
4. Pull the card out. Draw an arrow pointing downward on the part of the card that was exterior; write a math problem on the part of the card that was interior.
5. When you write the math problem color-coordinate them so that the questions and answers are the same color. This makes the activity self-corrective.
6. Follow the same pattern of tracing to see where to write until you can better judge. Be sure to put an arrow pointing downward on both the question and the answer cards to show direction.

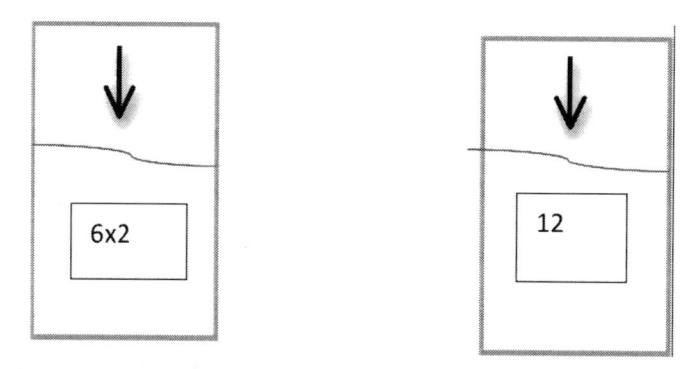

Figure 3.44. Math Card Insert Samples

Directions:
When your spyglass and cards are complete have one student load the cards placing the question in the front spot, closest to the end opening, and the answer directly behind it. Another student will read the question and try to answer it, then pull the first card out to check the answer. This is a partner activity. Hold cylinder a bit away from eye/face so card in first slot closest to your viewing eye can be easily seen. Then, 1.) Answer question orally; 2.) partner pulls out first card to reveal answer on second card that's in second slot.
  Questions:

1. What kind of math problems could you use this activity with?
2. How is this activity self-corrective? Why is that important?
3. What kind of learner does this activity appeal to? Why?
4. Why do you think hands-on partnered activities would benefit students in math?

39
IMMIGRATIONOPOLY (A New Twist on an Old Classic)
Erin Moroney

Immigrationopoly is a twist on the classic Milton Bradley game Monopoly. The object and rules of Immigrationopoly are the same as Monopoly. The object of the game is to become the wealthiest player through buying, renting, and selling property. You will also be given trivia questions in the Tenement Chest and Chance cards. The questions are in reference to our immigration unit and the book, *The Cat Who Escaped from Steerage*, by Evelyn Wilde Mayerson, for ages 8–years. The rules are explicitly outlined, so be sure to keep them out on your desk when you play the game. Unlike Monopoly, Immigrationopoly has a fifty-minute time limit. Before you begin, take a few minutes to thoroughly read through the instructions of the game with your classmates. You'll need to make the equipment cards and game pieces. You'll really need to use your imagination to create game pieces. A suggestion is to use places in the book by Wilde Mayerson. Questions have been provided.

Immigrationopoly Rules:

OBJECT: The object of the game is to become the wealthiest player through buying, renting, and selling of property.

EQUIPMENT: The equipment consists of a board, 2 dice, 8 tokens, 32 houses, and 12 Hotels. There are 16 Chance and 16 Tenement Chest cards, 28 Title Deed cards (one for each property), and play money.

PREPARATION: Place the board on a table and put the Chance and Tenement Chest cards face down on their allotted spaces on the board. Each player chooses one token to travel around the board. Each player is given $1,500 divided as follows: two $500s, two $100s, two $50s, six $20s, five $10s, five $5s, and five $1s. All remaining money and other equipment go to the Bank.

Before starting, the Banker shuffles and cuts the Title Deed cards and deals two to each player. Players immediately pay the Bank the price of the properties dealt to them.

BANKER: You will need to select a Banker who strictly works for the bank.

THE BANK: Besides the Bank's money, the Bank holds the Title Deeds, and the houses and hotels prior to purchase by the players. The Bank pays salaries and bonuses for all questions answered correctly. It sells and auctions properties and hands out the proper Title Deed cards when purchased by a player, it also sells houses and hotels to the players and loans money when required on mortgages.

The Bank collects all taxes, fines, loans, and interest, and the price of all properties it sells and auctions. The Bank *never goes broke*. If the Bank runs out of money, the Banker may issue as much as needed by writing on any ordinary paper.

THE PLAY: Starting with the Banker, each player in turn throws the dice. The player with the highest total starts the play. Place your token on the corner marked "GO," then throw the dice and move your token (*in the direction of the pink arrow*) the number of spaces indicated by the dice.

After you have completed your play, the turn passes to the left. The tokens remain on the spaces occupied and proceed from that point on the player's next turn. Two or more tokens may rest on the same space at the same time.

Depending on the space your token reaches, you may be entitled to buy real estate or other properties, or be obliged to pay rent, pay taxes, draw a Chance or Tenement Chest card, Get Deported, or obtain Free Citizenship.

If you throw doubles, you move your token as usual, the sum of the two dice, and are subject to any privileges or penalties pertaining to the space on which you land. Retaining the dice, throw again and move your token as before. If you throw doubles three times in succession, move your token immediately to the space marked "Get Deported."

GO: Each time a player's token lands on or passes over "GO," whether by throwing the dice or drawing a card, the Banker pays that player a $200 salary. *The $200 is paid only once each time around the board.*

BUYING PROPERTY: Whenever you land on an un-owned property you may buy that property from the Bank at its printed price. You receive the Title Deed card showing ownership. Place the title deed card face up in front of you. If you do not wish to buy the property, the Bank sells it through an auction to the highest bidder. The high bidder pays the Bank the amount of the bid in cash and receives the Title Deed card for that property.

Any player, including the one who declined the option to buy it at the printed price, may bid. Bidding may start at any price.

PAYING RENT: When you land on a property that is owned by another player, the owner collects rent from you in accordance with the list printed on its Title Deed card.

If the property is mortgaged, no rent can be collected. When a property is mortgaged, its Title Deed card is placed face down in front of the owner.

It is an advantage to hold all the Title Deed cards in a color-group (i.e., East Broadway and Park Avenue, or Allen St., East Houston St. and Essex St.) because the owner may then charge double rent for unimproved properties in that color-group. This rule applies to non-mortgaged properties even if another property in that color-group is mortgaged.

It is even more advantageous to have houses or hotels on properties because rents are much higher than for unimproved properties. The owner may not collect the rent if they fail to ask for it before the second player following throws the dice.

CHANCE AND TENEMENT CHEST: When you land on either of these spaces, take the top card from the deck indicated, follow the instructions, and return the card face down to the bottom of the deck.

INCOME TAX: If you land here you have two options: You may estimate your tax at $200 and pay the Bank, or you may pay 10 percent of your total worth to the Bank. Your total worth is all your cash on hand, printed prices of mortgaged and un-mortgaged properties and cost price of all buildings you own.

You must decide which option you will take before you add up your total worth.

GET DEPORTED: You get deported when:

(1) Your token lands on the space marked "Get Deported,"
(2) You throw doubles three times in succession.

When you are deported you cannot collect your $200 salary in that move since, regardless of where your token is on the board, you must move directly into the Great Room. Your turn ends when you are sent to the Great Room.

If you are not "sent to the Great Room" but in the ordinary course of play land on that space, you are "Just Visiting," you incur no penalty, and you move ahead in the usual manner on your next turn. You still are able to collect rent on your properties because you are "Just Visiting."

A player gets out of the Great Room by:

(1) Throwing doubles on any of your next three turns.

If you succeed in doing this you immediately move forward the number of spaces shown by your doubles throw. Even though you had thrown doubles, you do not take another turn.

(2) Paying a fine of $50 before you roll the dice on either of your next two turns.

If you do not throw doubles by your third turn, you must pay the $50 fine. You then get out of the Great Room and immediately move forward the number of spaces shown by your throw.

Even if you are in the Great Room, you may buy and sell property, buy and sell houses and hotels, and collect rents.

FREE CITIZENSHIP: A player landing on this place will receive $20 from the Bank.

HOUSES: When a player owns all the properties in a color-group they may buy houses from the Bank and erect them on those properties.

If you buy one house, you may put it on any one of those properties. The next house you buy must be erected on one of the unimproved properties of this or any other complete color-group you may own. The price you must pay the Bank for each house is shown on your Title Deed card for the property on which you erect the house. The owner still collects double rent from an opponent who lands on the unimproved properties of their complete color-group.

Following the above rules, you may buy and erect at any time as many houses as your judgment and financial standing will allow. But you must build evenly—that is, you cannot erect more than one house on any one property of any color-group until you have built one house on every property of that group. You may then begin on the second row of houses, and so on, up to a limit of four houses to a property. For example, you cannot build three houses on one property if you have only one house on another property of that group.

As you build evenly, you must also break down evenly if you sell houses back to the Bank (see SELLING PROPERTY).

HOTELS: When a player has four houses on each property of a complete color-group, they may buy a hotel from the Bank and erect it on any property of the color-group. They return the four houses from that property to the Bank and pay the price for the hotel as shown on the Title Deed card. Only one hotel may be erected on any one property.

BUILDING SHORTAGES: When the Bank has no houses to sell, players wishing to build must wait for some player to return or sell their houses to the Bank before building. If there are a limited number of houses and hotels available and two or more players wish to buy more than the Bank has, the houses or hotels must be sold at auction to the highest bidder.

SELLING PROPERTY: Unimproved properties, railroads, and utilities (but not buildings) may be sold to any player as a private transaction for any amount the owner can get. However, no property can be sold to another player if buildings are standing on any properties of that color-group. Any buildings so located must be sold back to the Bank before the owner can sell any property of that color-group.

Houses and Hotels may be sold back to the Bank at any time for one-half the price paid for them. All houses on one color-group may be sold at once, or they may be sold one house at a time (one hotel equals five houses), evenly, in reverse of the manner in which they were erected.

MORTGAGES: Unimproved properties can be mortgaged through the Bank at any time. Before an improved property can be mortgaged, all the buildings on all the properties of its color-group must be sold back to the Bank at half price. The mortgage value is printed on each Title Deed card.

No rent can be collected on mortgaged properties or utilities, but rent can be collected on un-mortgaged properties in the same group. In order to lift the mortgage, the owner must pay the Bank the amount of mortgage *plus* 10 percent interest. When all the properties of a color-group are no longer mortgaged, the owner may begin to buy back houses at full price.

The player who mortgages property retains possession of it and no other player may secure it by lifting the mortgage from the Bank. However, the owner may sell this mortgaged property to another player at any agreed price. If you are the new owner, you may lift the mortgage at once if you wish by paying off the mortgage plus 10 percent interest to the Bank. If the mortgage is not lifted at once, you must pay the Bank 10 percent interest when you buy the property and if you lift the mortgage later you must pay the Bank an additional 10 percent interest as well as the amount of the mortgage.

BANKRUPTCY: You are declared bankrupt if you owe more than you can pay either to another player or to the Bank. If your debt is to another player, you must turn over to that player all that you have of value and retire from the game.

In making this settlement, if you own houses or hotels, you must return these to the Bank in exchange for money to the extent of one-half the amount paid for them.

This cash is given to the creditor. If you have mortgaged property you also turn this property over to your creditor, but the new owner must at once pay the Bank the amount of interest on the loan, which is 10 percent of the value of the property.

The new owner who does this may then, at their option, pay the principal or hold the property until some later turn, then lift the mortgage. If they hold property in this way until a later turn, they must pay the interest again upon lifting the mortgage.

Should you owe the Bank, instead of another player, more than you can pay (because of taxes or penalties) even by selling off buildings and mortgaging property, you must turn over all assets to the Bank. In this case, the Bank immediately sells by auction all property so taken, except buildings. A bankrupt player must immediately retire from the game. The last player left in the game wins.

THE RICHEST PLAYER WINS!

The Cat Who Escaped from Steerage Trivia Questions:
1. Yonkel and his family traveled in this section of the steamship when they came to America.
    A. Steerage
    B. Third Class
    C. First Class
2. Another name for Grandmother's tale passed down from generation to generation.
    A. Bubbemesier
    B. Tall tale
    C. Bedtime Story
3. She was the nine-year-old girl who was always getting in trouble.
    A. Rifke
    B. Yonkel
    C. Chanah
4. The country which Yonkel and his family fled for America.
    A. Italy
    B. Germany
    C. Poland
5. Where the $5 was hidden when Yonkel and his family traveled to America.
    A. Yonkel's shoes
    B. A loaf of stale bread
    C. Rifke's purse

6. The family brought this pet in a basket when they were traveling to America.
   A. Dog
   B. Fish
   C. Cat
7. This adjective was used to describe Yonkel in the book.
   A. Mean
   B. Angry
   C. Funny
8. This adjective was used to describe Tante Mima.
   A. Forgetful
   B. Funny
   C. Sad
9. This adjective was used to describe Benjamin.
   A. Devious
   B. Kind
   C. Arrogant
10. The name of the cat who escaped from Steerage.
    A. Pistel
    B. Marty
    C. Fuzzy
11. Yaacov, Chanah's cousin, suffered from this disability.
    A. Autism
    B. Cerebral Palsy
    C. Deafness
12. Chanah threw this out in order to provide a place for Pistel to sleep.
    A. Blanket
    B. Pillow
    C. Coat
13. The place where Rifke washed laundry
    A. Washing machine
    B. Bathroom
    C. Wood Bucket
14. This was the family's eleventh English word.
    A. Boat
    B. Infirmary
    C. Thank you
15. The captain on the ship christened the Russian baby.
    True
    False
16. Who was the first person to step on American soil?
    A. Yonkel
    B. Rifke
    C. The Russian baby
17. Samuel, Chanah's brother, insisted on going with Chanah and Yaacov to the kennel to look for the cat
    True
    False
18. How did the officer at Ellis Island know Yaacov was deaf?
    A. He clapped his hands
    B. He threw a book
    C. He yelled at the boy

19. What did Schmuel steal a tin of and hide under his shirt?
    A. Cups
    B. Cats
    C. Biscuits
20. Kerosene was used in Chanah's hair to prevent ring worm.
    True
    False
21. Silver cups were tucked tightly into two loaves of bread when the family traveled to America.
    True
    False
22. The name of the woman holding a torch in one hand and clutching a book in the other
    A. Ellis Island
    B. Statue of Liberty
    C. Mona Lisa
23. Chanah and her family were taken to a ferry that would bring them to Ellis Island.
    True
    False
24. The ferry ride was about two hours long.
    True
    False (15 minutes)
25. The number of questions the inspector asked them in the great hall.
    A. 50
    B. 76
    C. 29
26. Spigot can be defined as
    A. A Basket
    B. A place for holding water
    C. A small peg or plug for stopping the vent of a cask.
27. Knickers can be defined as
    A. A shirt worn by men
    B. A baby's outfit
    C. Loose-fitting short trousers gathered in at the knees
28. Steerage can be defined as
    A. Where the cattle are held in a barn
    B. (In a passenger ship) the part or accommodations allotted to the passengers who travel at the cheapest rate
    C. The place where the wealthiest people sleep
29. Two reasons that people immigrated to Ellis Island during the turn of the century
    A. Religious freedom and job opportunities
    B. Vacation and relaxation
    C. Discovery and new inventions
30. Throng can be defined as
    A. A toy used at the turn of the century
    B. A part of the ship
    C. A multitude of people crowded or assembled together; crowd
31. Yaacov was returned to Poland because he was deaf.
    True
    False (He was not returned because Chanah intervened)
32. The officials questioned Yonkel and Rifke to confirm if they were married.
    True
    False

Playing-the-Pages Activities

33. Yonkel and his family stopped in this city before they left for New Jersey.
    A. Atlantic City
    B. New York City
    C. Boston
34. The place where Yonkel would work when he arrived in New Jersey.
    A. An office building
    B. A farm
    C. A movie theater
35. The number of years which Raziel had not seen her husband, Shimson.
    A. 10
    B. 5
    C. 2
36. Yonkel, unlike Shimson, wanted his daughters to get an education in America.
    True
    False
37. In the end, Pistel was returned to Chanah in New York in this item.
    A. A cardboard box
    B. A hat box
    C. A cigarette box

Ellis Island Book Questions:

38. This word best describes the steerage section.
    A. Beautiful
    B. Spacious
    C. Crowded
39. This is the first landmark most immigrants saw when they first arrived in New York Harbor.
    A. The Empire State Building
    B. Statue of Liberty
    C. Great Hall at Ellis Island
40. Black bread, boiled potatoes, and watery soup made up the diet for the population in steerage.
    True
    False
41. Over 1 million people immigrated through Ellis Island while its doors were open.
    True
    False
42. X marked on someone's collar was a sign for the doctor to check what?
    A. The immigrant had whooping cough
    B. The immigrant was lame
    C. The immigrant may have a mental defect
43. The highly contagious eye disease that doctors checked immigrants for when passing through Ellis Island.
    A. Trachoma
    B. Lice
    C. Heart Disease
44. The continent most immigrants came from during the turn of the century.
    A. North America
    B. Europe
    C. Asia
45. The age at which a child may be sent back to their country of origin alone.
    A. 5
    B. 10
    C. 15

46. About two out of every one hundred immigrants were sent home.
    True
    False
47. People's names were changed in the noise and confusion that took place on Ellis Island.
    True
    False
48. This was the name of Ellis Island before it became Ellis Island.
    A. Gull Island
    B. Island of Hope
    C. Gibbet Island
49. Ellis Island was named for this American merchant.
    A. Peter Ellis
    B. Mark Ellis
    C. Samuel Ellis
50. The reason why the Irish immigrated to America.
    A. Sheep were available in abundance
    B. The potato crop failed
    C. They wanted to join the army
51. The day Ellis Island opened its doors
    A. March 5, 1885
    B. August 10, 1895
    C. January 1, 1892
52. This was the cause of destruction to Ellis Island in 1897.
    A. Flood
    B. Fire
    C. Gas explosion
53. The year Ellis Island closed
    A. 1950
    B. 1975
    C. 1930

Photo 3.9. Immigrationopoly goes here

Playing-the-Pages Activities 105

The Answer Key is: A, A, C, C, A, C, C, A, C, A, C, B, C, B, True, A, C, True, True, A, True, False, C, B, C, B, A, C, False, True, B, B, C, B, C, B, True, True, C, A, B, B, True, True, C, C, B, C, B, A.

40
CHIRP GAME
Jennifer Herdmian

Materials and Directions: Mathematical strips, pen or pencil, scissors, and scrap paper. Setting up the game involves cutting out the strips of mathematical facts in the figure below. Once all of the strips are cut out, place the strips in a big pile, nonsequentially.

The first player will select a strip at random and solve the problem. All work must be shown on scrap paper and explained. If any player disagrees with the final solution, all players need to individually complete the problem. Then, all players will discuss their findings. Correct answers result in keeping the mathematical strip. Incorrect answers cause the players to place all of their strips back into the center.

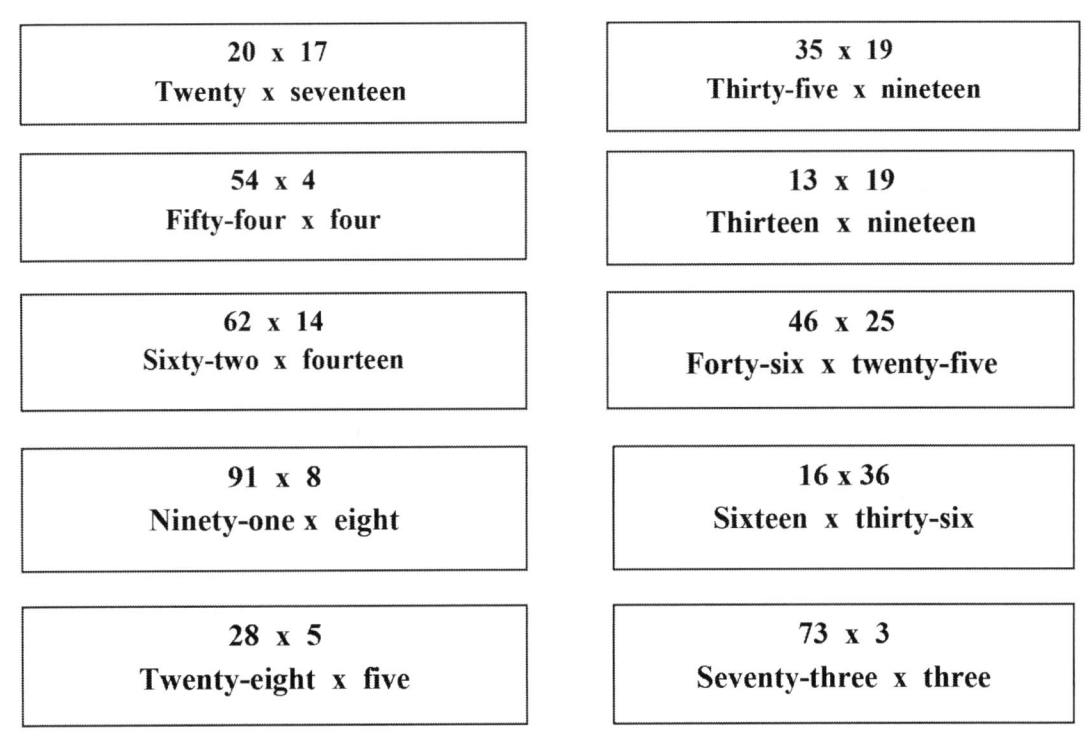

20 x 17 Twenty x seventeen	35 x 19 Thirty-five x nineteen
54 x 4 Fifty-four x four	13 x 19 Thirteen x nineteen
62 x 14 Sixty-two x fourteen	46 x 25 Forty-six x twenty-five
91 x 8 Ninety-one x eight	16 x 36 Sixteen x thirty-six
28 x 5 Twenty-eight x five	73 x 3 Seventy-three x three

Figure 3.45. Chirp Game

41
FROM EQUATIONS TO LETTERS TO MESSAGE
Marjorie Schiering

A Special Message from Max Lucado's book *You Are Special*

Add those Stars...Erase those Dots
MATH

Punchinello received a lot of dots from Wemmicks in his village. He didn't like this, as you know. Below are 13 addition and/or subtraction problems See how many you can solve and then match the answer numbers with the corresponding letters to receive a message all about you!

Key: a/1, b/2, c/3, d/4, e/5, f/6, g/7, h/8, i/9, j/10/ k/11, l/12/, m/13, n/14, o/15, p/16, q/17, r/18, s/19, t/20, u/21, v/22, w/23, x/24, y/25, z/26.

1. 10 + 15 = ___
2. 25 - 10 = ___
3. 17 + 4 = ___

4. 1 - 0 = ___
5. 9 + 9 = ___
6. 23 - 20 = ___

7. 30 - 11 = ___
8. 7 + 9 = ___
9. 51 - 46 = ___
10. 44 - 41 = ___
11. 4 + 5 = ___
12. 1 + 0 = ___
13. 6 + 6 = ___

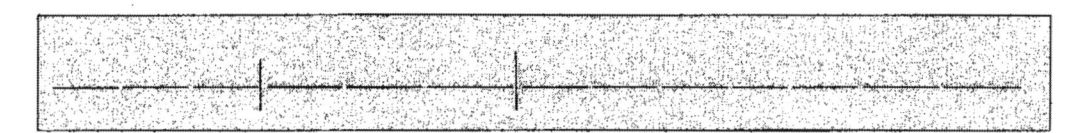

Figure 3.46. From Equations to Letters to Message

42
Electro-Board European Countries and Capitals
Blaire and Casi Borut

This educational game is a fun way for you to learn about Europe's geography. As the fifth activity in this IBR revolving around Roald Dahl's book *The BFG*, the third setting of the story is in the Queen of England's castle, as you know. The place where the story took place is important and the following Electro-Board gives you the chance to match places in Europe we've talked about in class with their capital cities. Use a continuity tester to make the match. If the light lights you are correct. To make your own Electro-board refer back to section 2 for directions.

This activity will give you the chance to reinforce your knowledge of these new places. The skills you'll be addressing are:

- *Realizing* and *recognizing* the places where this story took place;
- *Classifying* countries and capitals;
- *Initial* and *Advanced Deciding* which is a capital city and which is the country as you compare and contrast names of each location given;
- *Predicting* where to place the continuity tester to see if your answer is correct;
- *Communicating* with others as you are discerning the answer;
- *Evaluating* your familiarity and/or knowledge-base regarding the topic;
- *Generalizing* that these are countries and which are capitals;
- *Recalling* and reflecting on the names of the countries and capitals;
- *Self-actuating* when you play-the-page (Match 1, 2, 3, 4, 5 and 5, 4, 3, 2, 1).

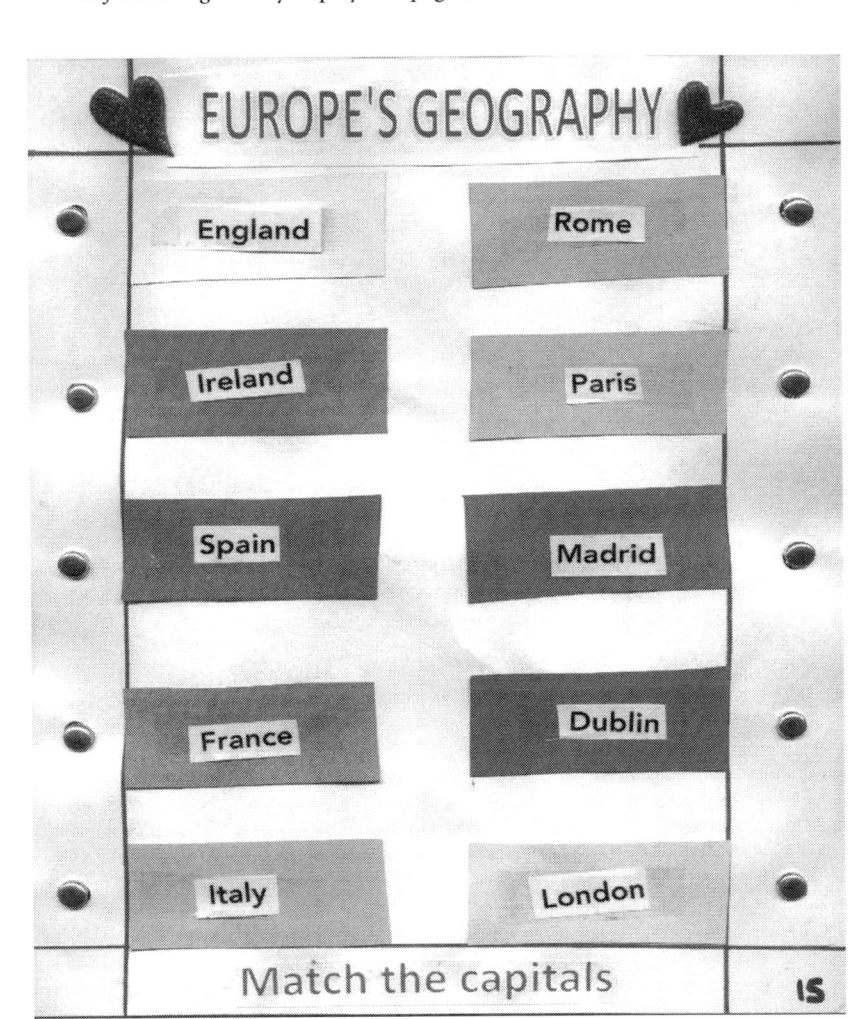

Figure 3.47. European Countries and Capitals

Playing-the-Pages Activities

43
Golden Star Graph Reading from *You Are Special* by Max Lucado IBR
M. Schiering

ONE CLASSROOM/LIFE RULE

NO put downs...ONLY LIFT UPS

GOLDEN STAR GRAPH

Punchinello received dots while other Wemmicks received Stars. If we all had a classroom or life rule of "No Put downs....ONLY Lift UPS (Schiering, 1976) think how positive our life would be! We could learn to make statements that made people feel better, or good about him/herself. There would be no grey dots for anyone; just stars!

On the back of this sheet are ten bar-graph questions. Use the graph below to find the answers to these questions. Then, on the graph paper provided, try making your own bar-graph. Of course you could make a circle/pie, or line graph. Remember to title your graph and label the "X" and "Y" axis. It's time to have fun practicing your graphing skills!

GOLDEN STARS ONLY

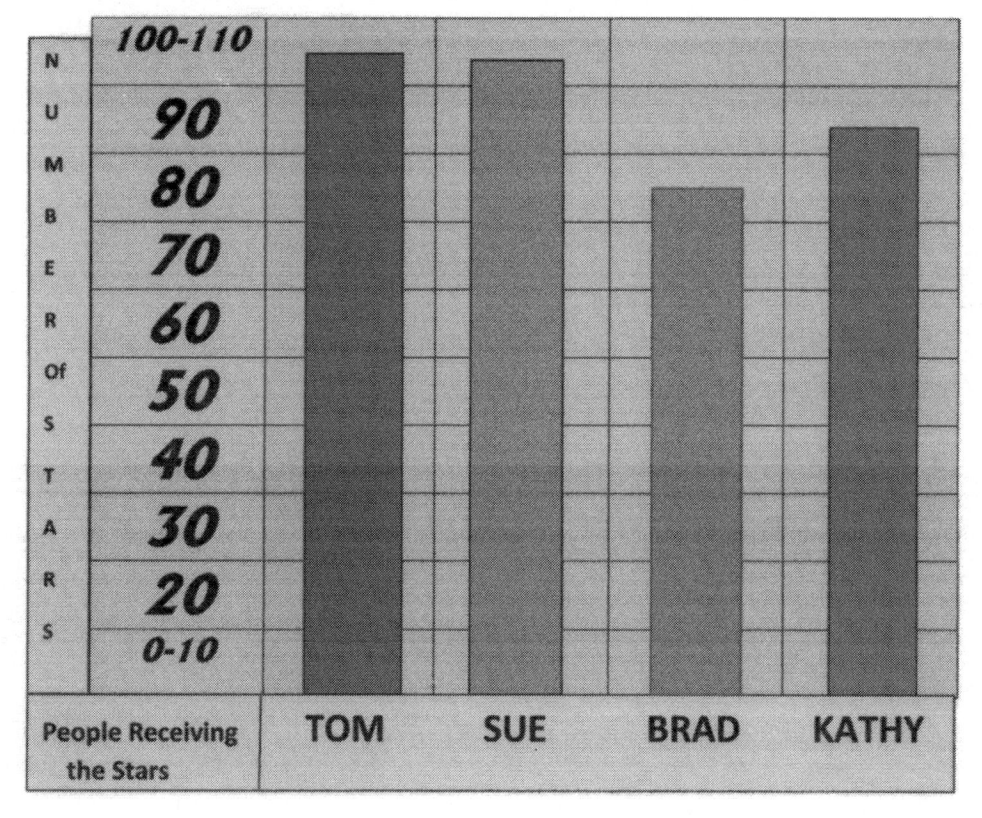

Number of Stars	TOM	SUE	BRAD	KATHY
100-110				
90				
80				
70				
60				
50				
40				
30				
20				
0-10				
People Receiving the Stars	TOM	SUE	BRAD	KATHY

Figure 3.48. Golden Star Graph

"GOLDEN STARS ONLY"

Directions: Use the graph on the previous page to answer these questions by filling in the blank spaces.

1. Tom has _____ stars, which is _____ stars more than Sue.

2. Brad has _____ stars, which is _____ less than Kathy.

3. Kathy has _____ stars.

4. If Brad were to have _____ stars, this would be 5 more than _____.

5. Tom received _____ stars.

6. Sue has _____ stars.

7. Kathy has _____ stars, which is _____ more than Brad.

8. _____ has the most stars.

9. If you were on this graph you'd have _____ stars. Why? _____

10. There are _____ stars in all represented on this graph.

(Answers to these questions appear below. Just lift the flap and see how it goes. If you disagree with an answer ask a friend to see if you can reach consensus. Explain your reasons for the answers you selected).

1). 105/1. 2). 85/7. 3). 93. 4). 98/Kathy. 5). 95. 6). 104. 7). 93/8 8). Tom. 9). 110 10. 387

Figure 3.49. Golden Star Graph Questions

44
SEASONS OF THE YEAR DRESS-UP
Danielle Voltmer and Dana Defliese

Do you know what clothing is appropriate to wear for different seasons of the year? Would you wear a raincoat in the summer when the sun is shining? Would you wear a snowsuit when it's the autumn season and the sun is shining? The answer to these questions is "No." How you know that is from experiences you've had since you were little and someone dressed you in accordance with the weather. Rainy weather means you'd be in a raincoat. A hot day in June would mean you'd be in shorts and a T-shirt or less clothing than you'd wear if it were snowing outside.

Not all of us live in an area that has four seasons of summer, fall, winter, and spring. Some areas have only a warm and cool season, or a wet and dry one. Regardless, let's review the weather and corresponding clothing type worn during the summer by using the dress-up cutout in figure 3.50. Then, using the Clothing Page figure 3.51, cut out the clothes the girl figure would wear during the summer season depending on a sunny weather condition.

On your own or with a small group make a few friend figures and draw clothing to match the fall, winter, and spring seasons. Now, dress the figures in those clothing cutouts you created. Share these with others. Another idea: Mount the people figures on a drinking straw and create a role-play puppet show for your class. See figure 3.16 for how to make a Puppet Theater.

Thinking skills used for this activity include: Recognizing the season and the clothing, realizing what's to be worn, classifying the seasons and types of clothing as you compare and contrast these. Then, there's communicating this by dressing the figures provided, inventing your own clothing for the additional seasons, initial and advanced deciding on what is to be worn, analyzing your selections, recalling and reflecting on the seasons, and self-actuating when dressing the figures.

Figure 3.50. Seasons of the Year Dress Up Holly

Figure 3.51. Season of the Year Clothing

45
THE FOUR SEASONS: CLOZE READING
Alexandra Falconieri and Michelle Gould

Directions: There are ten parts-of-speech words missing from these paragraphs. Look at the boxed words at the bottom of the page and see if you can select and fill-in the correct one for each missing Noun, Verb, or Adjective space. Correct answers appear at the bottom of Activity 51.

There are four seasons in the northeastern part of the United States. These are fall/autumn, winter, spring, and summer. Each season has its own holidays, holiday traditions, and typical weather conditions. In the fall/autumn season, one thinks of NOUN on the trees turning yellow, red, and ADJECTIVE, as they begin to fall from the trees.

In the USA, Thanksgiving is a well-known holiday that many people celebrate.

Winter means snow and cold weather. Most trees have lost their leaves and some NOUN have gone into hibernation, which is a ADJECTIVE winter's sleep. Holidays take place in the winter. One is New Year's Eve. One outside activity that children enjoy is making a NOUN.

Spring means large amounts of NOUN. Colorful NOUN are blooming, and leaves are appearing on the trees, which may have budding flowers. Baby birds are VERB. Summertime is next, as it is a favorite season of many children. It's a time to VERB in pools or ponds. And going to a NOUN is always fun if there is one around. In lots of places children look forward to going on vacation.

animals   rain   swim   flowers

long   Snowman   leaves   beach   hatched   orange

46
HANDS ON METHODS OF TEACHING GEOMETRY
Netta Riba, Retired NYC High School Mathematics Teacher

These activities provide students, whether children, teenagers, or adults with experience with geometric concepts; the activities can be used independently or to supplement classroom instruction. The topics covered here in these activities are:

1. How to read a ruler
2. What is meant by area?
3. How triangles can be determined to be congruent

Rulers rule: What is a ruler and how can I make one?
Vocabulary:

Ruler: An instrument that has a straight edge, marked in units of length, and is used to measure length.
Unit of length: A straight line of a particular length (a line segment). Common units of length are inches, feet, centimeters, and meters

Materials:

- A sharp pencil
- A sheet of cardboard
- A piece of paper
- Thin line colored makers
- Scissors

Directions:

1. Use the edge of the cardboard for the edge of the ruler.
2. Cut a strip off this side of the cardboard. Make it a little wider than your thumb. The edge of the cardboard that has been marked with the marker is your straight edge.

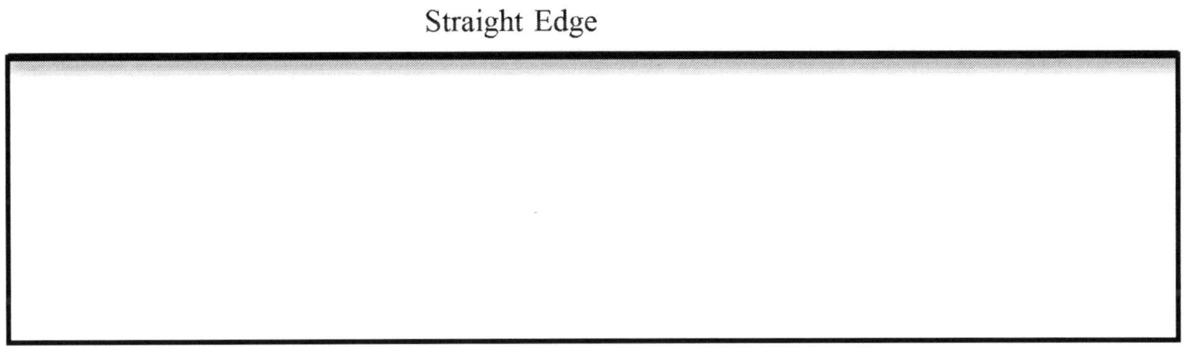

Straight Edge

Figure 3.52. Rulers Rule # 1

3. Now take out the piece of paper and use a marker to make a thin line along an edge of the piece of paper. You may choose to mark a length on this edge an inch long if you want your ruler to be in inches, or you may choose another length and call it your unit of measure. Make your unit small enough so that at least four or five of them will fit on your straight edge.
4. Cut out a rectangle with this length as its long side.

5. Go to the end of the cardboard strip, which is now your ruler, and mark this length on your straight edge. Put your unit of measure at the end of this marking and mark off another unit. Continue doing this until your ruler has been completely marked. Be sure to start each new unit where the previous unit ends
6. Make a thin line under the straight edge colored strip to show the length of each unit. You may use a color different from the one marking the edge of the straight edge. You may number the units.

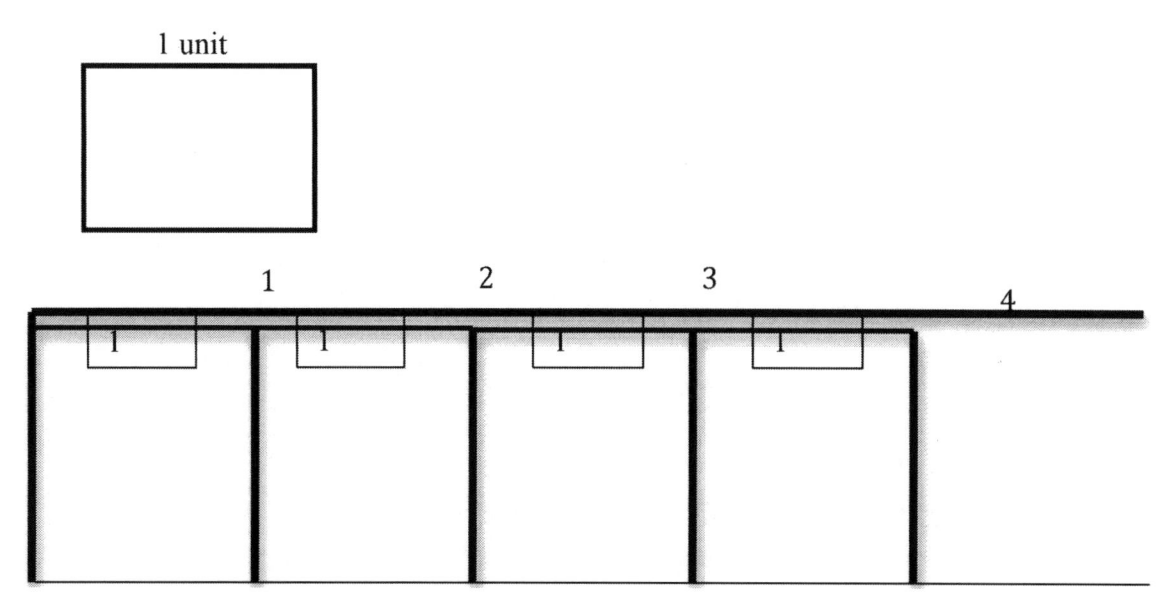

Figure 3.53. Rulers Rule 2

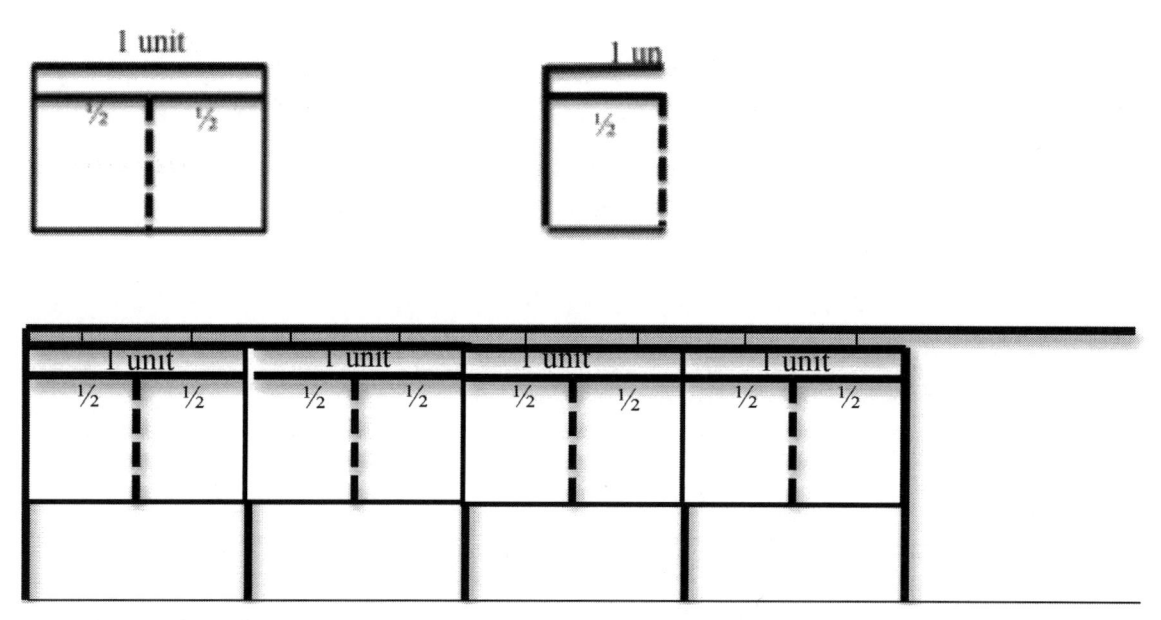

Figure 3.54. Rulers Rule # 3

116   SECTION 3

7. Fold the piece of paper that is your unit of measure very carefully in half along its long edge. This is now a ½ (half) unit.
8. Mark these half units along your straight edge. How many fit in 1 unit?
9. You may use a third color to mark each half unit.

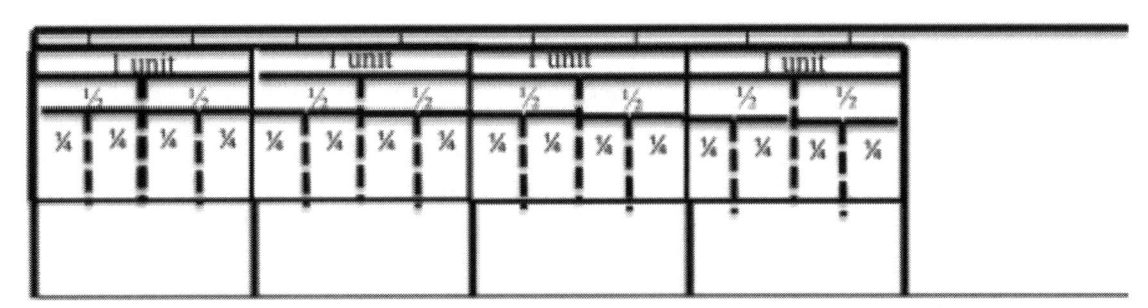

Figure 3.55.   Rulers Rule # 4

10. Fold your half unit again in half along the long edge. This is now a ¼ (one quarter) unit.
11. Mark these ¼ units along your straight edge.
12. You may use a fourth color to mark each quarter unit. How many ¼ units fit in 1 unit?

Line segment a

Figure 3.56.   Rulers Rule # 5

Playing-the-Pages Activities   117

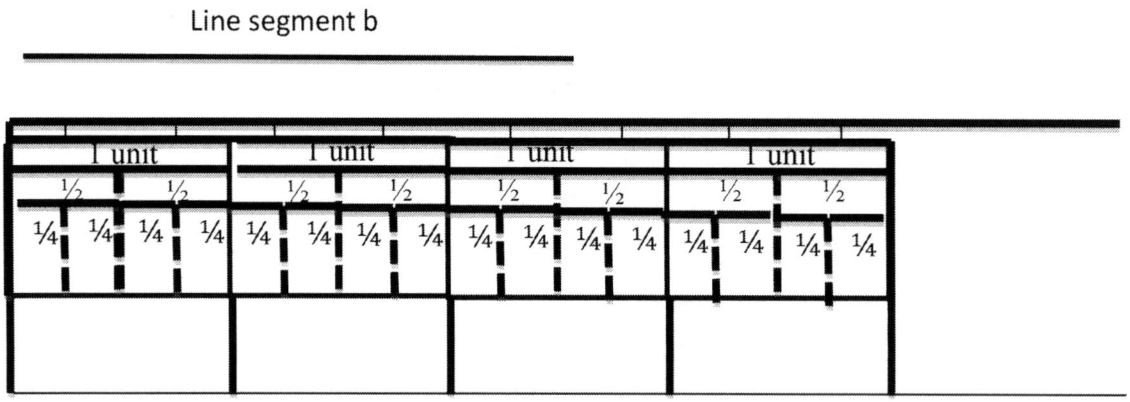

Line segment b
_____

Figure 3.57. Rulers Rule # 6

13. If you were to fold your ¼ unit in half, (it is likely difficult to actually do this), you would then have a ⅛ unit. How many eighth units would fit in 1 unit?
14. Draw a unit line with your ruler and, as carefully as you can, freehand, divide it in half, then each half in half again, then each section in half again. You should have eight sections. Each one would be called an eighth of your unit.
15. When you order a pizza, how many pieces is it usually cut into? What is each section of that pizza called?

118   SECTION 3

47
RULING WITH RULERS: HOW TO USE THE RULER
Netta Riba

1. Use the ruler shown to measure the line segment drawn below.
   Refer to figure 3.56 RULERS RULE
   How long is line segment above in figure 3.56?
   Refer to figure 3.56 RULERS RULE
   How many units fit in the line segment?
   How many half (½) units fit in the line segment?
   How many quarter (¼) units fit in the line segment?
   How many eighth (⅛) units fit in the line segment?
   Use the ruler shown to measure the line segment drawn in figure 3.57.
   Refer to figure 3.57 RULERS RULE
   How long is line segment b in figure 3.57?
   How many units fit in this line segment?
   How many half (½) units fit in this line segment?
   How many quarter (¼) units fit in this line segment?
   How many eighth (⅛) units fit in this line segment?
   The line segment in figure 3.57 is longer than 2 units, but smaller than 3 units.
   We can say it is 2 units and ½ or 2½.
2. Take your ruler and measure the line segment in figure 3.56 and figure 3.57. Do you get the same result? Why or why not?
3. Why do you suppose people all use the same unit to measure things?
4. Use your ruler to measure the following items and record your results.
   a) This book: length, width, thickness
   b) The table where you are seated
   c) Your index finger
   d) Your pencil
5. If your unit of measure is not an inch, use a standard ruler also. Write down both measurements.

48
SAME SIZE AND SHAPE: CONGRUENT TRIANGLE ACTIVITY
Netta Riba

This activity is about how many measurements you need to make to decide if two triangles are congruent. Foreknowledge of angles would be of assistance in doing this activity. Some of the activities you are going to do are:

1. Make a triangle.
2. Copy the sides and angles of the triangle.
3. Determine how many measurements you need to make to decide if the two triangles are congruent.

Vocabulary:

1. Triangle: A flat-plane closed figure formed by three line segments connected at their endpoints.
2. Scalene triangle: A triangle in which no two sides are equal.
3. Angle: A flat-plane figure formed by two lines (sides) connected at an endpoint.
4. Vertex of an angle: The endpoint where the two sides of the angle meet.
5. The measure of an angle: The amount of rotation needed to move a line segment from a position on top of one side of the angle to the other side, keeping the segment always connected to the vertex of the angle.
6. A complete rotation: The amount of rotation needed to move a line segment from a position on top of one line around in a circular motion until it returns to rest on the original line, keeping the lines always connected at the same end point, called the vertex. This is generally referred to as a 360 degree rotation.
7. Right angle: An angle equivalent to one-quarter of a complete rotation, or 90 degrees.
8. Right triangle: A triangle that contains a right angle.
9. Congruent triangles: Two triangles whose sides and angles are all exactly the same measure thus causing them to fit exactly one on top of the other.

Materials:

1. Two pieces of unlined paper
2. A sheet of medium-weight plastic (an overhead projector sheet, one side of a sheet protector, the plastic sheet from a new shirt or, about 10 inches of medium-weight plastic sheeting from a hardware store)
3. One thin-line permanent color marker. (If the marker is not permanent it will smear on the plastic. If needed, permanent marker can be erased with a tissue dampened with rubbing alcohol. Alcohol will also remove permanent marker from clothing.)
4. Scissors
5. A small bottle of rubbing alcohol
6. A ruler

How to prepare the materials:

1. Use a ruler to draw a triangle that does not have any equal sides on the paper. This is called a scalene triangle. Check that no sides are equal with the ruler. Avoid putting a right angle in your triangle, as this may lead to a special case.
2. When the triangle is to your liking, put the paper under the plastic so that the triangle is close to the top of the plastic and trace the triangle using the ruler and thin marker.
3. Cut off the top of the plastic sheet that contains the triangle. Do not cut on the lines of the triangle.
4. Put the plastic triangle under the bottom part of the plastic sheet and carefully trace each side of the triangle and each angle of the triangle separately with the marker. Do not try to make them into a triangle. Make the sides of the angles shorter than in the original triangle.
5. Make two long straight edges near the edge of the plastic with the ruler.
6. Cut around each line segment and angle leaving approximately a ¼-inch border. Do not cut on the lines. Cut out the straight edges the same way.

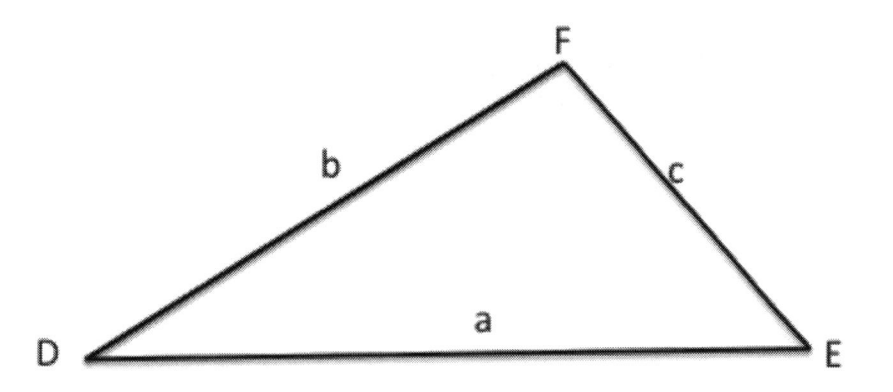

Figure 3.58. Same Size and Shape # 1

STRAIGHT EDGES

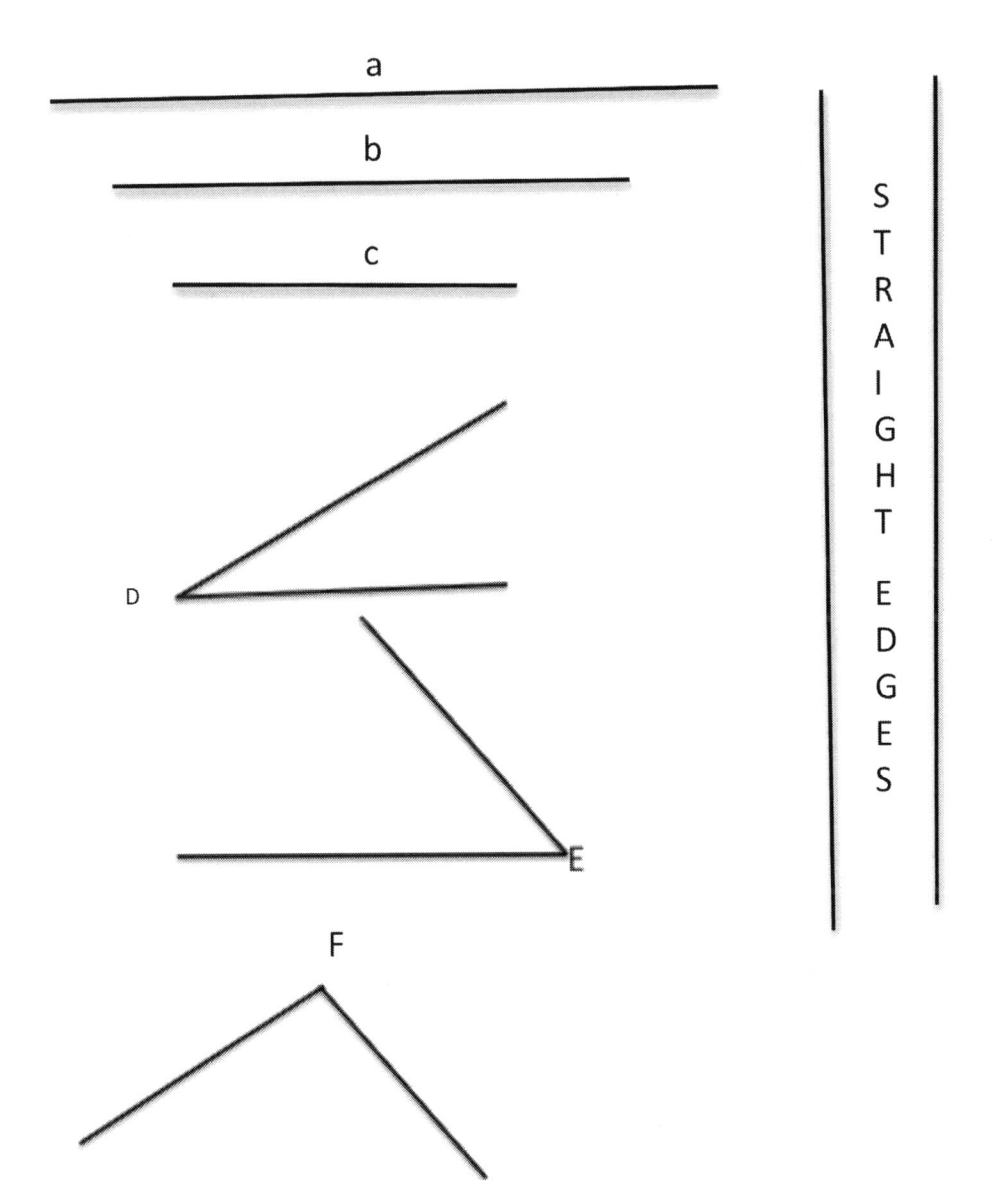

Figure 3.59. Same Size and Shape # 2

Playing-the-Pages Activities 121

b

a

cut

c

Straight Edges

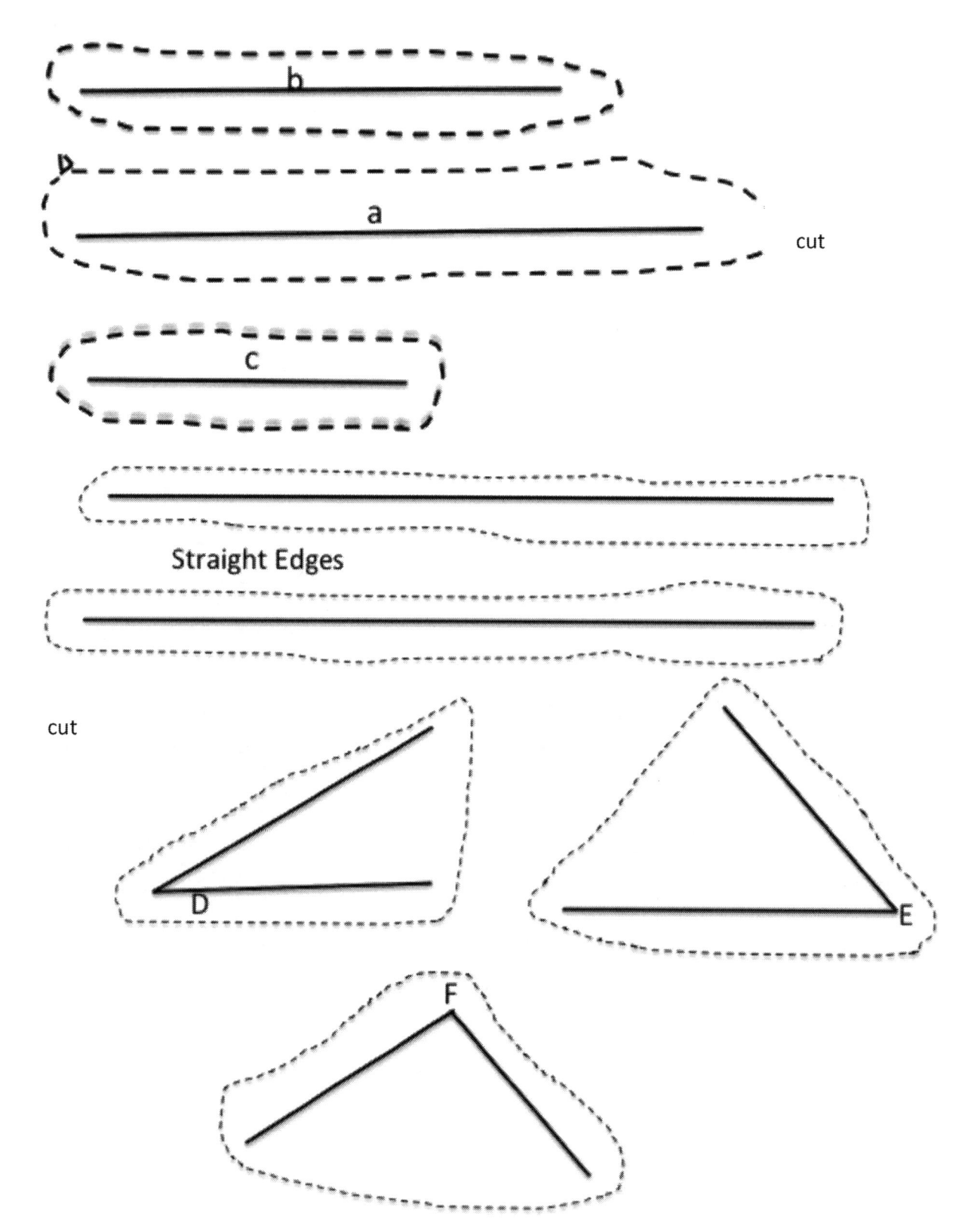

cut

D

E

F

Figure 3.60. Same Size and Shape # 3

122   SECTION 3

What to do:

1. You now have three line segments and three angles (the two straight edges may be used any way you like). Try to make a triangle exactly the same (congruent) to the original triangle with the pieces that you have. Ignore the cut edges. It is easier to work on top of the second piece of paper. Line segments must touch at the ends, and the vertex of the angles must be at the end of a line segment. The straight edges may be used to complete the triangle (For example: by lengthening the sides of the angles). Will the examples shown below result in a triangle congruent to the original triangle? Why or why not?

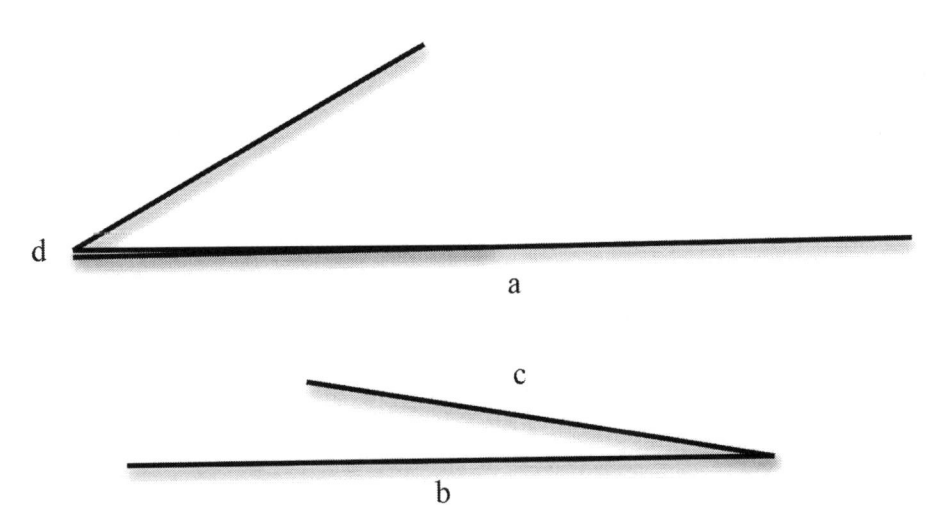

Figure 3.61. Same Size and Shape # 4

2. Check to see if you have been successful by putting the original triangle on top of the one you have made.
3. Now see if you can discover what would be the fewest number of pieces (angles and/or sides) you would need to make the original triangle. Straight edges do not count and can be used any way you like.
4. How many different ways can you make the original triangle without using all the pieces?
5. Explain how would you have to arrange the pieces.
6. Can you make a triangle congruent to the original triangle using only three pieces (angles and/or sides, not counting straight edges)?
7. Can you list all the different ways that you can make a triangle congruent to the original triangle using only three pieces plus straight edges?
8. Try making your original triangle a right triangle; copying the pieces of the right triangle, and see if you find another way to make a triangle congruent to the original right triangle.

Playing-the-Pages Activities 123

49
PLANE AREA ACTIVITY
Netta Riba

Definitions:

1. Square: A four-sided figure all of whose angles are right angles and all of whose sides are the same length.
2. Square unit: A square, the length of whose sides is the unit. A square whose sides are 1 inch is 1 square inch (1 in^2). A square whose sides are 1 centimeter is 1 square centimeter (1 cm^2).
3. Area: The number of square units that will fit inside a shape with no overlapping and no empty spaces.

Materials: Paper, harp pencil, ruler, a sheet of thin cardboard
How to prepare the materials:
Draw parallel horizontal lines on the cardboard all the same distance apart (you may pick any distance); then draw vertical lines on the cardboard the same distance apart as the horizontal lines.

1. You now have many little squares all the same size; cut them all apart.
2. Make a rectangle out of twelve of the squares. The rectangle must be filled with squares and they should not overlap.
3. Count the number of squares in the rectangle.
4. This is called the area of the rectangle. Your squares are called square units.
5. How could you figure out how many squares there are without counting all of them?
6. Using the same number of squares, make a different rectangle.
7. How many rectangles can you make using the same number of squares? (These rectangles all have the same area.)
8. Draw or record your results.
9. Make another rectangle with forty-eight squares.
10. How many rectangles can you make with forty-eight squares?
11. Draw or record your results.
12. Choose a different number of squares and make another rectangle.
13. How many different rectangles can you make with this number of squares?
14. Draw or record your results.

(Technical support: Benjamin Riba, retired, Haverstraw-Stony Point Central School District, Joseph Riba, Pasco County Florida School District, Rebecca Riba-Wolman, MD, Connecticut Children's Hospital).

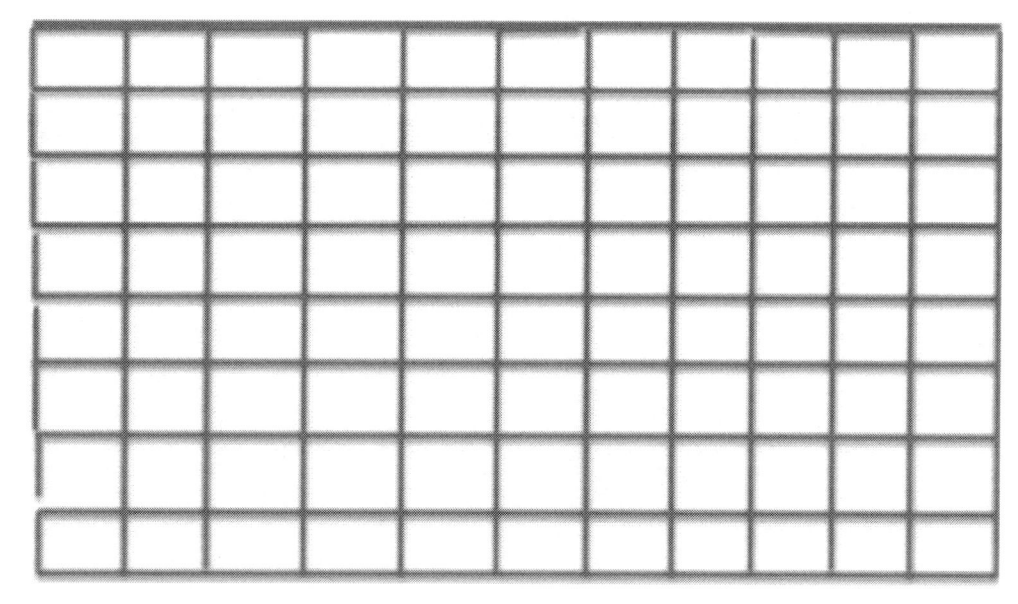

Figure 3.62. Plane Area Activity Goes Here

50
Create a Postcard
Lucia Sapienza

Directions: Now that you have visited Narnia, create a postcard explaining your journey to anyone you choose. Pretend that you traveled with Lucy, Susan, Edmund, and Peter. Be sure to describe your surroundings and the different creatures you encountered in Narnia. After writing your message, draw a picture of Narnia on the other side of the postcard. A sample postcard is displayed (to be used with the book, *The Lion, the Witch, and the Wardrobe* by C. S. Lewis).

While this postcard activity is for the book mentioned above, you can do it for any book you read. Use a 5 × 7 index card and draw a picture on the front of the postcard. This should represent a setting or idea from the book you have read. Notice that the picture I did was the castle from Narnia. I used the Insert icon on the computer and then selected "shapes" to make the castle. However, you might just draw the picture or use clip art or decorate the front of the postcard with figures from the story.

Then, make the writing on the other side be from one of the story characters and reflect what one of the characters in the story might say about something that happened in the book. See the backside of the postcard from Narnia for an example of this.

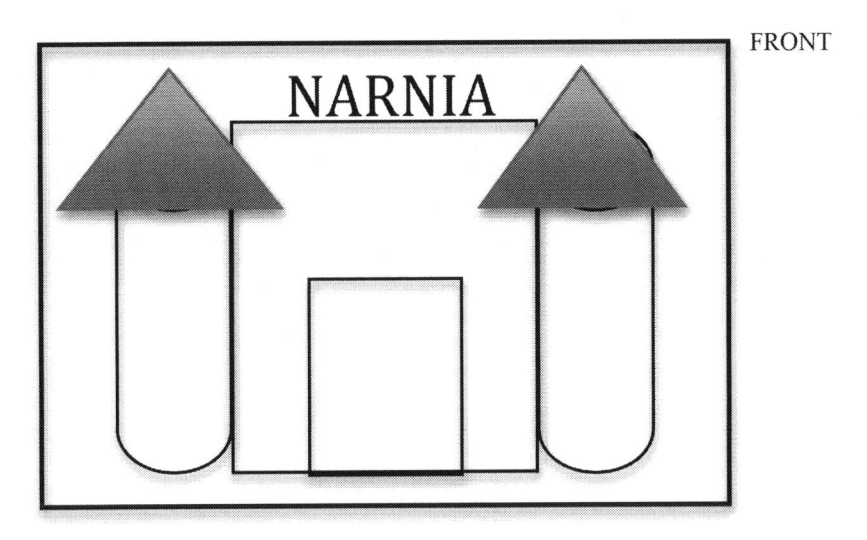

FRONT — NARNIA (castle illustration)

BACK:

Dear Mom,
I'm having so much fun with Peter, Edmund, Lucy, and Susan. I met a baby deer, dwarf and some nice beavers. Narnia is cold with a lot of snow, but I'm having fun. See you soon!
Love, Laura

Maria Sapienza
14 Dreamland Avenue
Dreamland, NY 11267

Stamp goes here

Figure 3.63. Create a Post Card

51
VENN DIAGRAM for MEXICO and CALIFORNIA + VENN DIAGRAM STATEMENTS
Alyssa Ferrandino

In the book *Esperanza Rising* the main character faces numerous challenges. In her home country of Mexico she has a charmed life with her Papa, Mama, Abuelita, and several servants and workers. Esperanza's father teaches her to listen to the heartbeat of the earth on their huge farm. A series of immediate and disruptive incidents cause Esperanza and some of her family members to move to California where Esperanza and her family now live at a work camp.

Directions: Use two hula hoops and place them on the floor overlapping one another. If you don't have hula hoops then make two large string circles overlapping one another and place them on the floor. The left side at the top of the circle is to be labeled "Mexico Differences" and the top of the right side circle is to be labeled "California Differences." The overlap part is labeled "Mexico and California Similarities." Using the previous brief scenario, the object of this interactive and kinesthetic activity is to find similarities between California and Mexico, as well as differences.

Following, are the sentence strips you are to place in what you think is the correct section of the circles on the floor. Decide if what you are placing is something Mexico has and California doesn't (left side); something California has and Mexico doesn't (right side), or something both countries have (center section).

Place the information provided in the list below on index cards or poster board cutout pieces or use oak tag paper. Make the print large, as the space on the floor for the overlapping circles is big, or cut out the sentences provided for you. Then, put the index cards on the correct section of the Venn diagram. Decorate your Venn diagram by putting a flag of Mexico on the left side and one of California on the right side.

Esperanza Rising statements for the Venn diagram:

1. Esperanza wears fancy clothes.
2. Esperanza wears working clothes.
3. Esperanza was wealthy.
4. Esperanza lives at a work camp.
5. Esperanza became poor and did farm work.
6. Esperanza lived with her Mama, Papa, and Abuelita.
7. Esperanza maintains her culture in both places.
8. Esperanza was with Mama.
9. Esperanza was with Miguel.
10. Esperanza had to adjust to a new life style.
11. Esperanza lived on her family's ranch, El Rancho de las Rosas.

The big challenge of this activity is to do it with a partner and compare your choices. Then check the numbers to see if you're correct. Left: 1, 3, 6, 11; Right: 2, 4, 5, 10; Middle: 7, 8, 9.

Four Seasons: Cloze Reading Answers: leaves, orange, animals, long, snowman, rain, flowers, hatched, swim, beach.

52
ECOSYSTEM MATH STICKS
Jessica Hurley and Julia Nackenson

Directions: For this activity you will need scissors to cut out each strip that has a math word problem on it. Start with the "START" strip. Solve the math problem and then, find the answer to that problem on the far left side of another strip. Place that strip under the one that had the problem. Continue this process.

You will notice that on the right side of the strip there is a letter. If you follow the strips by answering each problem correctly, these letters will spell out a biome. Spell out the word on the spaces provided at the end of this activity in figure 3.64.

| ¼ | Finish | D |

| 72 | $32 \div 8 = ?$ | R |

| 4 | The difference between 32 and 18? | A |

| 1/3 | The divisor in 64 divided by 8 is? | L |

| START | $9 \times 8 = ?$ | G |

Figure 3.64. Ecosystem Math Sticks

Playing-the-Pages Activities 127

600 Change .25 into a fraction. **N**

8 What is 649 rounded to the nearest 100th? **A**

14 The sum of 73 and 29 is? **S**

102 Put 20/60 into the simplest form **S**

The name of the Biome is:

__ __ __ __ __ __ __ __

128   SECTION 3

53
FOOD CHAIN STACKING CUPS
Jessica Hurley and Julia Nackenson

Directions: A food chain shows the path from one living thing to another. Use your knowledge of the food chain to stack cups in the correct order from producer to carnivore consumer. To play the game, always begin with the producer. The top cup will always be the carnivore consumer.

Photo 3.10. Food Chain Stacking Cups # 1

Photo 3.11. Food Chain Stacking Cups # 2

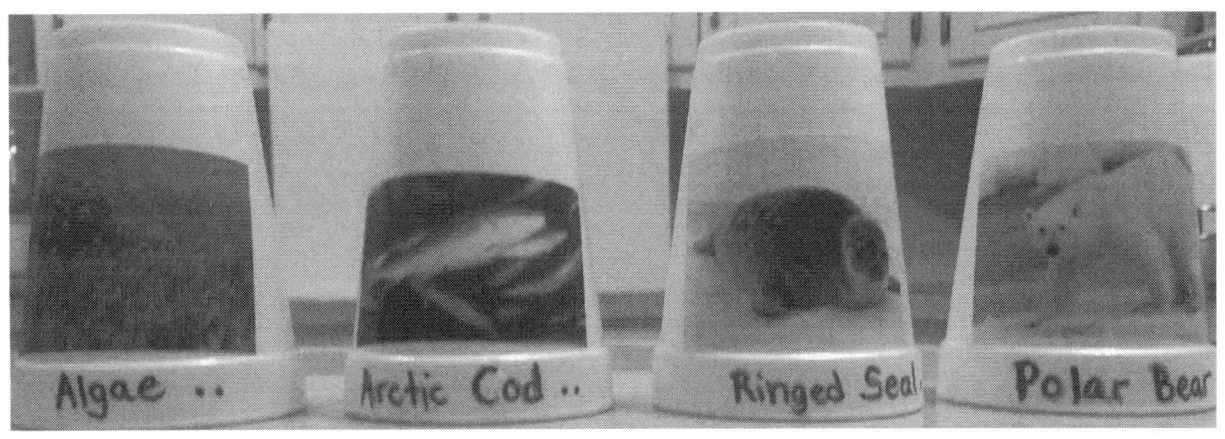

Photo 3.12. Food Chain Stacking Cups # 3

Playing-the-Pages Activities 129

Photo 3.13. Food Chain Stacking Cups # 4

130   SECTION 3

54
RECEPTIVE and EXPRESSIVE LANGUAGE THROUGH PUPPETRY
Carolina Schiering (MS, CCC-SLP (Bilingual speech-language pathologist-Early Intervention)

The puppets seen in photo 3.14 were made by Carolina Schiering, a speech pathologist practicing in Chula Vista, California. These puppets are used in conjunction with the book and/or animated music video for the *Five Little Monkeys Jumping on the Bed* to target a variety of receptive and expressive language skills.

The activity is adaptable depending on the needs of the child. First there's the making of the puppets to match a book's characters, as was done in this scenario along with the identification with the song by the same title. The second idea is to use the puppets to target a variety of skills.

One might be identification of concepts, such as what the monkeys are doing and what's the result of their actions. Then there's answering simple questions that involve literal comprehension. An example would be, "What are the names of the monkeys?" The answer would be the numbering of each one through five. Next might be for following commands, labeling, and increasing the phrase length for a response to the questions. These are ways to have children express themselves and be receptive to language development by using the puppets to stimulate thinking.

Working with children in this field for many years, Carolina states, "I strongly believe children need to be active participants in the learning process. That is the reason I adapt the books I use in my therapy sessions to engage them in learning for the development of receptive and expressive language."

Photo 3.14. Monkey puppets in Bed

Photo 3.15. Monkey Puppets

55
CHARLOTTE'S WEB TASK CARDS
Alexa Alongi

Using 5 × 8 index cards of the same color, on one side write a comprehension question from the book you've read and on the other side write the answer to that question. Next, separate each card by cutting it in half using a different shape for each card cut. The ones in figure 3.65 are from *Charlotte's Web* by E. B. White.

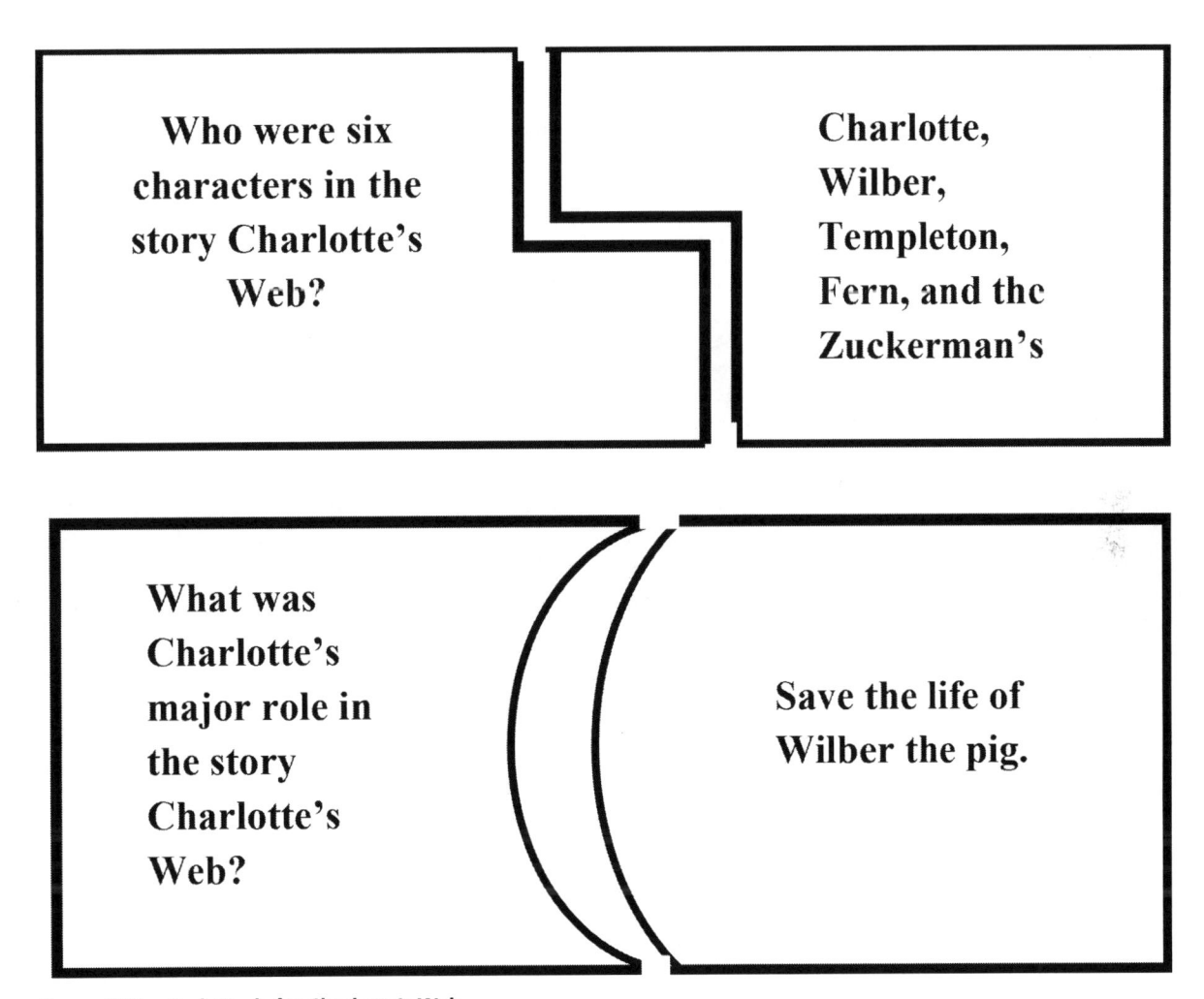

Who were six characters in the story Charlotte's Web?

Charlotte, Wilber, Templeton, Fern, and the Zuckerman's

What was Charlotte's major role in the story Charlotte's Web?

Save the life of Wilber the pig.

Figure 3.65. Task Cards for Charlotte's Web

56
DAUGHTER'S BOOK REPORT
Joshua and Landyn Schiering

My daughter, nine-year-old Landyn, from Center Elementary School in Stow, Massachusetts. was assigned a book report. She seemed uninspired until we saw the Interactive Tri-fold Board by Lucia Sapienza in *Learning and Teaching Creative Cognition: The Interactive Book Report*. Getting materials together, as her father, I spent time helping her with this first big assignment. It's important to help set the bar high and impress upon the children the importance of quality work. A lesson I hope will carry over with her for life, and certainly into her next project.

I think Landyn also learned and retained a lot about her book using this three-dimensional method. It caused her to *think* about what she read. When all was said and done she was one proud nine-year-old. In fact, her older sisters read through her report and said, "I want to read this book now!" What more could you want, I thought, as Landyn responded with "I'm so happy because the report came out so good. I'm proud of myself and look forward to showing it to my teacher and classmates."

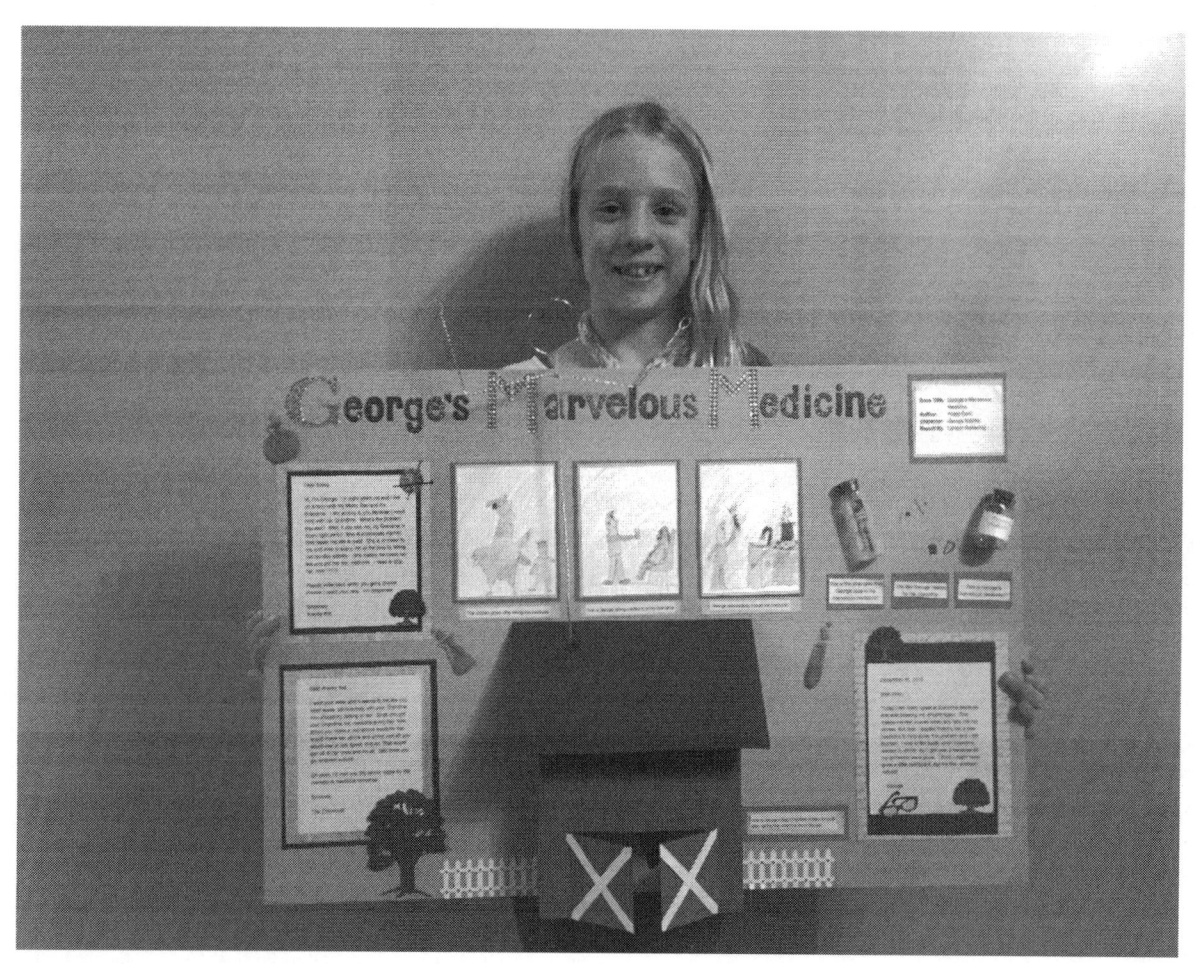

Photo 3.16. Landyn Book Report

The materials for this three-dimensional and Interactive Book Report are glitter letters, computer paper to write about the story elements of characters, setting, mood, events, problem, and solution. Then, the barn and story-related artifacts pasted on the board with sections bordered make the board's design pop-out at the viewer.

57
MATH WITH JUNIE B.
Danielle Collins and Vivian Stein

Directions: Junie B. has the cutest polka dots on her shirt, but she thinks she needs more. You'll need to cut out some circles as seen in photo 3.17, and Velcro tab each one as well as put a Velcro Tab on the shirt. To begin, take off all the Velcro tabs from the shirt. Then, answer the math problems on the worksheet and Velcro the amount of polka dots to the shirt! Velcro the problem you're answering to the top of the shirt, as seen in the illustration. When you get a chance add some questions for your friends and classmates to answer using the Junie B. shirt.

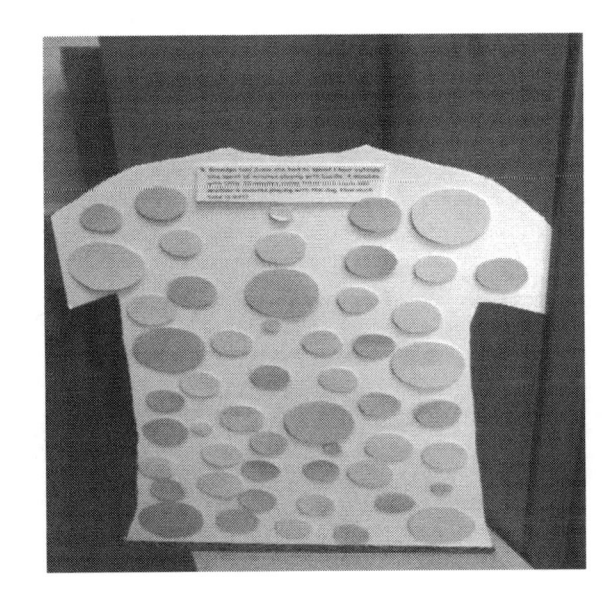

Photo 3.17. Math with Junie B.

Math Questions:

1. Junie B. has 10 grapes, 4 apples, and 3 oranges. How many does she have in all?
2. Mrs. A. has 25 students in the class, but 3 are at band practice and 4 are absent. How many students are in class right now?
3. Junie B. needs to invite her friends to her birthday party. There are 5 boys and 12 girls. How many gift bags for her guests is she going to need?
4. Junie B.'s mom has three trays of cookies. She is placing six cookies on each tray. How many cookies does she have in all?
5. Mrs. A needs to order buses for a field trip next week. If she has 40 students and 6 chaperones with ten people on each bus, how many buses does she need in all?
6. Junie B. has 20 toys in her room. If she put away 13 how many toys does she still have?
7. Grace has seven more books than Junie B. on her bookshelf. If she multiplies that by 4, how many books would be on the bookshelf?
8. Lucille has 5 different colors of M&M's in the package. There are 3 of each color. How many pieces of candy are there in all?
9. Lucille and Junie B. wanted to earn some money for toys. So, they decided to run a snack stand. They sold lemonade for 20 cents and cookies for 30 cents. If they sold 10 cups of lemonade and 10 cookies, how much money did they make?
10. Now it's your turn to make questions. Cut out a strip of cardstock paper and print a question on it. Or you may use the computer and using a large font write your questions there. Then cut them out and Velcro them to the shirt, as you see has been done in photo 3.17. Have fun, you can do this!!! Try to have one of the following represented on each of four question cards: addition, subtraction, multiplication, and division.

58
SINK OR FLOAT SCIENCE EXPERIMENT
James Fitzpatrick

Directions: When Columbus sailed the ocean blue in 1492, he traveled in a large ship. That boat had to float. This is a science experiment for you to chart things that sink or float. Get a bowl and fill it with water, or get a large pot and put water in that. Now, find objects you might carry with you or are around the classroom or at home. You may have some coins, paper money, keys, a toy boat, eye glasses, a rock, or other objects. Use the chart below to record, with a check mark, what you predicted and then what actually happened.

OBJECT	Prediction of Sink	Prediction of Float	What Actually Happened	
			SUNK	FLOATED

Figure 3.66. Sink or Float Science Experiment

59
LET'S KEEP OUR EARTH CLEAN
Lauren Spotkov

Earth Day began on April 22, 1970, and has been an important day ever since. It's a day to reflect on our planet and our environment, and what we can do to help keep them healthy. On a piece of paper, make a poster advertising keeping our planet clean. The space provided below serves as an example.

Everyone needs to join in to

Always keep our planet clean

Right now think about the trees

That provide us with a

Home for our happiness

Yes, we need to keep our

Earth clean and green

As much as possible

Right now and always……

Figure 3.67. Poster: Clean Earth Poem

Playing-the-Pages Activities 137

60
THE KINDNESS TREE
Kathy Carter

First grade teacher, Kathy Carter, explains how she begins each morning with an activity to involve everyone in her class thinking positive things. "I have this 'Kindness Tree' on the wall (see photo 3.18). Each morning we begin with everyone getting a leaf template and either having me write a kindness shown to him/her within the past day, or the student printing that on the leaf by him/herself and pasting this to the tree. Then, we read the leaves of the tree. It's a feel-good activity, but more importantly it starts the day by realizing kindness is all around us in our classroom and outside of it as well." This works for any grade level or even at a workplace. A kindness leaf example might be. "You held the door open for me."

Photo 3.18. Kindness Tree

RECIPROCAL THINKING PHASES SKILLS: IDENTIFICATION AND APPLICATION FOR FIFTEEN ACTIVITIES FROM SECTION 3

1. **Things We Like Quilt:** Initially, the *recognizing* thinking skills are apparent with the concept of creating a quilt addressing things individuals like. *Realizing* is also evident, as classifying occurs when *organizing* the pictures to be inserted into the baggies. *Comparing and contrasting* happens when the quilt is observed and viewers come to *realize* the differences in preferences by *analyzing* the work represented on the quilt. *Prioritizing* is evident when the drawings or clip art pictures are selected for the quilt, and *communicating* is done when explanation of the pictures is provided. There's *generalizing* that many of the pictures may address the same or similar topics, cued to the age of the contributors. *Sequencing* the pictures and *initially deciding* which goes where occurs when the pictures are placed in the baggies. This activity also involves *advanced deciding* for the same reason.

Whenever anyone shares a personal preference there is *risk taking* that their contribution will be accepted. *Recalling and reflecting* are done with the selection of which illustration is representative of the individual sharing. *Active listening* happens when the performance-based sharing is done and *self-actuating/doing the work* is a major utilized thinking skill throughout the creation and sharing of the project.

2. **Sailboat with Geometrical Shapes:** *Recognizing* the six geometrical shapes and *comparing* and *contrasting* these while *prioritizing* and *organizing* the shapes, as well as *predicting* the overall design. *Generalizing* occurs when *realizing that initial deciding* and *problem solving* occur, simultaneously, before *self-actuating* by completing the sailboat configuration using the geometrical shapes by *analyzing* the general structure of the design. A minimum of twelve cognitive and metacognitive skills were used to play this page.

    Communicating is done when working with a partner to select the words by placing the rubber bands around the pins or nails. *Sequencing* occurs with the letters on the cardstock paper and organizing is realized at the same time. *Evaluating* the geo-board is done when the words are selected for rubber band placement, and so is self-actualizing.

3. **Making Compound Words:** *Evaluating* is a primary thinking skill used when *analyzing* the words that are presented as being able to join over twenty of them together. *Recognizing* some words more easily than others while *comparing and contrasting* word meanings seems to be a very natural thinking process. The learner is *sequencing* when doing this *generalization* of words joining together to form new ones. *Reflection* on known vocabulary helps to bring about the *initial* and later *advanced problem solving* of *creating* compound words.

    This activity is creative in the sense that such is what's happening with the *identification/beginning awareness* of words that match easily. Active listening occurs when one mentally relates the words that join. There may be *prioritizing* as the person joining the words decides which goes first and the overall *sequencing* of these compound words. Tremendous *discernment* is necessary when trying to find the two words that are used two times to form new words. *Tolerating* one's own ability to join words may come into play, but overall *risk taking* for *self-actuating* is evident.

4. **Decision-Making Graphic Organizer:** First there are *identifying* and *recognizing* the problem, and ultimately *realizing* that it's solvable; *critical and creative thinking* along with *inventing* are realized when *initially deciding* on three choices. Such thinking also encompasses the selecting of the possible three choices, and possible positive and negative outcomes. The Final Decision calls for *advanced decision making* and *problem solving*, as well as *sequencing* the material to be put on the Board respective of choices and possible outcomes being numbered. And before that, thinking skills regarding *inferring* the possible outcomes occurs. Metacognitive skills of *evaluating the choices and outcomes*, *organizing* the material on the graphic organizer, *synthesizing* the material to be concise, *analyzing* the final components, *recalling* any personal experiences and *reflecting* on these comes into play, simultaneously, while making/filling-in the organizer's sections. That last component is very important to remember: reciprocal thinking evidences all these skills occurring at the same time or close to that.

5. **Math Floor or Wall Game:** This activity allows for tremendous kinesthetic involvement and relies heavily on *realizing* that in conjunction with *classifying* various geometrical shapes. To solve the math equation word problems there's *awareness* and *generalizing* of what's to be done for solving addition, subtraction, multiplication, and division problems. *Sequencing* is realized when moving from one geometrical shape to another by answering the math questions. It's *recognized* even more when *reflecting* on the process of *problem solving*. *Risk taking, initial deciding, and problem solving* are equally evident when supplying an answer to the questions asked. *Reflecting* on math functions already known and *recalling* these is most readily *analyzed* for *self-actuating*.

6. **Portrait of Adjectives:** *Recognizing* through differentiation of parts of speech is evidenced with basic awareness and acknowledging of the special components of adjectives. Then, *communicating* this happens with the listing of adjectives along the picture frame; *self-awareness* occurs with the *creating* of the portrait; and *communicating* is made obligatory when viewing the frame. Hopefully *predicting* that others may see the same qualities in you as you see occurs by chance. However, *deciding* initially and in advanced formats occurs when selecting the adjective to represent your personality qualities. Most often there is *risk taking* when revealing thoughts about oneself and ongoing *analyzing* what adjectives apply happens, as *recalling* one's character by *creating* the frame and portrait shows *self-actuating*.

7. **Spyglass Math:** Perhaps the *creative and critical thinking skills* are most used for this activity. Certainly, *inventing* is a predominate utilized skill, as the idea of a spyglass shows *imagination* and use of a variety of materials. *Deciding* on the math problems to be used calls for this cognitive/metacognitive skill to be evidenced when choosing the equations. *Risk taking* is involved when selecting an answer for the problem and *collaborating* occurs when one works with a partner for insertion of the math problem and removal of it to reveal the answer.

Playing-the-Pages Activities

8. **Match That Word:** *Realizing* in this activity requires matching everyday vocabulary words with their definitions. In an alphabet-letter match between word and definition, when applied as an Electro-Board or Wrap-Around, there is *comparing and contrasting* these words and definitions. *Organizing* occurs when these words are placed *sequentially* to represent everyday vocabulary. *Synthesizing* occurs with the brevity of definitions and, deciding which word matches the definitions on the right side of the page. And *recalling* along with *reflecting* on these matches happens before doing the self-actuating Wrap-Around. *Collaborating, communicating, generalizing* what match goes where, and *predicting* happens then as well. *Deciding* before doing the wrap, which is *self-actuating* is continuously occurring.
9. **Wrap-Around Timeline:** *Realizing* is in knowing this is a timeline dealing with political events in history, and *comparing and contrasting* these events. *Organizing* occurs when these events are put into *sequential* order. *Synthesizing* is relating historical events to six important ones that took place during the story *Number the Stars*. *Deciding* which events takes place in matching the dates on the right side of the Wrap-Around, *recalling* the historical events, and *reflecting* on these before doing the *self-actuating* wrap.
10. **Name That U.S.A. State and Its Capital:** Through identification, the states and their capitals are *realized* and *recognized* by name. *Classifying* is done by state and corresponding capital. The *sequencing* and *organizing* may be experienced by the order of the states, alphabetically, or if one chooses, by region. *Recalling* and *reflecting* on the state names and capitals is done when the Flip-Chute card is inserted in the top slot and the name of the capital is said, orally or only mentally. *Generalizing* is in the idea that all states have capital cities. *Collaborating* is experienced when partnerships do this activity. *Initial and advanced deciding* are *realized* when the state name or capital is said, and so is *self-actuating* done at that time.
11. **Literary Elements:** *Recognizing and realizing* the story elements is perhaps the first of these cognitive skills to be in play, then *classifying* these elements into six sections and comparing *and contrasting* each element's requirements, then *sequencing* the events of the story in order and *prioritizing* which event came first, second, third, etc. By *analyzing* the mood of the story there is *deciding* which element belongs where. *Recalling* the story elements and events and filling in each section makes it possible to *self-actualize*. *Deciding* comes into play with the *realization* of the story message and *problem solving* is evident as it's one of the story elements.
12. **Metamorphosis of a Butterfly:** *Realizing* occurs with discovery of this being the process of a caterpillar changing into a butterfly, which is called metamorphosis; *comparing and contrasting* with each stage of the butterfly's life cycle; *prioritizing and sequencing* with affixing the stages to the template. *Generalizing occurs with knowing* that metamorphosis is a process. *Deciding* on colors to be used for the butterfly and where each stage should be placed is part of the process. Completion of the construction directions equates with *self-actualizing*.
13. **Mathematic Flash Cards:** *Inventing* the Flash Cards is realized when putting complicated as well as easy math problems on the not-numbered side of the playing cards. *Recognizing* each card has a value and *initial* as well as *advanced deciding* as to what multidimensional equations go on the card. Combining multiplication with division and/or other math functions requires *evaluating, organizing, critiquing,* and possibly *communication* if done with a partner. *Synthesizing* material for the card, *analyzing* the equations for exactness and *self-actuating* when selecting the answer to the numerical problem.
14. **Chirp:** *Recognizing and realizing* these are math equations written in numerical and word formats. *Collaborating* with a partner on *problem solving* and *decision making* by *communicating* the steps taken regarding how one got the answer to it. *Active listening* comes with *communicating* and *sequencing* the process of obtaining an answer, which called for *initial deciding* and *evaluating* the aforementioned process. *Recalling* and *reflecting* accompanying *analyzing* the problems and *self-actualizing* happens when the problem is solved.
15. **Number to Letters:** *Problem solving* comes with *realizing and recognizing* that each number in the math equation's answer has a letter equivalent. *Comparing and contrasting* occurs with varied looking at the different equations. *Evaluating* the letter happens with determining and *organizing* the letters to create a word message. *Analyzing* one's work comes with predicting the words will be familiar and are connected to the Lucado book. *Sequencing* the letters to spell words goes with deciding if the answer to the math problem is correct. *Critiquing* one's work is part of the *problem-solving* experience, and producing the number to letter to word is *self-actualizing*.

LEARNING STANDARDS FOR TWENTY-THREE ACTIVITIES FROM SECTION 3: NICOLE DIBLASIO

A. Flip-Chute: Standards

New York State P–12 Common Core Learning Standards for English Language Arts & Literacy
Language Standards K–5

GRADES K–5:

1. Use words and phrases acquired through conversations, reading and being read to, and responding to texts.
2. Use words and phrases acquired through conversations, reading and being read to, and responding to texts, including using frequently occurring conjunctions to signal simple relationships (e.g., because).
3. Use words and phrases acquired through conversations, reading and being read to, and responding to texts, including using adjectives and adverbs to describe (e.g., When other kids are happy that makes me happy).
4. Acquire and use accurately grade-appropriate conversational, general academic, and domain-specific words and phrases, including those that signal spatial and temporal relationships (e.g., After dinner that night we went looking for them).
5. Acquire and use accurately grade-appropriate general academic and domain-specific words and phrases, including those that signal precise actions, emotions, or states of being (e.g., quizzed, whined, stammered) and that are basic to a particular topic (e.g., wildlife, conservation, and endangered when discussing animal preservation).
6. Acquire and use accurately grade-appropriate general academic and domain-specific words and phrases, including those that signal contrast, addition, and other logical relationships (e.g., however, although, nevertheless, similarly, moreover, in addition).

Indicator: *This will be evident when students acquire the new vocabulary from the Flip-Chute activity that is appropriate for the students' grade level.*

Reading Standards: Foundational Skills (K–5)

GRADES K–5:

1. Read emergent-reader texts with purpose and understanding.
2. Read with sufficient accuracy and fluency to support comprehension.

Indicator: *This will be evident when students read the directions in order to create the Flip-Chute activity correctly re-reading the directions if necessary for understanding.*

B. Constellation and Creative Writing: Standards

New York State P–12 Common Core Learning Standards for English Language Arts & Literacy
Writing Standards K–5

TEXT TYPES AND PURPOSES, GRADES 3, 4, AND 5:

1. Write narratives to develop real or imagined experiences or events using effective technique, descriptive details, and clear event sequences.
   a. Orient the reader by establishing a situation and introducing a narrator and/or characters; organize an event sequence that unfolds naturally.
   b. Use narrative techniques, such as dialogue, description, and pacing, to develop experiences and events or show the responses of characters to situations.
   c. Use transitions and temporal words and phrases to signal event order.
   d. Use concrete words and phrases and sensory details to convey experiences and events precisely.
   e. Provide a conclusion that follows from the narrated experiences or events.

Indicator: *This is evident when the students write their creative story that describes why their constellation is in the sky.*

RESPONDING TO LITERATURE, GRADES 3, 4, AND 5:

1. Create and present an original poem, narrative, play, art work, or literary review/critique in response to a particular author or theme studied in class.
   a. Recognize and illustrate social, historical, and cultural features in the presentation of literary texts.

Indicator: *This is evident when the students write their own story after being shown the model.*

C. Learning the Literary Elements: Story Map Standards

New York State P–12 Common Core Learning Standards for English Language Arts & Literacy
Reading Standards for Literature K–5

GRADE 1: DESCRIBE CHARACTERS, SETTINGS, AND MAJOR EVENTS IN A STORY, USING KEY DETAILS

Indicator: *This is evident when the students describe the characters, settings, and major events in a story using evidence from the text in the story map graphic organizer.*

Reading Standards: Foundational Skills (K–5)

FLUENCY, GRADE 1:

1. Read with sufficient accuracy and fluency to support comprehension.
   a. Read grade-level text with purpose and understanding.
   b. Use context to confirm or self-correct word recognition and understanding, rereading as necessary.

Indicator: *This is evident when the students read the story in order to fill out the story map graphic organizer.*

D. Literary Elements Story Map: Standards

New York State P–12 Common Core Learning Standards for English Language Arts & Literacy
College and Career Readiness Anchor Standards for Reading

KEY IDEAS AND DETAILS

1. Read closely to determine what the text says explicitly and to make logical inferences from it; cite specific textual evidence when writing or speaking to support conclusions drawn from the text.
2. Determine central ideas or themes of a text and analyze their development; summarize the key supporting details and ideas.

Indicator: *This is evident when students read closely to determine the characters and their character traits, the setting, the mood, the sequence of events, the problem and the solution, and citing textual evidence.*

Reading Standards for Literature K–5

KEY IDEAS AND DETAILS, GRADE 3 STUDENTS:

1. Describe characters in a story (e.g., their traits, motivations, or feelings) and explain how their actions contribute to the sequence of events.

Indicator: *This will be evident when students complete the character section in the graphic organizer. Students will relate the characters to other characters in the story and describe them based on evidence in the text.*

E. Picture Match: Standards

New York State P–12 Common Core Learning Standards for English Language Arts & Literacy
Language Standards K–5

GRADES 3 AND 4:

1. Determine or clarify the meaning of unknown and multiple meaning words and phrases based on grade 3 reading and content, choosing flexibly from a range of strategies.

a. Use context as a clue to the meaning of a word or phrase.
   b. Use a known root word as a clue to the meaning of an unknown word with the same root (e.g., company, companion).
   c. Use glossaries or beginning dictionaries, both print and digital, to determine or clarify the precise meaning of keywords and phrases.
   Indicator: *This is evident when the students clarify the meaning of the words using multiple methods and place the corresponding picture next to the vocabulary word.*
2. Acquire and use accurately grade-appropriate conversational, general academic, and domain-specific words and phrases, including those that signal spatial and temporal relationships; including those that signal precise actions, emotions, or states of being (e.g., quizzed, whined, stammered) and that are basic to a particular topic (e.g., wildlife, conservation, and endangered when discussing animal preservation).

Indicator: *This will be evident when students acquire the new vocabulary by matching the picture with its corresponding vocabulary word.*

F. Portrait of Adjectives: Standards

New York State P–12 Common Core Learning Standards for English Language Arts & Literacy
College and Career Readiness Anchor Standards for Writing

PRODUCTION AND DISTRIBUTION OF WRITING

1. Use technology, including the Internet, to produce and publish writing and to interact and collaborate with others.

Indicator: *This is evident when students use the computer to create their portrait.*

Writing Standards K–5

RANGE OF WRITING, GRADES K–2

1. Create and/or present a poem, dramatization, art work, or personal response to a particular author or theme studied in class, with support as needed.

Indicator: *This will be evident when students create a portrait.*

Language Standards K–5

GRADE 1:

1. Demonstrate command of the conventions of Standard English grammar and usage when writing or speaking.
   a. Use frequently occurring adjectives.

Indicator: *This will be evident when students create a portrait using different adjectives.*

G. Sandwich-Board Guess What or Guess Who: Standards

New York State P–12 Common Core Learning Standards for English Language Arts & Literacy
Language Standards K–5

GRADES K–5:

1. Use words and phrases acquired through conversations, reading and being read to, and responding to texts.
2. Use words and phrases acquired through conversations, reading and being read to, and responding to texts, including using frequently occurring conjunctions to signal simple relationships (e.g., because).

3. Use words and phrases acquired through conversations, reading and being read to, and responding to texts, including using adjectives and adverbs to describe (e.g., When other kids are happy that makes me happy).
4. Acquire and use accurately grade-appropriate conversational, general academic, and domain-specific words and phrases, including those that signal spatial and temporal relationships (e.g., After dinner that night we went looking for them).
5. Acquire and use accurately grade-appropriate general academic and domain-specific words and phrases, including those that signal precise actions, emotions, or states of being (e.g., quizzed, whined, stammered) and that are basic to a particular topic (e.g., wildlife, conservation, and endangered when discussing animal preservation).
6. Acquire and use accurately grade-appropriate general academic and domain-specific words and phrases, including those that signal contrast, addition, and other logical relationships (e.g., however, although, nevertheless, similarly, moreover, in addition).

Indicator: *This will be evident when students acquire the new vocabulary from the sandwich-board activity that is appropriate for the students' grade level.*

Reading Standards: Foundational Skills (K–5)

GRADES K–5:

1. Read emergent-reader texts with purpose and understanding.
2. Read with sufficient accuracy and fluency to support comprehension.

Indicator: *This will be evident when students read the definitions on the back to their partner.*

H. Sequence of Events Story Game: Standards

New York State P–12 Common Core Learning Standards for English Language Arts & Literacy
College and Career Readiness Anchor Standards for Reading

KEY IDEAS AND DETAILS

1. Analyze how and why individuals, events, and ideas develop and interact over the course of a text.

Indicator: *This will be evident when the students read the text and analyze it to order the sequence of events.*

Reading Standards: Foundational Skills (K–5)

FLUENCY

1. Read with sufficient accuracy and fluency to support comprehension.
   a. Read grade-level text with purpose and understanding.
   b. Use context to confirm or self-correct word recognition and understanding, rereading as necessary.

Indicator: *This is evident when the students read the story to order the sequence of events.*

I. Solving Easy Puzzles: Standards

New York State P–12 Common Core Learning Standards for English Language Arts & Literacy
College and Career Readiness Anchor Standards for Reading

KEY IDEAS AND DETAILS

1. Read closely to determine what the text says explicitly and to make logical inferences from it; cite specific textual evidence when writing or speaking to support conclusions drawn from the text.

CRAFT AND STRUCTURE

1. Analyze the structure of texts, including how specific sentences, paragraphs, and larger portions of the text (e.g., a section, chapter, scene, or stanza) relate to each other and the whole.

Indicator: *This is evident when the students must thoroughly analyze an essay to figure out the order of the paragraphs.*

Reading Standards for Informational Text

CRAFT AND STRUCTURE, GRADES 6–12:

1. Determine an author's point of view or purpose in a text and analyze how the author distinguishes his or her position from that of others.
2. Determine an author's point of view or purpose in a text in which the rhetoric is particularly effective, analyzing how style and content contribute to the power, persuasiveness, or beauty of the text.

Indicator: *This will be evident when the students determine what the authors are trying to convey to their readers and arranging the order of the essay to match that point of view.*

J. Things We Like Quilt: Standards

New York State P–12 Common Core Learning Standards for English Language Arts & Literacy
Writing Standards K–5

TEXT TYPES AND PURPOSES, KINDERGARTEN:

1. Use a combination of drawing, dictating, and writing to compose opinion pieces in which they tell a reader the topic or the name of the book they are writing about and state an opinion or preference about the topic or book.

Indicator: *This will be evident when the students write what they like including a drawing of what that is. (See Activity 1 in this section.)*

PRODUCTION AND DISTRIBUTION OF WRITING; RESEARCH TO BUILD AND PRESENT KNOWLEDGE:

1. With guidance and support from adults, recall information from experiences or gather information from provided sources to answer a question.

Indicator: *This will be evident when the students recall from their experiences things that they like.*

K. Three-Dimensional Work Search Geo-Board: Standards

New York State P–12 Common Core Learning Standards for English Language Arts & Literacy
Reading Standards: Foundational Skills (K–5)

KINDERGARTEN:

1. Demonstrate understanding of the organization and basic features of print.
    a. Recognize that spoken words are represented in written language by specific sequences of letters.

Indicator: *This is evident when students solve the word search sequencing the letters to form words.*

Language Standards K–5

1. Demonstrate command of the conventions of Standard English capitalization, punctuation, and spelling when writing.
    a. Spell simple words phonetically, drawing on knowledge of sound-letter relationships. Use conventional spelling for words with common spelling patterns and for frequently occurring irregular words.
    b. Consult reference materials, including beginning dictionaries, as needed to check and correct spellings.
    c. Spell grade-appropriate words correctly, consulting references as needed.

Indicator: *This is evident when students use their knowledge of spelling words to solve the word search and consult references as needed.*

L. Word Family Picture and Word Match: Standards

New York State P–12 Common Core Learning Standards for English Language Arts & Literacy
Reading Standards: Foundational Skills (K–5)

PHONICS AND WORD RECOGNITION, KINDERGARTEN:

1. Know and apply grade-level phonics and word analysis skills in decoding words.
    a. Demonstrate basic knowledge of one-to-one letter-sound correspondences by producing the primary sound or many of the most frequent sounds for each consonant.
    b. Associate the long and short sounds with common spellings (graphemes) for the five major vowels.

Indicator: *This is evident when students read the vocabulary words that all share the same family in order to match it to the corresponding picture.*

Language Standards K–5

VOCABULARY ACQUISITION AND USE, KINDERGARTEN:

1. Determine or clarify the meaning of unknown and multiple-meaning words and phrases based on kindergarten reading and content.
    a. Identify new meanings for familiar words and apply them accurately (e.g., knowing duck is a bird and learning the verb to duck).

Indicator: *This is evident when students match the vocabulary word with the corresponding picture.*

M. Chirp: Standards

New York State P–12 Common Core Learning Standards for English Language Arts & Literacy
Speaking and Listening Standards K–5

GRADE 5:

1. Engage effectively in a range of collaborative discussions (one-on-one, in groups, and teacher-led) with diverse partners on grade-5 topics and texts, building on others' ideas and expressing their own clearly.
    a. Follow agreed-upon rules for discussions and carry out assigned roles.
    b. Pose and respond to specific questions by making comments that contribute to the discussion and elaborate on the remarks of others.
2. Summarize the points a speaker makes and explain how each claim is supported by reasons and evidence.

Indicator: *This is evident when the students work together to come up with the right answer and if there is debate students will problem solve between differences of opinion.*

New York State P–12 Common Core Learning Standards for Mathematics
Number and Operations in Base Ten 5. NBT

PERFORM OPERATIONS WITH MULTI-DIGIT WHOLE NUMBERS AND WITH DECIMALS TO HUNDREDTHS

1. Fluently multiply multi-digit whole numbers using the standard algorithm.

Indicator: *This will be evident when the students multiply the strips and show all of their work.*

N. Math Word Problem Constructing Answers: Standards

New York State P–12 Common Core Learning Standards for English Language Arts & Literacy
Reading Standards: Foundational Skills (K–5)

GRADE 5:

1. Read with sufficient accuracy and fluency to support comprehension.
   a. Read grade-level text with purpose and understanding.
   b. Use context to confirm or self-correct word recognition and understanding, rereading as necessary.

Indicator: *This will be evident when the students read the questions carefully in order to figure out what to do to solve the word problem.*

New York State P–12 Common Core Learning Standards for Mathematics
Number & Operations in Base Ten 5.NBT

PERFORM OPERATIONS WITH MULTI-DIGIT WHOLE NUMBERS AND WITH DECIMALS TO HUNDREDTHS

1. Fluently multiply multi-digit whole numbers using the standard algorithm.

Indicator: *This will be evident when the students multiply to solve the equations.*

GEOMETRY

1. Understand that attributes belonging to a category of two-dimensional figures also belong to all subcategories of that category. For example, all rectangles have four right angles and squares are rectangles, so all squares have four right angles.

Indicator: *This will be evident when the students describe the shape and answers geometry questions about a golden ticket.*

O. Mathematics Flashcards: Standards

New York State P–12 Common Core Learning Standards for English Language Arts & Literacy
Reading Standards: Foundational Skills (K–5)

GRADES K–5:

1. Read emergent-reader texts with purpose and understanding.
2. Read with sufficient accuracy and fluency to support comprehension.

Indicator: *This will be evident when students read the directions in order to create the flashcards.*

New York State P–12 Common Core Learning Standards for Mathematics
Operations & Algebraic Thinking 3.OA (Since this activity can be used for a variety of different math topics there are a variety of standards that correspond)

1. Multiply and divide within 100. Fluently multiply and divide within 100, using strategies such as the relationship between multiplication and division (e.g., knowing that 8 × 5 = 40, one knows 40 ÷ 5 = 8) or properties of operations. By the end of Grade 3, know from memory all products of two one-digit numbers.

Indicator: *This will be evident when the students practice their multiplication facts in the flashcard activity.*

P. Spyglass Multiplication: Standards

New York State P–12 Common Core Learning Standards for English Language Arts & Literacy
Speaking and Listening Standards K–5

GRADES K–5:

1. Participate in collaborative conversations with diverse partners about kindergarten topics and texts with peers and adults in small and larger groups.
2. Engage effectively in a range of collaborative discussions (one-on-one, in groups, and teacher-led) with diverse partners on grade 3 topics and texts, building on others' ideas and expressing their own clearly.

Indicator: *This will be evident when the students work together to play the activity.*

New York State P–12 Common Core Learning Standards for Mathematics
Operations & Algebraic Thinking 3.OA (Since this activity can be used for a variety of different math topics there are a variety of standards that correspond)

1. Multiply and divide within 100. Fluently multiply and divide within 100, using strategies such as the relationship between multiplication and division (e.g., knowing that 8 × 5 = 40, one knows 40 ÷ 5 = 8) or properties of operations. By the end of Grade 3, know from memory all products of two one-digit numbers.

Indicator: *This will be evident when the students practice their multiplication facts in the spyglass activity.*

Q. Community Match: Standards

New York State P–12 Common Core Learning Standards for English Language Arts & Literacy
Reading Standards for Informational Text K–5

INTEGRATION OF KNOWLEDGE AND IDEAS, GRADE 3:

1. Use information gained from illustrations (e.g., maps, photographs) and the words in a text to demonstrate understanding of the text (e.g., where, when, why, and how key events occur).

Indicator: *This will be evident when the students use the different pictures and information from the definitions to fill out the chart.*

New York State Common Core Social Studies Framework Grades K–8

COMMUNITIES AROUND THE WORLD: GEOGRAPHY, HUMANS, AND THE ENVIRONMENT, GRADE 3:
Geographic factors often influence where people settle and form communities. People adapt to and modify their environment in different ways to meet their needs.
Geographic factors influence where people settle and their lifestyle. Some factors are more suitable for settlement while others act as a deterrent.

1. Investigate the lifestyle of the people who live in each selected world community and how the lifestyle has been influenced by the geographic factors.

Indicator: *This will be evident when the students learn about the different communities and fill out the chart to show their understanding.*

R. Map the Electro-Board! Map Matching: Standards

New York State P–12 Common Core Learning Standards for English Language Arts & Literacy
Reading Standards: Foundational Skills (K–5)

GRADE 3:

1. Read with sufficient accuracy and fluency to support comprehension.

Indicator: *This will be evident when the students read the directions in order to put the electro-board together.*

New York State Common Core Social Studies Framework Grades K–8

COMMUNITIES AROUND THE WORLD: GEOGRAPHY, HUMANS, AND THE ENVIRONMENT, GRADE 3:

The location of world communities can be described using geographic tools and vocabulary.
World communities can be located on globes and maps.

1. Examine where each selected world community is located.

Indicator: *This will be evident when students locate different cities and geographic features in China and Brooklyn on a map.*

S. Biodegradable Electro-Board: Standards

New York State P–12 Common Core Learning Standards for English Language Arts & Literacy
Language Standards K–5

GRADES K–3

1. Use words and phrases acquired through conversations, reading and being read to, and responding to texts, including using frequently occurring conjunctions to signal simple relationships (e.g., because) and including using adjectives and adverbs to describe (e.g., When other kids are happy that makes me happy).
2. Acquire and use accurately grade-appropriate conversational, general academic, and domain-specific words and phrases, including those that signal spatial and temporal.

Indicator: *This will be evident when the students learn the vocabulary terms "biodegradable" and "non-biodegradable."*

Elementary Science Core Curriculum Grades K–4

MAJOR UNDERSTANDINGS:

1. Identify ways in which humans have changed their environment and the effects of those changes. Humans, as individuals or communities, change environments in ways that can be either helpful or harmful for themselves and other organisms.

Indicator: *This will be evident when the students discuss and learn about what is biodegradable and what is not.*

T. Phases of the Moon: Standards

New York State P–12 Common Core Learning Standards for English Language Arts & Literacy
Reading Standards for Informational Text K–5

KEY IDEAS AND DETAILS, GRADE 4 STUDENTS:

1. Determine the meaning of general academic and domain specific words or phrases in a text relevant to a grade 4 topic or subject area.
2. Describe the overall structure (e.g., chronology, comparison, cause/effect, problem/solution) of events, ideas, concepts, or information in a text or part of a text.

Indicator: *This will be evident when the students use an informational text to order the phases of the moon and recreate the cycle with cookies and cream.*

Elementary Science Core Curriculum Grades K–4

MAJOR UNDERSTANDINGS:

Natural cycles and patterns include: the appearance of the Moon changing as it moves in a path around Earth to complete a single cycle.

Indicator: *This will be evident when the students create the phases of the moon with cookies and cream.*

U. Skeletal System: Standards

New York State P–12 Common Core Learning Standards for English Language Arts & Literacy
Language Standards K–5

VOCABULARY ACQUISITION AND USE, GRADES K–2:

1. Determine or clarify the meaning of unknown and multiple-meaning words and phrases.

Indicator: *This will be evident when students match the skeletal vocabulary with the correct part.*

Elementary Science Core Curriculum Grades K–4
Standard 4: The Living Environment

1. Describe how the structures of plants and animals complement the environment of the plant or animal. Each animal has different structures that serve different functions in growth, survival, and reproduction.

Indicator: *This will be evident when the students label the parts of a skeleton of a human body and discuss why the skeleton is important.*

V. Task Cards by M. Schiering: Standards

New York State P–12 Common Core Learning Standards for English Language Arts & Literacy
Language Standards K–5

GRADE 4:

1. Acquire and use accurately grade-appropriate general academic and domain-specific words and phrases, including those that signal precise actions, emotions, or states of being (e.g., quizzed, whined, stammered) and that are basic to a particular topic (e.g., wildlife, conservation, and endangered when discussing animal preservation).

Indicator: *This will be evident when students complete the Task Cards and use them to learn the vocabulary for ecosystems.*

Elementary Science Core Curriculum Grades K–4

1. Describe how plants and animals, including humans, depend upon each other and the nonliving environment.

MAJOR UNDERSTANDINGS:
An organism's pattern of behavior is related to the nature of that organism's environment, including the kinds and numbers of other organisms present, the availability of food and other resources, and the physical characteristics of the environment.

Indicator: *This will be evident when the students learn about ecosystems and how all living things and non-living things affect each other through vocabulary.*

W. Understanding the Metamorphosis of a Butterfly: Standards

New York State P–12 Common Core Learning Standards for English Language Arts & Literacy
Language Standards K–5

GRADE 3:

1. Acquire and use accurately grade-appropriate conversational, general academic, and domain-specific words and phrases, including those that signal spatial and temporal relationships.

Indicator: *This will be evident when students acquire the new vocabulary through constructing the metamorphosis butterfly and labeling the stages.*

Elementary Science Core Curriculum Grades K–4

1. Describe the major stages in the life cycles of selected plants and animals.

MAJOR UNDERSTANDINGS:
Plants and animals have life cycles. These may include beginning of a life, development into an adult, reproduction as an adult, and eventually death.
Each generation of animals goes through changes in form from young to adult. This completed sequence of changes in form is called a life cycle. Some insects change from egg to larva to pupa to adult.
Indicator: *This will be evident when the students construct the metamorphosis butterfly showing the four stages.*

ADDENDUM TO SECTION 3: "A GUIDE TO KICKING IT UP A NOTCH!" BY JOSHUA SCHIERING
I have been in the youth services business, pretty much my entire life, and nothing beats the look on the faces of the children after you take an everyday project and "kick it up a notch!" Everyone these days can Google projects and worksheets to do with their classes. At the LINX Afterschool Enrichment Center in Wellesley, Massachusetts, I challenge our instructors to "kick it up a notch!"
You may be asking, "What does that mean?" Well, it means taking an ordinary idea or activity and using your *creative cognition* for finding a way to make it more magnificent. It means being inspiring by using imagination, challenging yourself and learners to be thinkers and doers. *It means showing the students that the only limits we have are the ones we set for ourselves.* When your students or those you're teaching see you, their role model and example setter, testing the boundaries of a project, the end results far exceed meeting state guidelines and standards. The result is a room full of supportive and energized doers and thinkers—and students who have learned more and who become eager to learn even more after that! By "kicking it up a notch" you call on individuals to imagine, invent, explore, and engage themselves to create and enjoy a learning experience.

How to Do It

When you look at your textbooks or search the Web for ideas or worksheets, don't stop there! Ask yourself the Kick It Up a Notch six questions:

1. What can I do to make this more spectacular?
2. What can I do to get the kids' eyes to pop?
3. What if we _____?!!!
4. Could we _____?!!!
5. Imagine if we _____?!!!
6. How would the kids react if we _____?!!!

Of course, you might be faced with limitations—budgetary constraints, space constraints, practicality, weather, etcetera. That's okay! Work around those limitations and get creative yourself. It will rub off on the students and pay you back tenfold.

Working Backwards

Sometimes working backwards gets you *exactly* where you want to go! Imagine starting with the craziest idea and project, then construct and frame how you will present it. Your last move is to make the list of principles/concepts the students will learn from the project (hence working backwards by not starting first with the concepts to teach). This approach has proven to help inspire the imagination at the LINX Enrichment Center. It gets the creative juices flowing and fosters a "can do" attitude among leaders and students. It also enables leaders to be creative and not only focus on how to get everything to fit into the box (state frameworks/standards). Remember, the last step is figuring out how to make the frameworks/standards apply. Believe me, if you use this approach, you will have the creative skills needed to make it fit!

Examples of Success

At the LINX Enrichment Center in Wellesley, Massachusetts, part of my responsibilities is overseeing the science department, which includes the summer camps, year-round classes, and in-school science fairs. I met with two talented instructors, Chris Dumais and Chris "Cornbread" Coimbra and I asked them to develop an in-school science presentation that would take the everyday science class and "Kick It Up a Notch." We looked at several worksheets involving gravity, chemical reactions, friction, flight, and Newton's laws of physics. The two experienced teachers started by using the Kick It Up a Notch method:

STEP 1: Think of (or research) a cool project (working backwards).
STEP 2: Ask yourself the six Kick It Up a Notch questions (and record your answers).
STEP 3: Decide on a project.
STEP 4: Make a list of supplies needed.
STEP 5: Figure out your presentation method.
STEP 6: Determine the principles that will be taught as a result of this project/presentation.

Dumais and Cornbread far exceeded my expectations with a show that rocked the stage at a regional science fair. The audience (parents and children) laughed and cheered as the two made a mess of everything on their stage while inspiring and expanding the creative minds of those in attendance.

WORKBOOK PAGE: KICKING IT UP A NOTCH: DIALOGUE

Dumais: What if we made a machine that could hurl a roll of toilet paper across the room and cover the entire place?

Schiering: What if we made a giant contraption and instead of just one roll we launched six rolls?!!!

Cornbread: How much power (electricity) would it take?[constraint identified]

Dumais: Let's design it on paper first, then figure out the supplies needed, the project requirements, and then the principles that apply!

END RESULT

At the Science Fair, Dumais and Cornbread started with a challenge. They asked for a volunteer to see who could unroll the toilet paper the fastest, the volunteer or Dumais (man vs. science). The volunteer could only use his hands, while Dumais could use science. Well, what Dumais and Cornbread had done to attach a paint roller to the end of an electric leaf blower. They then slipped a roll of toilet paper onto the paint roller and the race began. Within seconds the volunteer was covered in the unrolled paper from Dumais's roll while continuing to manually unroll, square by square.

Well, for veteran teachers and entertainers Dumais and Cornbread this was not enough! After the crowd settled down, they wheeled out the Toilet Paper Party Machine, a diaper-changing station retrofitted with six electric leaf blowers and over six thousand squares of toilet paper. What a mess! And what a great way to learn about Bernoulli's Principle! You can see a clip here: http://www.linxcamps.com/SpecialtyCamps/Toilet_Paper_Party

Photo 3.19. Science Principles The T- Party Machine

During the development phase of our project planning, I tell my staff to:

1. "Go big or go home."
2. If we cannot "kick it up a notch," then we don't do it!

I will often suggest the name of a made-up contraption (e.g., a water-breathing Minian Squasher). Once you say something that may sound ridiculous, it inspires an image or an idea, or it generally gets the group/individual thinking, "What does that character look like and what does it do and, then, how can we do/show that?" Next thing you know, you have the makings for a cool project the kids are gonna love!

SCIENCE PRINCIPLES: PHYSICS, ELECTRICITY, FLIGHT

Materials: 1 hair dryer, 6 leaf blowers, 30 toilet paper rolls, 1 extension cord (20 ft), 1 power strip (6 outlets), 8 paint rollers (2 mini, 6 jumbo), 1 tarp to cover project (10 × 20 ft), tape measure (30 ft)

Scientific Questions:
- **Math (approximating):**
  - How many squares are in a roll of toilet paper?
  - How many squares are in 20 rolls of toilet paper?
  - How far can you throw a roll of toilet paper?
  - Can you throw the toilet paper in different ways to get it to unroll faster?
- **Challenge:**
  - Have each group discuss and brainstorm ways they can unroll a roll of TP the fastest.
  - Give each group a roll of TP and see who can unroll the TP the fastest.
  - What are ways we can get to unroll the toilet paper faster in the future?

Description: Get ready to make a mess, with toilet paper! Ever wonder how many sheets of toilet paper are in a roll of toilet paper? Ever wonder how fast you could unroll toilet paper off its roll? Wonder if there is science in unrolling a roll of toilet paper? Get ready to see the fastest way to unroll toilet paper using physics, electricity, and principles of flight!

Science Principles: The flying toilet paper is a wonderful example of Bernoulli's Principle, the same principle that allows heavier-than-air objects like airplanes to fly. Bernoulli, an eighteenth-century Swiss mathematician, discovered something quite unusual about moving air. He found that the faster air flows over the surface of something, the less the air pushes on that surface (and so the lower its pressure).

The fast moving air from the leaf blower flies above the toilet paper roll, causing an area of low pressure. The slower moving air under the roll causes an area of higher pressure. The difference in pressure between the fast moving air above the roll and the slower air underneath it creates "lift." This "lift" causes the toilet paper to fly off of the roll. Now you are challenged to make your own science principles activity!

(Airplanes can fly because of Bernoulli's Principle. Air rushing over the top of airplane wings exerts less pressure than air from under the wings. So the relatively greater air pressure beneath the wings supplies the upward force, or lift, that enables airplanes to fly. That's why airplanes have to "drive" down the runway and gain speed before they lift off the runway. The jet engines keep the airplane moving through the air continuously creating lift.)

SECTION 4

IM and IBR

Summing Up the Method and Strategy

OVERVIEW

In the previous sections, definitions of creativity have been given attention along with information about the advantages of using the IM and IBR. The development and teaching of thinking has been addressed through the illustration and definitions of cognitive and metacognitive skills in figure 1.3 relating to the Reciprocal Thinking Phases. Then, examples of interactive instruction resources for use in an IBR or as activity centers were provided, at length.

This section commences with the key points on how this IM and, specifically, the IBR develops "leadership." Then, in alignment with the examples given of possible IBR pages, step-by-step information is provided on how to make an IBR for literature and then a thematic unit of study. This is followed by "Overall IBR Important Messages," and an actual complete IBR example by Liz Struzzieri (2015).

Professor Laura Shea Doolan's "Intertwining Creativity and Innovation for Classroom Success: The IBR as Inspiration for Learning Achievement" is provided. Having taught the EDU 506A course for many years, this author and international presenter gives her perspective on the IBR regarding "the need to adapt to the legitimate, diverse needs of college level students' learning to better ensure their academic success to be the best teachers of those who are entrusted to their care."

A photographic and narrative section titled "The IBR and IM within and beyond the College Classroom" comes directly before the "Author's Closing Thoughts."

CREATIVE COGNITION'S IBR: LEADERSHIP BUILDING: MATTHEW SCHEIRING

Let's take a look at leadership development when using the IM to design an IBR with the use of creative cognition. First there is a *singularity of purpose*, as the method and IBR are intended to develop innovative thinking through imagining and inventing the pages to be played. Next there is *encouragement and reassurance* when making and/or playing the pages of an IBR, which involves the IM.

When working on the IBR in a classroom setting or elsewhere, at any age/grade level, there is the overall concept of *one's being successful* built into the project. This is accomplished by the *overriding emphasis on accepting one's inspired work*. Consequently, the making of an IBR is heartening and provides desire to *continue being creative*, due to the triumphant experience being supportive of one's efforts!

In advance of working on the IBR, whether alone or with another or others, there is the idea that this IBR can be accomplished. Examples are provided by the teacher, and this *builds self-confidence*. When working with others, *discussion ensues* and this allows for *assurance and support of ideas and inventions*. This promotion serves to reassure endeavors of creative cognition applications.

Collaboration and reassurance of this project *leads naturally to presenting ideas and images* in a linear or reciprocal format while calling for others' reaction and possible input. Assistance may be given and *cooperation builds strength in purpose*.

Yet another leadership quality of the IBR is that it provides an *optimistic perspective*. The IBR promotes and supports *positive thinking* with the idea that this making of pages/learning-through-play can be accomplished with *good planning*. This preparation is evidenced as the IBR pages are designed to address varied disciplines. Therefore, the connection between the topics of the pages to be reviewed, learned, or taught must be subject to *comprehension* of them. This requires *scheduling and arrangement*, as well as *sequencing for a comprehensive scope* of the project.

The final leadership quality that comes to mind is that of *persistence*. Whether making an IBR by oneself or working with a partner or even in a small group, there is *an end product* that needs to be present. This requires *goal setting* and working to complete the project, which encourages continually moving forward with purpose to produce or reach a target (M. R. Schiering, 2015).

THE IBR FOR REVIEW OR INTRODUCTION TO A PIECE OF LITERATURE

Step-by-Step IBR Directions

Materials: For the IBR that reviews of piece of literature, you'll need a binder (3–4 inches), page protectors, laminate, markers, construction paper, continuity tester, index cards, cardstock paper, 12-inch ruler, masking tape, aluminum foil, top-lid box, and brass fasteners.

General Directions: This IBR is designed to review a piece of literature, and the major requirements include: "About the Author" page, story summary, Invitation page, six interactive pages with one for each major discipline (reading, ELA, math, social studies, and science) and creative page. While you may have more than six pages, the main requirement is at least six tactile and/or kinesthetic activities pages. What follows is the sequence for making this type of IBR:

1. Select a piece of literature that's either a children's picture book or chapter book for children or adolescents. The latter is recommended for grades two through twelve.
2. Read the book, and, using Post-It notes or regular note paper, tag the sections of the story you want represented in your IBR.
3. Using the Internet and available resource books, research the author and create an Author Page that gives information about the book(s) this author has written and important facts about his/her life.
4. Again, using the Internet or your own awareness of the book's storyline, create a Summary of the Story page.
5. Write an *Invitation to Play-the-Pages of* the IBR that welcomes learners to engage in the activities you create.
6. Create a minimum of six interactive pages that require tactile and/or kinesthetic involvement. You may have pages that require more passive involvement, such as making an audiotape or doing a crossword puzzle, but there should be six definite get-up-and-move pages.
7. The interactive pages need to be in each of the five major disciplines of reading, math, science, social studies, and English language arts, and then the creative page could address art, music, construction, dance, or one of the other disciplines already provided.
8. For the creative page you may design something new that is in the format of an educational game. This may be a board, wall, or floor game or one that requires movement, or a role-play activity, a Puppet Theater with puppets, or making of a quilt, or a specific drawing that is possibly three-dimensional, such as a diorama.
9. Decide which activities are going to be represented for each discipline and plan out your IBR.
10. Plan to number each page in the IBR.
11. Create a table of contents.
12. Make the interactive/game pages using your own ideas.
13. Title each page of the IBR.
14. Create a Chart that lists the activities and corresponding cognitive and metacognitive skills you think are used when playing the page. Use the *Reciprocal Thinking Chart* to do this. A sample chart is provided in figure 4.1.
15. Put the pages in page protectors, or laminate them for multiple use, and place in the binder.
16. On the back-side of some activity pages, you might have encouragement statements, or information related to the book, and/or an example of how the page would look if not already self-corrective.
17. Have a *Congratulations Certificate* at the close of the IBR. You may want to include a *Your Comment Page* where learners may express their opinions about the IBR (Schiering, 1996).

THE IBR FOR A REVIEW OR INTRODUCTION TO A THEMATIC UNIT OF STUDY

Step-by-Step IBR Directions

Materials: For the IBR that reviews or introduces a thematic unit of study, you'll need a binder (3 to 4 inches), page protectors, laminate, markers, construction paper, continuity tester, index cards, cardstock paper, 12-inch ruler, masking tape, aluminum foil, top-lid box, and brass fasteners.

General Directions: This IBR is designed to address a specific area of the grade-level curriculum. This may be something like ecosystems, or body systems, such as the skeletal, respiratory, nervous, and circulatory systems. Or your unit of study may be on planets in our solar system, explorers, feelings, character development, or a period of history such as the time of the pioneers. The major requirements include: a title page, a page inviting the students to play the pages, and a minimum of six interactive pages with one for each major discipline and a creative page. While you may have more than six and include sedentary activities, such as a Word Search, the main requirement is at least six pages of tactile and/or kinesthetic activities. What follows is the sequence for making this type of IBR:

1. Select a topic that you are either interested in studying or, in a classroom, is part of the grade-level curriculum.
2. Using first- and secondhand resources, such as someone's addressing the topic from firsthand knowledge; using the Internet as a research guide, or gathering information from books on the topic, take notes (audio or handwritten) on the topic.
3. When using a book for information use Post-It notes or regular note paper, tag the important points you want represented in your IBR.
4. Discuss this with others in your group, or, if in a partnership, discuss your findings with your partner. Try to stay on-topic.
5. Beginning construction of the IBR includes an outside cover page and inside title page for the binder. Then, write an *Invitation to Play-the-Pages* of the IBR that welcomes learners to engage in the activities you create. Remember that all activity pages need to be self-corrective, or show an example on the flip-side of the instruction page.
6. All activities need a title. Try to make this title appealing. An example would be "Math Mania."
7. There are to be a minimum of six interactive pages that require tactile and/or kinesthetic involvement. You may have pages that require more sedentary involvement, such as making an audiotape or doing a Word Search or Word Jumble or even a Maze, but there should be six definite "get-up-and-move" pages.
8. The interactive pages need to be in each of the five major disciplines of reading, math, science, social studies, and English language arts, as well as the aforementioned creative page.
9. The creative page is where you design something new that is in the format of an educational game. This page may be a board, wall, or floor game, or creating a map where cardinal directions are in play. You may choose to have directions for a role-play activity, Puppet Theater with puppets, or making of a quilt out of large baggies with drawings on paper inserts and colorful duct tape to bind the quilt together, or a specific drawing that is possibly three-dimensional, or making of a diorama that would be engaging and a point for discussion of the topic being addressed.
10. Activity pages: other suggestions may include Flip-Chute, Pic-A-Dot, Wrap-Around, Electro-Board, or graphic organizers that require Velcro match. Most importantly, use your own imagination to design and then create pages for self-actualizing.
11. Decide which activities are going to be represented for each discipline, and plan out your IBR.
12. Number each page in the IBR.
13. Create a table of contents.
14. Create a chart that lists the activities and corresponding cognitive and metacognitive skills you think are used when playing the page. Use the *Reciprocal Thinking Chart* to do this. A sample chart is provided in Figure 4.1.
15. Put the pages in page protectors, or laminate them for multiple use, and place in the binder.
16. On the back-side of each activity page, you might have encouragement statements or information related to the book and/or an example of how the page would look in case you've not developed a self-corrective page.
17. Have a *Congratulations Certificate* at the close of the IBR. You may want to include a *Your Comment Page* where learners may express their opinions about the IBR (Schiering, 1996).

EXAMPLE OF AN IBR: *THE GRUFFOLO*: A FIRST-GRADE IBR, *ELIZABETH STRUZZIERI*

On the following pages one entire IBR is presented so you may see the flow and structure of this IM project- and performance-based work. This IBR was originally made by Elizabeth Maria Struzzieri and classmate for an Integrated Reading and English Language Arts course at Molloy College (EDU. 506A: Spring, 2015) and was then re-created by Elizabeth for this publication.

The IBR is partially made in class, with a good deal of it being constructed in after-school hours. Overall, it serves as a prototype when presented in the grade-level classroom for which the selected book is appropriate. It also gives students the opportunity to *review* or be *introduced* to a piece of literature, or in some cases to a thematic unit of study. Pages may be removed and returned, as each is numbered and in a clear plastic page protector with the activity inside that.

Playing a page, whether at one's desk or sitting in a group or experiencing through a Learning Center, allows the students to be personally involved in the topic. Retention of material is at an optimum, because learning is through doing/self-actuating!

Take a look back at the addendum to section 3 and reread the psychology of the activity "Kicking It Up a Notch." The principle used there by this Linx V.P. and summer camp director, Joshua Schiering, has the same idea as an IBR. This concept is that those engaged in learning will remember the material, the thoughts, ideas, opinions, and feelings when playing the pages, due to the significance of being involved.

When you've examined the pages of the following literature-based IBR please give some thought, when you have made your own IBR, to exchanging it with other classes of student-learners who might enjoy the IBR you created. Then, when you or your students make an IBR on a book or thematic unit of study at any grade level, you may exchange the IBRs with other classes of students. That way, students are teaching students. Remember, the IBR may be in any discipline or area of work (nursing, business, sciences, history, etc.). You continually have the opportunity to learn-through-play by addressing varied literature and/or themes.

Photo 4.1. IBR Cover

Title Page
The Gruffalo
Written by Julia Donaldson
Illustrated by Axel Scheffler
***An Interactive Book Report for
1st Graders***
Interactive Book Report Author:
Elizabeth Maria Struzzieri

Welcome Page
Welcome, First Grade Explorers! Let's take a stroll through the deep, dark woods as you review the story about the Gruffalo, or take a look to discover the story content before reading this book. There are all sorts of activities for you to play on each page; one in each discipline of reading, English language arts, social studies, math, and science. As you play the pages you'll visit story themes and discover the use of the main character, the mouse's cleverness and creative thinking to make it safely through the forest and home for dinner. Have fun!

There's adventure in this IBR
As you are learning through play
There are pages with activities
To use every day.

You'll discover the Gruffalo, and a mouse
Oh so fine
It meets an owl, fox, and snake
It will need to outshine

As
That mouse travels through the woods
Trying to get home for dinner
It escapes the scary forest creatures
by being quite clever.
Enjoy playing these pages and do remember
Return them to their place
For someone else's later playing-pleasure.

Table of Contents
Materials Needed for Playing or Making IBR Pages
Reciprocal Thinking Phases Identification Chart
Author Study
Book Summary
Reading/ELA: Character Thought Cloud Activity
Reading: Vocabulary Flip-Chute Activity with F.C. Cards
Reading: Comprehension Pic-A-Dot Holder Sample with Sample Question Cards
ELA: Character Headband Activity
ELA: Rhyming Word Wrap-Around
Social Studies: Story Wheel Character Sequence Spinner Game
Social Studies: Character Puppet Show
Math: Size Ordering: Question and Answer Key
Science: Build or Draw Your Own Gruffalo
Science: Find That Footprint Activity
Creative Page 1: Invent Your Own Imaginary Creature and Its Purpose!
Creative Page 2: Build Your Own Gruffalo
Congratulations Certificate and Reference Page

IBR Materials

In order to play the pages of this IBR you will need the following materials. Not every page requires the use of all the materials, and some pages may not need any of them. Still, it's best to be prepared, so here they are listed for you: scissors, pencil, paper, glue, ruler, dark color string or yarn, black marker, paper fastener, magnifying glass, card stock paper in different colors, tongue depressors, white construction paper, colored pencils, crayons, and/or markers, and cotton balls.

The Reciprocal Thinking Phases Cognition and Metacognition Identification Chart

This chart addresses the thinking skills involved in playing each of the IBR activity pages. As you know, self-actuating means to go forward and do something. It means to take action. Therefore, when each page is played you are self-actuating. Most of the time, you are also deciding. Examine the chart to see what thinking skills are utilized when playing the IBR pages.

Author Study

Julia Donaldson was born on September 16, 1948, in London, England. She attended Bristol University, where she studied drama and French. She first worked in publishing and as a teacher, and spent her free time performing street theater with her husband, Malcom. She performed the songs that she personally wrote and even directed musicals for children, which soon led to a career in writing songs for children's television. In 1993, after one of her songs was made into the book *A Squash and a Squeeze*, Donaldson continued to write over one hundred children's books as well as plays for both children and teenagers.

Donaldson is an English writer, playwright, street theater performer, and the 2011–2013 Children's Laureate. She is well-known for her popular rhyming children's stories such as *The Gruffalo, Room on the Broom, The Snail and the Whale,* and *Zog*, which are all among England's best-selling picture books. In total, she has 184 published works, which include 120 educational titles. Donaldson describes "Songbirds" as her proudest achievement, a complete phonics reading scheme of sixty books for children and a part of the Oxford Reading Tree. Donaldson is now a patron of the charity "Artlink Central," which engages artists to work in hospitals, prisons, and schools. Julia enjoys writing poetry and encouraging children to act and read aloud!

Figure 4.1. Reciprocal Thinking Identification Chart (Schiering, 2000)

Activities	Phase 1	Phase 2	Phase 3
Flip Chute and Definitions	Realizing Classifying	Communicating Inferring Predicting Generalizing Initial Deciding Initial Problem-solving	Evaluating Collaborating Advanced Deciding Problem-solving Analyzing Synthesizing Self-actualizing
Draw Your Own Imaginary Creature	Realizing Classifying Comparing Contrasting	Prioritizing Inferring Predicting Initial-deciding Initial Problem-Solving Communicating	Evaluating Problem Solving Analyzing Inventing Synthesizing Self-actualizing
Pick-A-Dot	Recognizing Realizing Classifying Comparing Contrasting	Active Listening Prioritizing Inferring Predicting Initial-deciding Initial Problem-Solving	Problem-solving Analyzing Synthesizing Self-actualizing
Character Headbands	Recognizing Realizing Classifying Comparing Contrasting	Prioritizing Inferring Communicating Predicting Active Listening Initial-deciding Initial Problem-Solving	Advanced Problem-solving Evaluating Analyzing Collaborating Synthesizing Self-actualizing
Rhyming Wrap Around	Realizing Classifying	Prioritizing Inferring Predicting Initial-deciding	Problem Solving Analyzing Synthesizing Self-actualizing
Story Wheel	Recognizing Realizing Classifying Comparing Contrasting	Prioritizing Inferring Predicting Initial-deciding Initial Problem Solving Organizing	Problem Solving Analyzing Synthesizing Recalling Self-actualizing Evaluating

Character Puppet Show	Recognizing Realizing Classifying	Active Listening Prioritizing Inferring Predicting Organizing Initial-deciding Initial Problem Solving	Collaborating Problem Solving Analyzing Synthesizing Self-actualizing
Size Ordering	Recognizing Realizing Classifying Comparing Contrasting	Prioritizing Inferring Predicting Organizing Initial-deciding Initial Problem Solving	Problem Solving Analyzing Synthesizing Self-actualizing
Measuring Characters	Recognizing Realizing Classifying Comparing Contrasting	Prioritizing Inferring Predicting Initial-deciding Initial Problem Solving Organizing	Problem Solving Analyzing Synthesizing Self-actualizing
Gruffalo Spinner Game	Recognizing Realizing Classifying	Prioritizing Inferring Predicting Organizing Initial-deciding Initial Problem Solving	Problem Solving Collaborating Analyzing Synthesizing Recalling Self-actualizing Evaluating
Foot Print Identification	Recognizing Realizing Classifying Comparing Contrasting	Prioritizing Inferring Predicting Initial-deciding Initial Problem Solving Organizing	Problem Solving Analyzing Synthesizing Recalling Self-actualizing Evaluating
Gruffalo Body Part Wheel	Recognizing Realizing Classifying Comparing Contrasting	Prioritizing Inferring Predicting Initial-deciding Initial Problem Solving	Problem Solving Analyzing Synthesizing Recalling Self-actualizing Evaluating

Figure 4.1. *(continued)*

| Build Your Own Gruffalo | Recognizing Realizing | Prioritizing Inferring Predicting Initial-deciding Initial Problem Solving | Problem Solving Analyzing Synthesizing Recalling Self-actualizing Evaluating |

Book Summary

The Gruffalo is an exciting and silly rhyming story about a mouse's stroll through a forest. On his walk, the mouse comes across a snake, a fox, and an owl. Although the mouse is small and knows that he could be eaten by all the other big animals, he is not the least bit afraid! The mouse is confident in his own intelligence and uses his very *big* imagination to make it through the forest safely just in time for dinner.

He tells the snake, fox, and owl that he is going to meet the Gruffalo for lunch. The Gruffalo, however, is an imaginary creature! The mouse knows that the other animals are big enough to eat him, so he decides to use his brains to overcome their brawn. Just hearing about the Gruffalo's terrible tusks, claws, and teeth in his jaws, is enough to help the animals decide to let the mouse be on his way.

This clever creative-thinking mouse's journey with a humorous twist takes us along his road of trials quite literally. Imagine the mouse's surprise when he comes across a real, live Gruffalo! He has "big orange eyes, knobby knees, and purple prickles all over his back," just like he imagined!

Although the Gruffalo is ten times his size, the mouse's courage is even *more* powerful. To avoid becoming the Gruffalo's lunch, the mouse takes him for a stroll through the woods and passes by the homes of the owl, the fox, and the snake. The Gruffalo suddenly sees that all the other animals would not dare to bother the mouse, and suddenly thinks that the mouse must be the *strongest* animal in the woods! Suddenly, the roles are reversed and the brilliant mouse safely walks home just in time for dinner, while the fox, owl, snake, and Gruffalo are left believing that they escaped the most ferocious creature in the woods, *the mouse*!

The mouse's physical strength is slim in comparison to the other animals. Still, he uses his wits to convince all of them that he is indeed a force with which to be reckoned.

In my opinion, children reading this book learn about creative thinking and apply it to courage, bravery, standing up for one's self, survival, and that by utilizing his/her mind, it is possible to overcome even the most difficult obstacles. Although the Gruffalo may appear to be scary and the mouse very meek, Donaldson's, "brains over brawn" theme comes shining through along with the mouse's active thinking, as the Gruffalo humorously hurries home to escape the mouse.

The rhymes and repetitive language in this story encourage reading aloud and, overall, provide readers with a message of how *mighty* the imagination truly is.

Reading/ELA: Character Thought Cloud Activity

Directions:

- Put the pictured page in a clear page protector so you can write on the page protector with a dry-erase marker and later remove what you've written and play the page again at a later time.
- Write two words in each of the thought bubbles that describe the character at the bottom of the worksheet.
- Continue writing describing words in the thought clouds until you have run out of room.
- Review your descriptive/adjective words with a friend who had read the book. See if this collaboration finds you agreeing, making corrections, and/or finding more words,
- Take one or two of the words and construct a sentence or two at the bottom of the page.

Example Gruffalo Picture and Character Cloud: The words "scary" and "ferocious" might be used in the Character Cloud.

Example of Sentence at Bottom of Character Cloud Page: The Gruffalo was scary because it looked so different from other forest animals. It seems ferocious because of its huge pointed teeth and purple prickles on its back.

Photo 4.2. Gruffalo Thought Cloud

Descriptive Sentences:

Photo 4.3. Owl Thought Cloud

Photo 4.4. Mouse Thought Cloud

166 SECTION 4

Photo 4.5. Fox Thought Cloud

Descriptive Sentences:

Photo 4.6. Snake Thought Cloud

168　SECTION 4

Reading Vocabulary Flip-Chute Activity with F. C. Cards

Directions:

The Gruffalo is hungry for some . . . VOCABULARY!

You'll need a Flip-Chute to do this activity. A picture of one is in photo 4.8. Perhaps you can make one that looks like this one. If not, use the directions and template from section 2 of this Interactive Workbook and make your own Flip-Chute.

- Cut out the Flip-Chute Card with the meaning of the word facing up and the notch in the upper right corner. Fold the card along the dotted line and use wide clear tape to fasten the cards together all the way around.
- Feed the card to the hungry Gruffalo by placing it in its mouth = the upper slot. Be sure the Flip-Chute Card has the notch in the upper right corner. Think of the answer before the card appears in the bottom slot.
- When the card comes out of the Flip-Chute, you will see the name of the vocabulary term or, in two cases, comprehension question answers. Continue feeding the cards to the Gruffalo until there are no more to be fed into it. He won't be full until you are familiar with all of your vocabulary words and meanings, so keep going until you know them all! And, you may want to make ten Flip-Chute Cards to add to the ones provided for you in photos 4.10A and 4.10B.
- If the cards provided in the photos 4.10A and 4.10B aren't big enough for you, then use these as a guide to make your own Flip-Chute cards. And, when you get a chance, add to these with other vocabulary cards that are of words you want to learn and/or are in your textbooks in reading, science, social studies, or language arts.

Photo 4.7. Gruffalo Flip-Chute

IM and IBR 169

A very big meal is a _____	An animal that slithers on its belly and makes a hissing sound is called a _____	A body of water that is surrounded by land is a _____
feast	snake	lake
One of the orange colored animals with a white tipped long tail that the mouse met when going through the forest was the	A relaxing walk is called a _____	Branches of a tree that are cut into rectangular pieces and used for a fireplace are called _____
	stroll	logs

Photo 4.8. Flip-Chute Cards # 1

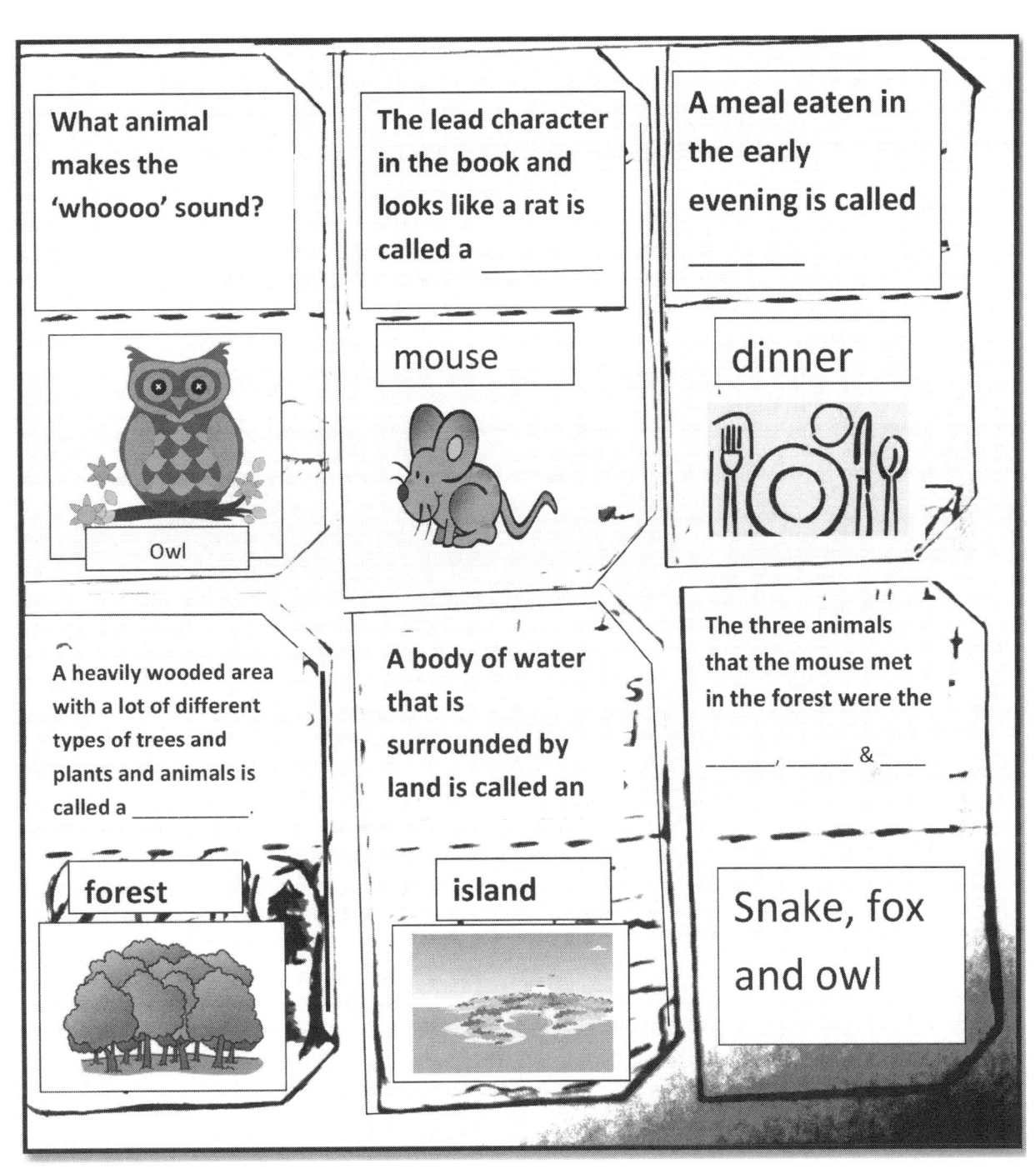

Photo 4.9. Flip-Chute Cards # 2

Reading: Comprehension Pic-A-Dot Holder Sample with Sample Question Cards

Directions:

- Open up your Pic-A-Dot.
- Next, read the question on the card and think to yourself what the answer might be.
- Use a pencil to pick the "dot" or circle that is under the answer you think is correct.
- Now, try lifting-up/pulling-out the card while keeping your pencil in the open space! If your card comes out, your answer is correct! If your card does not come out, read the question at the card's top again and try picking another answer with your pencil. Keep going until all of your cards lift-up and remember to have fun!
- Use the Pic-A-Dot Template from section 2 to make your own and view the one in photo 4.11. Then, use the information on the "cards" from xfigures 4.12 and 4.13 to put on your cards.

Photo 4.10. Pic-A-Dot Holder (Sample)

PIC-A-DOT : The following are 6-Pic-A-Dot cards you'll need to make on 5x8 index cards. Let the ones on this page and the next serve as a guide for literal comprehension questions about the Gruffalo book.

Who is the second character the mouse meets in the Gruffalo story?	What color are the prickles on the Gruffalo- back?
Gruffalo Snake **Owl**	Red **Purple** Yellow

What did the mouse eat at the end of the Gruffalo story?	What meal dos the mouse-character say he is going to eat with the Gruffalo?
A nut Cheese Breakfast	Lunch Dinner Breakfast

Where does the Owl-character live?	Who is the first character the mouse meets?
Swamp Lake **Treetop**	**Fox** Snake Owl

Photo 4.11. Pic-A-Dot Cards 1–6

PIC-A-DOT (continued): The following are six Pic-A-Dot cards you'll need to make on 5 x 8 index cards. Let the ones on this page serve as a guide for literal comprehension questions about the Gruffalo book.

PIC-A-DOT (continued): The following are 6-Pic-A-Dot cards you'll need to make on 5x8 index cards. Let the ones on this page serve as a guide for literal comprehension questions about the Gruffalo book.

The story about the Gruffalo is what genre of book? History　　Realistic Fiction　　Fiction 　○　　　　○　　　　○	Where did the mouse take a stroll? Pond　　　Woods　　　Pool 　○　　　　○　　　　○
The mouse took a stroll in the _____, dark woods. deep　　　flower　　　tree 　○　　　　○　　　　○	What color is the Gruffalo- tongue? Purple　　　Black　　　Orange 　○　　　　○　　　　○
Which character does the Gruffalo think is the scariest? Snake　　　Fox　　　Mouse 　○　　　　○　　　　○	Where does the snake think the mouse Is going? It is to a _____ Feast　　　mountain　　　snowstorm 　○　　　　○　　　　○

Photo 4.12. Pic-A-Dot Cards 7–12

ELA: Character Headband Activity

Directions:

- Find four friends and working together make five headbands with one of each of the following names on one of the headbands: Gruffalo, Owl, Mouse, Fox, Snake
- Put all the headbands on the floor with the names facing down.
- Close your eyes and take turns picking character headbands. Put yours on your head without turning it over. Remember, keep your eyes closed until the headband is on your head and do not peek at it!
- Now you will try to guess what character you are from the book using clues from your friends!
- You can now take turns asking one friend one question that will help you figure out who you are (For example: What color am I? Do I have fur? Am I big or small? Where do I live? Did I meet the Gruffalo first?). The only question you cannot ask your friends is "Who am I?"
- Continue taking turns asking each friend a question until everyone has guessed which characters they are.
- Close your eyes and put your character headbands on the floor again.
- Pick a new headband without peeking and play again until everyone has had a turn being each character. Have fun!

ELA: Rhyming Wrap-Around

Directions:

- Find the blue yarn in the top corner of the Wrap-Around.
- Turn the paper around and look for the green "Start" arrow.
- Line up the blue yarn with the "Start" line and hook it onto the first hole.
- Flip the paper back over!
- You have started your rhyming Wrap-Around with the word "wood." Move the blue yarn over to a word on the right that rhymes with "wood" and hook it onto the hole.
- To get to the next word ("toes"), move the yarn behind the paper and hook it onto the hole for "toes" on the left.
- Keep matching the words that rhyme until there are no more open holes.
- Flip the paper over and check if your ending yarn lines up with the red "End" arrow and black line. Check if your blue yarn lines up with the black lines on the back of the paper! If they don't line up try again . . . and have fun!

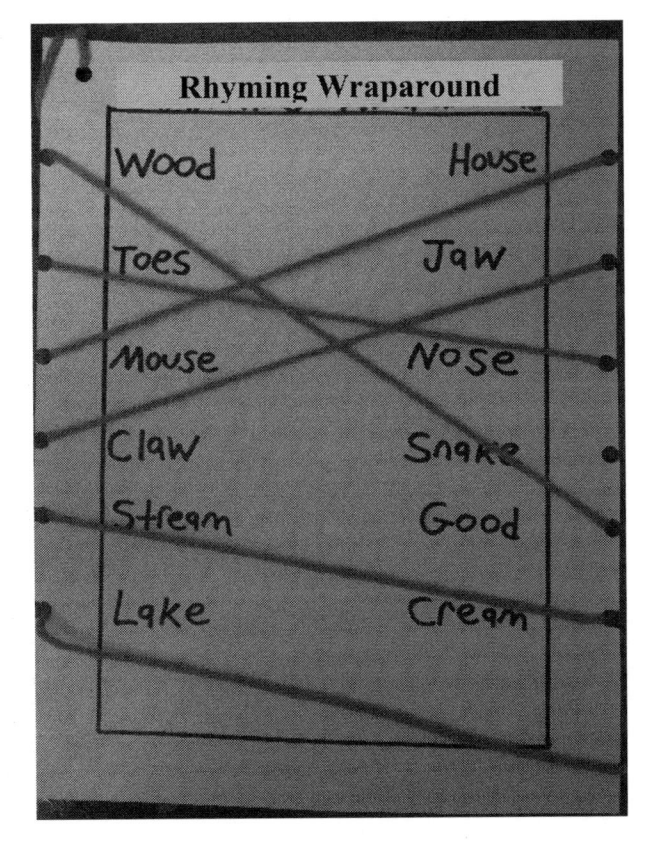

Photo 4.13. Rhyming Wraparound

IM and IBR 175

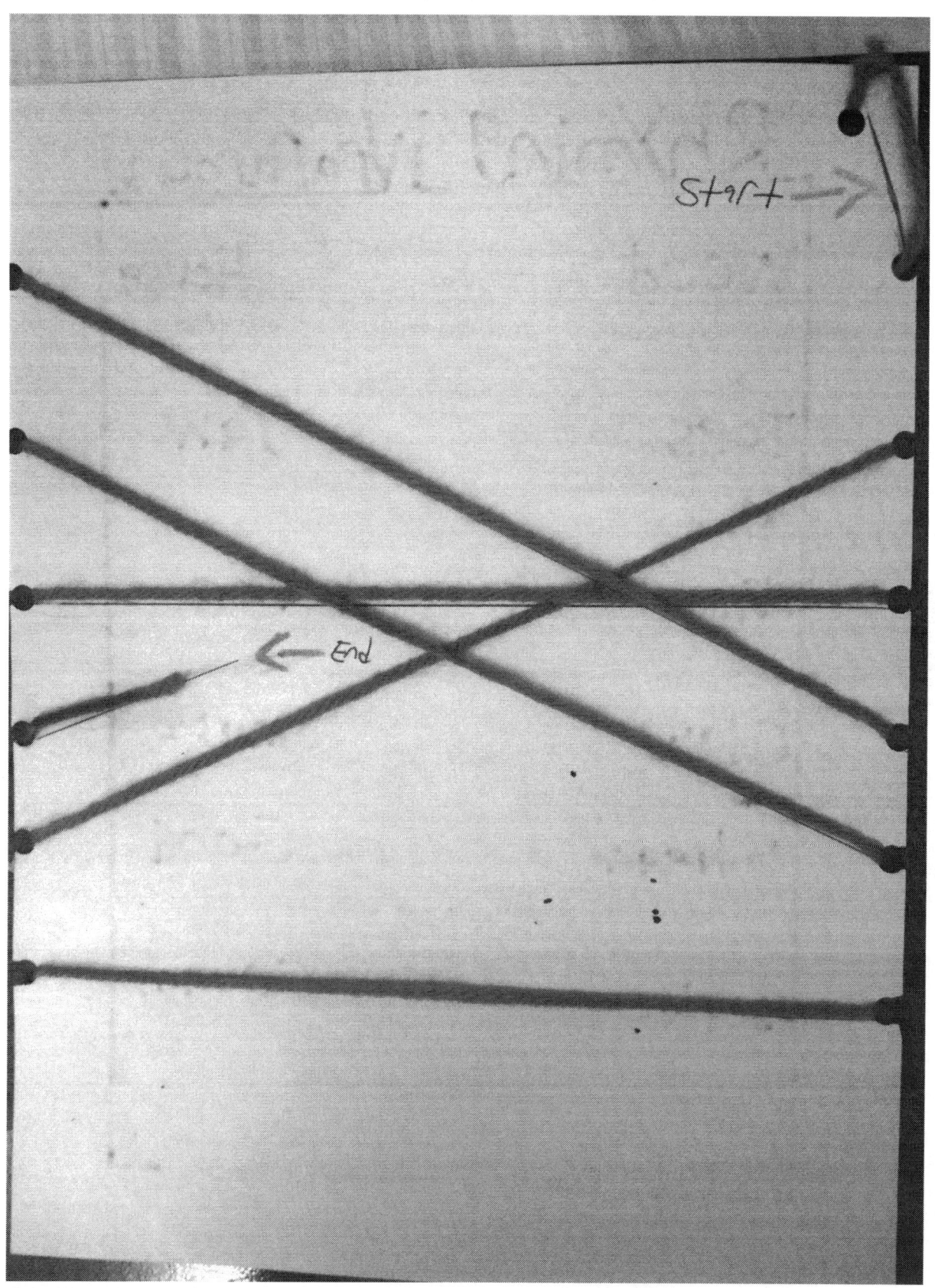

Photo 4.14. Wraparound Key

Social Studies: Story Wheel Character Sequence Spinner Game

Inner Circle/Wheel

Outer Circle/ Wheel

1

← Brass fastener →

STORY WHEEL CHARACTER-SEQUENCE-SPINNER GAME

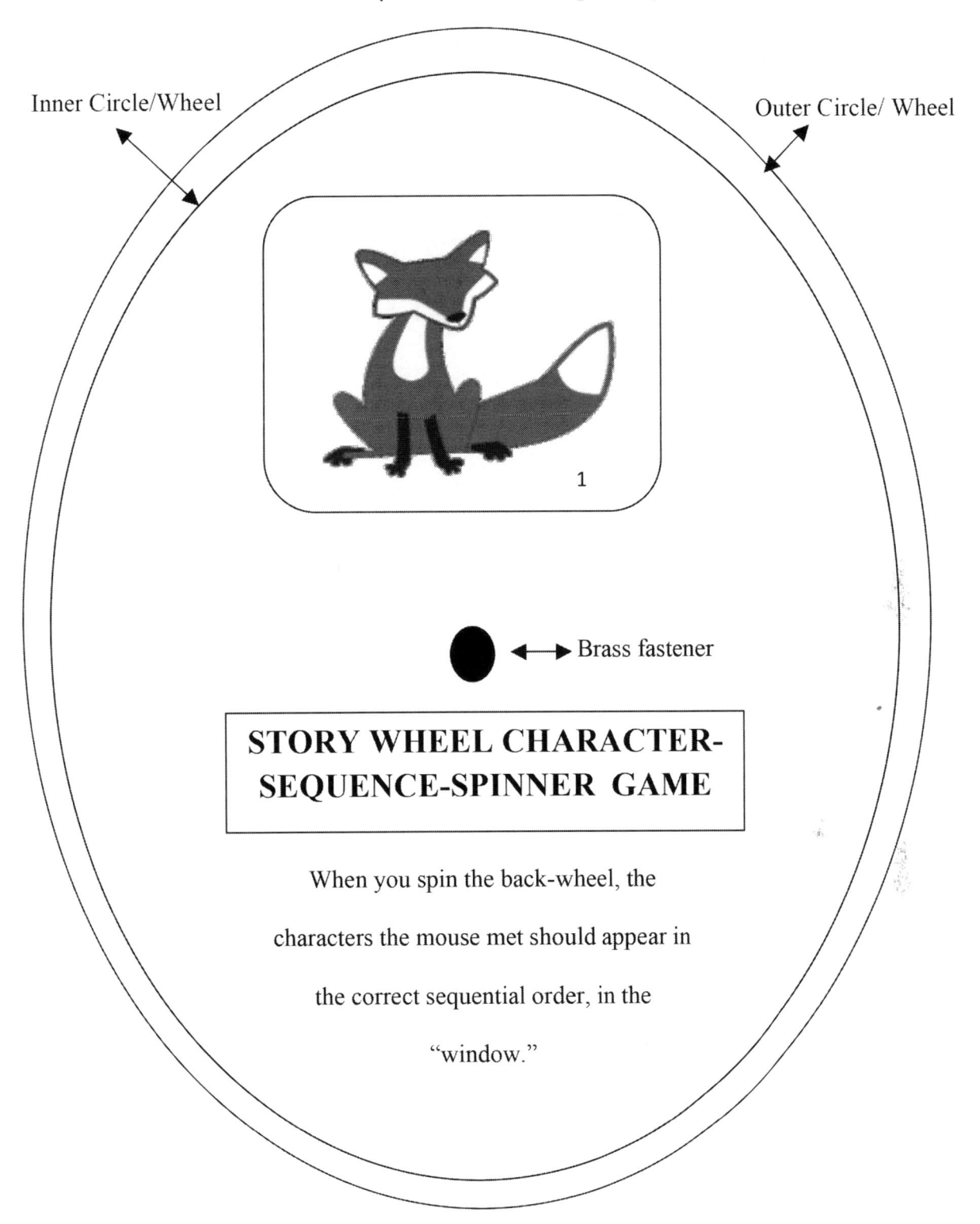

When you spin the back-wheel, the characters the mouse met should appear in the correct sequential order, in the "window."

Photo 4.15. Story Wheel Character-Sequence Spinner Game

Directions:

- You'll need two cutout circles that we are calling "wheels." These are approximately 12 × 12 inches for the inner wheel/circle and 12 × 12¼ or 12 × 12½ inches for the outer wheel/circle. Or, you could use a paper dinner plate and trim off about a quarter of an inch for the inner wheel/circle
- The larger wheel/circle, which is also the "outer" one, will have four pictures on it in the cardinal direction places of north/top-of-circle, south/bottom of circle, east/right side of circle, and west/left side of circle.
- At the top of the larger wheel/circle, glue or draw a picture of the fox. And, in the far right corner of the picture put the number 1. See figure 4.16.
- Glue or draw a picture of the owl in the east/right position of the larger wheel/circle, and the number 2 in the bottom right corner.
- Glue or draw a picture of the Snake on the bottom of the larger wheel/circle and the number 3 in the bottom right corner.
- Glue or draw a picture of the Gruffalo on the west/left side of the larger wheel/circle and the number 4 in the lower right corner.
- On the smaller or inner wheel/circle cut out a square opening about 4 × 4 inches on the top of the wheel/ circle.
- Attach the outer and inner circles with a brass fastener in the center. The smaller of the two circles goes on the inside while the larger one is the outer circle. Now spin the outer circle (wheel) "*counter-clockwise*" and watch the Gruffalo story characters appear one-by-one in the cutout space of the inner circle. These will be in the sequential order that the mouse met these characters in the story.
- If you get a chance, do this activity with a friend and make up or recall dialogue to share about what the characters said when meeting the mouse.

Social Studies: Character Puppet Show

Directions:

- Find four friends and make a Puppet Theater like the one shown in section 3 and titled Puppetry Theater (activity 14).
- Each friend will play one character using a stick puppet.
- Each friend will draw a different background, to help show where the mouse met each character in the story (forest, lake, stream, trail).
- Act out the mouse's journey in the correct order from the book with the stick puppet and backgrounds.
- When you are done, switch character puppets with your friends and perform another show.

(These Character Pictures were hand drawn using the illustrations from the book.)

Photo 4.16. Puppet Samples: Owl, Mouse, Fox

IM and IBR 179

Photo 4.17. Puppet Samples: Gruffalo and Snake

Math: Size Ordering: Question and Answer Key

Directions:
Snake

- Find the snake tiles.
- Spread the tiles out on the floor.
- Put the snakes in order from biggest to smallest.
- Turn the tiles over when you are done. If you see the word: **SNAKES** and the numbers **1, 2, 3, 4, 5, 6** in order, you are correct!

Gruffalo

- Find the Gruffalo tiles.
- Spread the tiles out on the floor.
- Put the Gruffalos in order from smallest to biggest.
- Turn the tiles over when you are done. If you see the word: **FOREST** and the numbers **1, 2, 3, 4, 5, 6** in order, you are correct!

Mouse

- Find the mouse tiles.
- Spread the tiles out on the floor.
- Put the mice in order from biggest to smallest.
- Turn the tiles over when you are done. If you see the word: **CHEESE** and the numbers

Photo 4.18. Size Ordering Picture of Character Pieces

Photo 4.19. Size Ordering Word Key

182   SECTION 4

Science: Build or Draw Your Own Gruffalo

Directions:

- Make an outline of a Gruffalo, and then make a Spinner Wheel like the one in Figure 4. Spin the spinner and look at the number of dots where the spinner is pointing.
- Find the picture of what the spinner arrow is pointing to on the "Gruffalo Spinner Game Board." Now, put your finger on it.
- Move your finger across the row and choose one body part you would like to draw on your Gruffalo's body.
- Keep spinning until you have drawn one Gruffalo body part on your Gruffalo drawing that is from each row on your Gruffalo Spinner Game Board!
- Give your unique Gruffalo a name and write three sentences that describe what it looks like.

Keep up the great work you are doing!

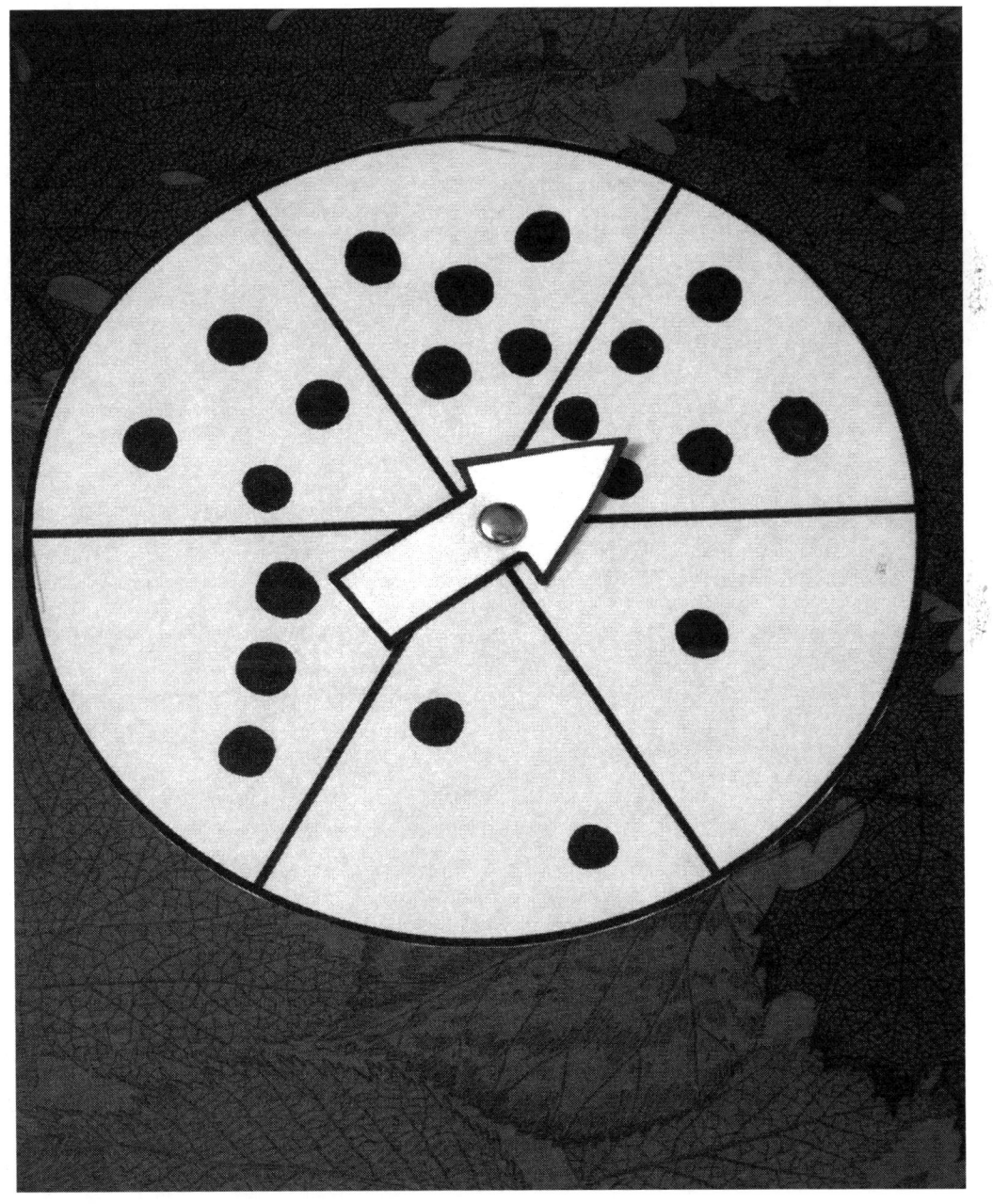

Photo 4.20.   Gruffalo Spinner

IM and IBR   183

Gruffalo Spinner Answer Key

	Brown eyes	Big eyes	Tiny eyes	Red eyes	Spooky eyes	Yellow eyes
(eyes)						
(nose)	Hairy nose	Dog-shaped nose	Round nose	Square nose	Big nose	Oval nose
(ear)	Human-type ear	Elephant ear	Three tiny ears	Four orange ears	Two pointy ears	One big ear with dots on it
(hand)	Two hands with ten fingers on each hand	Three Mitten-covered hands	Two hands with pointed nails	One hand with claws	Four bear-paw hands	Two Webbed Hands
(mouth)	One-tooth open mouth	Spiky-teeth open mouth	Tongue sticking out of mouth	Two mouths with smiles	One big frown mouth	Bat-teeth mouth
DOTS	1	2	3	4	5	6

Photo 4.21. Gruffalo Spinner Answer Key

Directions

- Take out your animal footprints, scientists! These are on Figure 4.23.
- Look very carefully at the animal footprints.
- If you need some clues to find out who the footprint belongs to, read the description above, below or next to the footprint. The arrow points you in the correct direction.
- Make a prediction as to which footprint(s) belong to the characters of the human being, fox, mouse, Gruffalo, snake, and owl. Be sure to write your answer on the provided line and check figure 4.24 to check if the answer you selected is correct.

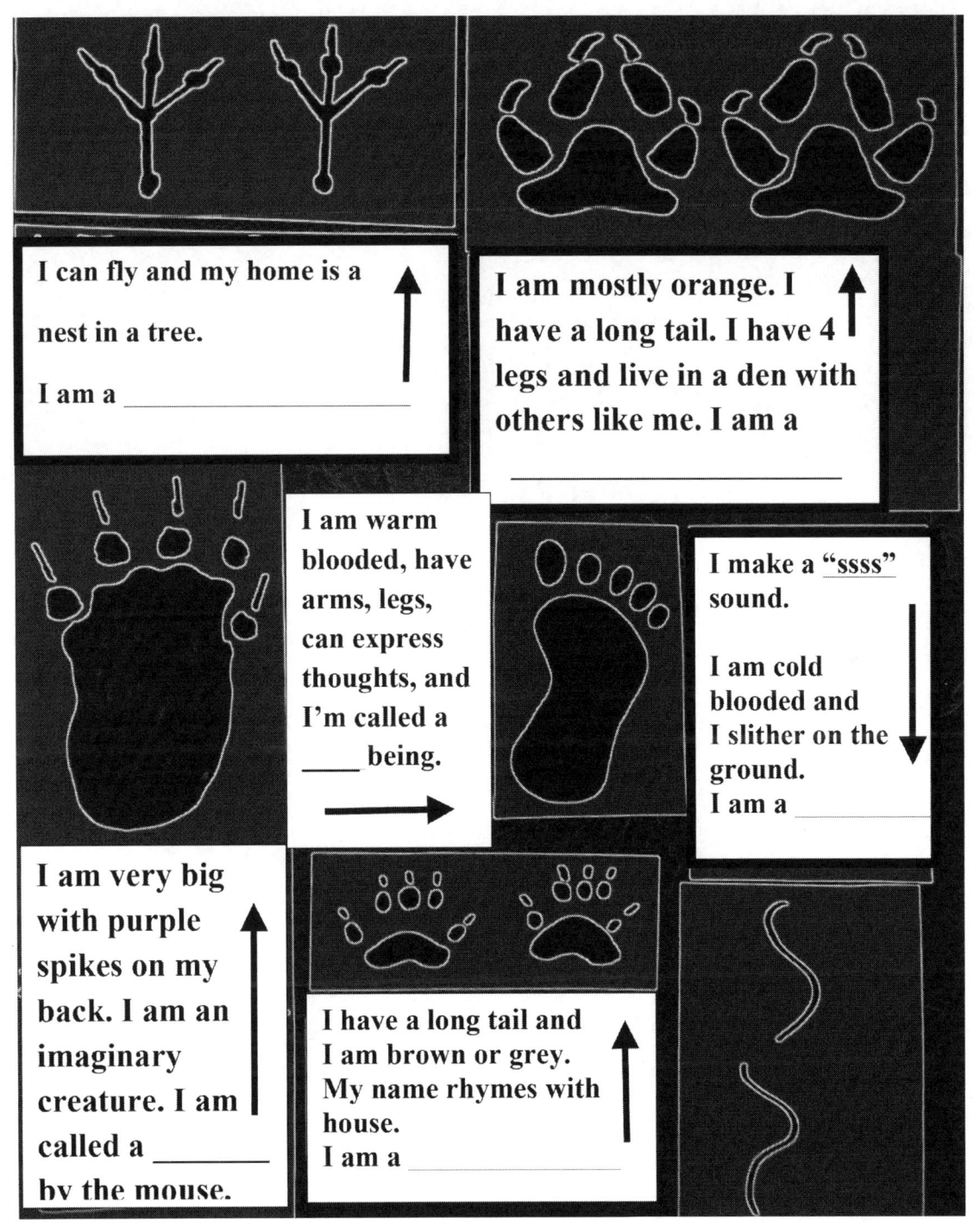

I can fly and my home is a nest in a tree.
I am a _____

I am mostly orange. I have a long tail. I have 4 legs and live in a den with others like me. I am a _____

I am warm blooded, have arms, legs, can express thoughts, and I'm called a ____ being.

I make a "ssss" sound.

I am cold blooded and I slither on the ground.
I am a _____

I am very big with purple spikes on my back. I am an imaginary creature. I am called a _____ by the mouse.

I have a long tail and I am brown or grey. My name rhymes with house.
I am a _____

Photo 4.22. Footprint Identification Activity

IM and IBR 185

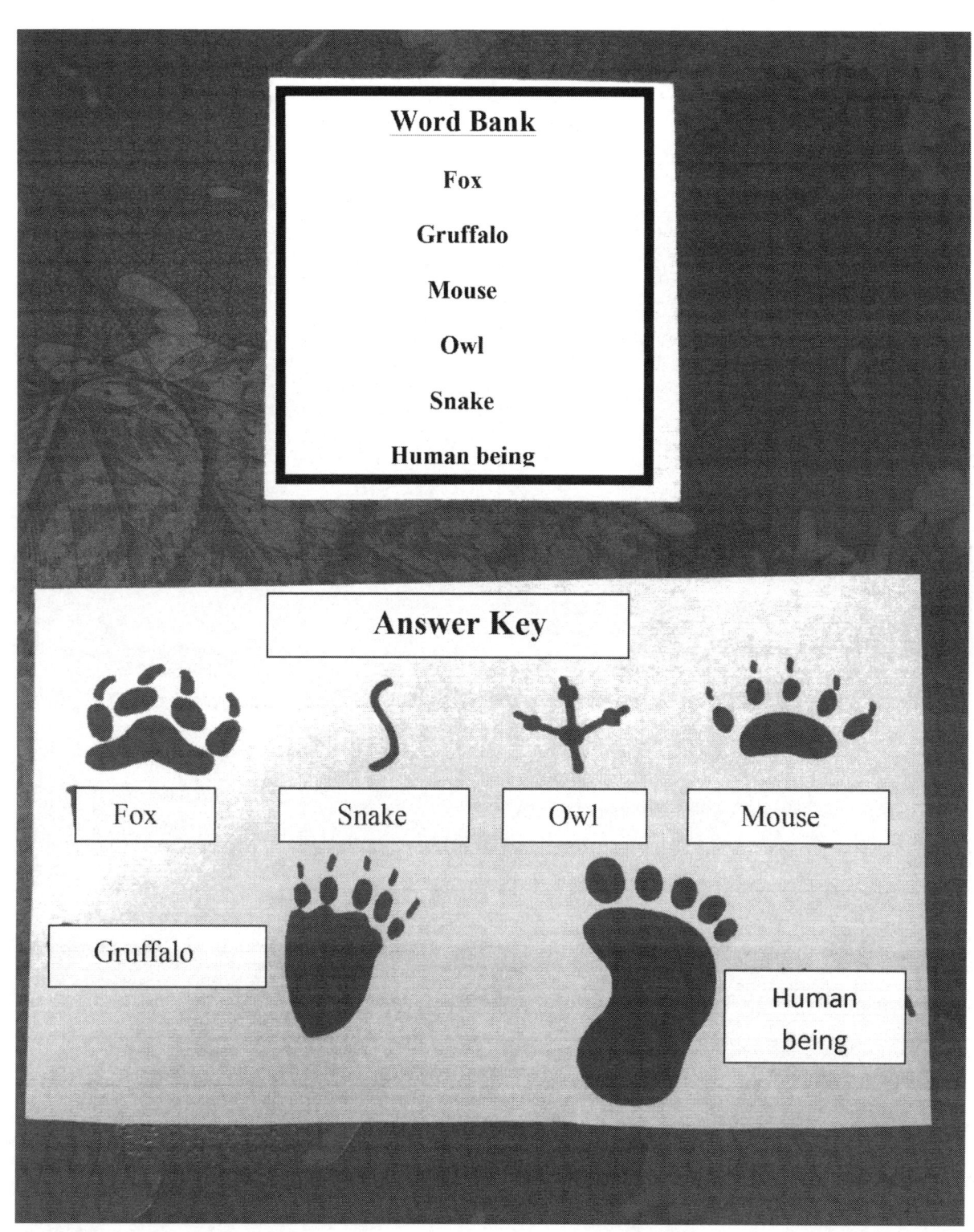

Photo 4.23. Footprint Answer Key

Creative Page 1: Invent Your Own Imaginary Creature and Its Purpose!

Directions: This activity requires you to use your imagination to design and create. Remember that one's imagination is a powerful learning tool!

1. Think about inventing an imaginary figure or creature. What is its size and shape? What special features does it have? Does it have arms and feet? Does it look human or more like a woodland, flying, water animal, or outer space alien?
2. Think about the purpose of this creature or figure that you are about to invent.
3. Draw your special invented creature.
4. Write five to ten sentences that help describe the figure and its purpose for being. Try to make this a "helpful-to-others" purpose.
5. Give your creature a name.
6. Share your picture and sentences with a classmate and see if the two of you can create a story to role-play about the creature or figure drawing you invented.

1. Draggy can breathe fire from its nose.
2. Draggy can fly when it is happy.
3. Helping others makes Draggy happy.
4. Draggy loves to eat spicy food.
5. Draggy's purpose is to help people cook outdoor Bar-B-Q dinner meals.

Photo 4.24. Imaginary Creature Sample: Draggy

Creative Page 2: Build Your Own Gruffalo

Directions:

- Take out some glue and your brown Gruffalo, he is waiting to be brought to life!
- Use orange pom-poms or cotton balls and glue them where you think the Gruffalo's eyes should be. Use a black marker to make a pupil in the center of each eye. Great! Now your Gruffalo can see!
- Use scissors to cut out a long, black tongue and glue it where you think the Gruffalo's tongue should be. Great! Now your Gruffalo can taste!
- Use scissors to cut out white construction paper triangles and glue them where you think all of the Gruffalo's claws belong. Great! Now your Gruffalo can dig!
- Use scissors to cut out purple construction paper prickles and glue them all over your Gruffalo's back. Great! Now your Gruffalo is safe!
- Cut out construction paper horns and glue them where you think the Gruffalo's horns should be. Great! Now your Gruffalo is very tall!
- Glue some black beads onto them where you think the knobby knees belong on the Gruffalo. Great! Now your Gruffalo can walk!
- Use a green marker to draw a wart at the end of the Gruffalo's nose. Great! Now your Gruffalo is colorful!
- Use scissors to cut yarn and glue it all over your Gruffalo. Hooray! Now your Gruffalo is furry and complete!

Photo 4.25. Build Your Own Gruffalo

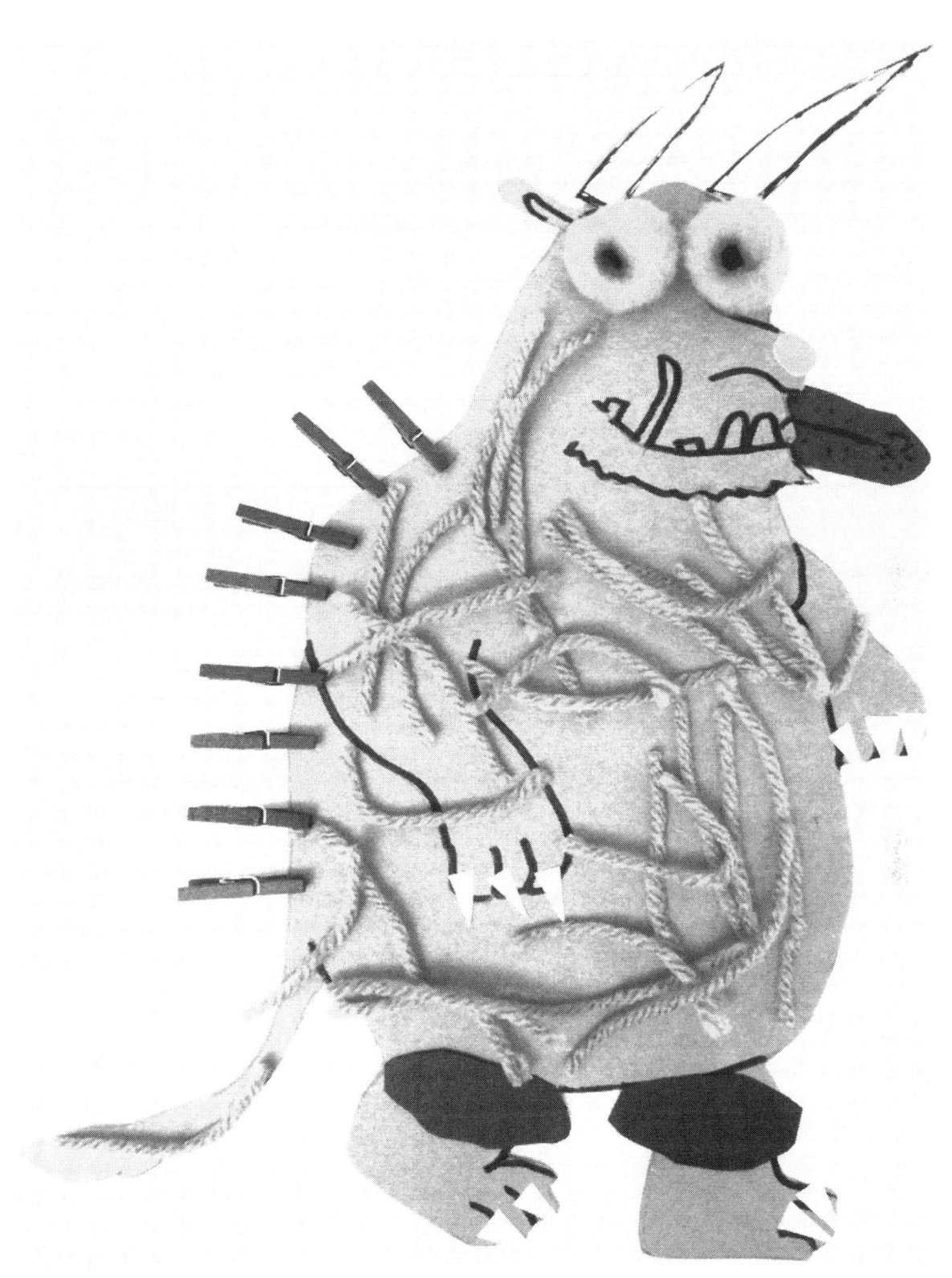

Photo 4.26. Build Your Own Gruffalo: Example

Congratulations

You have successfully played all of the pages in this Interactive Book Report! By doing this you reviewed the book and realized how imaginative and clever the "mouse" character was. While you were playing the pages of this IBR you used many thinking skills. These were outlined for you at the start of the IBR on the Reciprocal Thinking Pages. Take a look at those pages and discover how much thinking you did by playing the pages of this IBR.

You are very smart, I'm sure you'll agree. And, I am very proud of you for completing each of these activities. As you reviewed this Gruffalo book or maybe used this IBR to learn about it before reading it you gained information and saw creative thinking shown! Also, you have studied reading, English language arts, math, social studies and science by playing the pages. With your good fun work the mouse made it home to have a hazelnut for dinner. Yummy!

Perhaps you'd like to make some pages to add to this Interactive Book Report. If so, do that! And, remember this: you are never too small or too young or old to be imaginative and creative!

Fill in the part below that asks for your name. I have already signed this certificate. Cut out the part below along the provided dotted line.

— — — — — — — — — — — — —

IBR Completion Certificate

Student's Name: _____

IBR Author: Elizabeth Maria Struzzieri

INTERTWINING CREATIVITY AND INNOVATION FOR CLASSROOM SUCCESS: THE IBR AS INSPIRATION FOR LEARNING ACHIEVEMENT

Dr. Laura Shea Doolan

"What do you mean by the Interactive Book Report (IBR)?" asked the professor.

"Well, it's a creative cognition, perceptual preference component of learning styles, metacognitive resource that our graduate students who are enrolled in the Integrated ELA and Reading for the Diverse Learner in the Inclusion Classroom create," replied the director.

The professor took the challenge, and it became one of her and the teacher-candidate's favorite courses. The designing and making of an IBR assignment aligned with state standards enhanced everyone's ability to provide the best researched-based instruction to meet the learning needs of diverse students, which are imperative to foster graduate students' ability to meet required outcomes in conjunction with their own student-learners' outcomes that would best be incorporated into all teaching repertoire (Burke and Shea Doolan, 2006).

But why did this motivating enjoyment of the course happen? One might question. Shockingly, although most teachers know students learn differently, alarmingly, many continue to adopt a single, scripted reading approach, usually targeting only the auditory/visual modalities. Such limitation is done in hopes of best facilitating student mastery of the complex aspects of reading, regardless of learners' age, interests, gender, and so forth. In contrast, the IBR (Schiering 1996; ©2003; 2015), diverges from these approaches by appealing to all strands of the Dunn and Dunn (1992) Learning Style Model (Environmental, Emotional, Sociological, Psychological, Physiological), with the added components of using one's imagination and the application of creativity in design and self-actualization.

Why? Learning to read is a very difficult process and cannot be accomplished, optimally, by a large percentage of those who wish to read—regardless of age—when the identical approach to reading is adopted for all. This is because each person's brain is receptive in varying ways. Interestingly, research has revealed that many youngsters become absorbed in appealing learning endeavors (Dunn and Burke, 2007). Yet, different activities attract different students. According to Dunn and Griggs (2008), "Learning to read is the most important school-related accomplishment. However, how children master reading varies substantially, by each individual's academic achievement, age, brain processing, inclination, gender, and interests" (p. 3).

By addressing processing style, which is accommodated by the IM and IBR strategy, Dunn (2008) explains that standardized achievement test scores are literally reversed if previously they'd been poor. Treffinger, Schoonover, and Selby (2013) explain that creative learning should involve teaching that leads to student higher-level thinking. The Reciprocal Thinking Phases Cognition to Metacognition Identification Chart (Schiering 2000b) addresses that nicely. Consequently, teachers creating or having their student learners design and create IBRs on literature or a thematic unit of study to master content in all subjects and to meet rigorous learning standards facilitates their and their learner's creativity and innovation, which are vital characteristics in this rapid-paced technological world.

All in all, the IBR helps to establish a culture of high teaching and learning expectations with project- and performance-based work being the end product. As I reported in 2013, "Research studies, on the relationship between teaching strategies that foster student engagement, motivation, and empowerment (SEME) reveal a dramatic influence on positive student learning—academically and socially—that might also support the development of life-long learning communities" (p. 179). The IBR underscores a teaching commitment to provide an exceptional, instructional strategy facilitating all ages of learners to meet expected outcomes.

You might wonder what the graduate students "really" thought of the overall IBR assignment. It could be summed up with this quotation, "At first creating the IBR was challenging, and I thought I couldn't meet the requirements. Then, I got into planning it and making it. Now, I think, I'll start to create them to have students learn the most difficult material."

As for my own reaction to teaching this course that had the IBR as one assignment, "Well, it was one of my favorites, because it made me even more creative, innovative and continually aware of my need to adapt to the legitimate, diverse needs of college level students' learning to better ensure their academic success to be the best teachers of those who are entrusted to their care."

The Interactive Book Report attached to the Interactive Method allows its creators and those who use it to learn to flourish, and Plato would approve, as he stated, "Do not train youths to learning by force and harshness, but direct them to it by what amuses their minds, so that you may be better able, to discover with accuracy, the peculiar bent of the genius of each (Wandberg and Rohwer, 2003, p. 127). From my readings, Confucius also would agree.

THE IBR AND IM WITHIN AND BEYOND THE COLLEGE CLASSROOM

Within the Classroom: Fall Semester 2015 EDU. 506A

Photo 4.27 is of the IM being utilized through IBRs made by teacher candidates during the fall semester of 2015. The course is titled, Integrated Reading and ELA for the Diverse Learner in the Inclusion Classroom (EDU. 506A). Each one pictured is showing a personally designed and created IBR that will be or is being used in a classroom outside the college, within the Long Island community. The teacher candidates, in an end-of-semester course "Reflection Paper" commented on their reaction to this project.

Some Teacher Candidate Course "Reflection Paper" IBR Comments

Danielle Bowker: "At first my partner, Andrea Policastro, and I were completely overwhelmed. However, as we began to do the project and create the activities it really was an enjoyable and worthwhile experience. The IBR is something we'll be able to use in our future classrooms. I never imagined we'd finish this assignment and be proud of our work, but we are beyond proud.

Lauren Spotkov: "I think my favorite part of the IBR was when creativity was linked to the human experience, because it made it clear that we are all creative regardless of our life experiences. All the assignments, as we presented each one, helped with public speaking skills. Additionally, filling in the Reciprocal Thinking Skills Chart the IBR page player got to see what cognitive and metacognitive skills were used when playing the page. An example would be realizing this activity is about identifying parts of an ecosystem, and deciding what words are related to ecology and sustainability."

Vivian Stein: "Overall, my favorite class project would be the IBR, because I can't imagine a better assignment to help me in my future teaching."

James Fitzpatrick: "The IBR taught me that I can craft games that my students will enjoy. By sharing our IBRs in the classroom I gained information on other ideas to use for IBR pages. I think students frequently look for an experience where the teacher instructs them on how to do things. The structure of school seems as such that it inhibits creativity and forces children to second-guess themselves. We often, I think, convince ourselves that the work we produce on our own is not good enough unless we are told exactly what to do. The fact of the matter is we, as human beings, learn by doing."

Caitlin Kellegher: "Out of all the assignments, the IBR was my favorite. I worked with Nicole Kearns and we brainstormed ideas . . . bouncing off one another's inventions. This project offered us a way to collaborate. The activities are self-corrective and this means the teacher takes an indirect role and students benefit by teaching themselves, as they are self-reliant."

Carli Palladino: "If I am being completely honest I didn't think I was going to enjoy the IBR project. But, working with Kristin Rochford I learned what creativity can really accomplish! Overall, the IBR was an uplifting assignment as it showed me I could do anything I put my mind to, and that included using my imagination to invent things."

Photo 4.27. IBRs from EDU. 506A Fall Semester 2015

Beyond the Classroom: Fall Semester 2015 Children's Literature

In Schiering's English Children's Literature (ENG 262.03) course in the Freshman Learning Community section, an assignment designed to bring the IM into use through the construction of interactive Tri-fold Boards was given. The purpose of the assignment was to create interactive instructional resources as a strategy involving project and performance-based learning.

The second reason for this assignment was to use one's creative cognition to design educational games, as a *Service Learning* experience. This means that the class knowingly would be giving these boards they designed using their creative cognition to a school for use in an elementary classroom. The idea was to select a piece of children's literature and in the center of the board design a Story Map graphic organizer. Then, using the same concept of the IBR, but on a smaller scale, these college freshmen were creating educational games that addressed the story in the board's center for student learners' learning-through-play.

At the semester's end the boards were put on display in the second floor of Kellenberg Hall. The boards were then donated to the college's newly formed Circle K Club, student president Asad Moughal. The aforementioned club is sponsored by Peninsula Kiwanis, Hewlett, New York, with its past president and present secretary, Kevin Cooney, serving as the liaison between the two organizations. The focus of Circle K and Kiwanis is community involvement through varied types of service learning.

Consequently, with the donation of these Tri-fold Boards there is an established connection between the course, the college, and surrounding community in an outreach to assist student learners' instruction through an interactive learning endeavor. Support for this service project was continually given by English Department professors Drs. Robert Kinpoitner and Katheen Conway, in their respective responsibility areas of department chair and director of the Freshmen Learning Community. Support from Drs. Maureen Walsh and Joanne O'Brien, dean and associate dean of the Division of Education was provided regarding letters being sent to all book contributors from Molloy College. (Contributing course members are listed by photograph location).

Photo 4.28. Eng. 262.03: Freshmen Learning Community Children's Literature Course-Mates. Back Row: Gia Negron, Kelly Cassidy, James Snell, Brianna White, Vanessa Wiegman, Alyssa Soldano, Laura Drew, and Alexa Miritello. Front Row: Dominique Capolongo, Jess D'Amprisi, Sophia Moore, Brooke Gardner, and Mary Malinowski.

Photo 4.29. Sample of Three Eng. 262.03 Interactive Tri-Folds Boards

Photo 4.30. Closeup of Interactive Tri-Fold Board: Laura Drew

194   SECTION 4

Beyond the Classroom: Children Using Interactive Instructional Resource

Throughout this book and specifically in this section, the idea of having IBRs address a piece of literature or thematic unit of study has been given attention. To give you, the reader, an example of children using IBR interactive instruction resources, photo 4.32 is provided to show the addressing of a unit of study. These children are using a Pic-A-Dot, Task Cards, and Electro-Board to learn about how an individual may process, retain, and use new and difficult information with respect to components of the Dunn and Dunn Learning Style Model.

Photo 4.31. Children Using the IM and IBR Activities: Sam, Eliana, and Jonas

AUTHOR'S CLOSING THOUGHTS

Over the expanse of my teaching career I have thought there is one very important component aside from creating a warm, inviting-to-learn, safe classroom community. And it is this next component I'm going to addresses here, as it leads to creating that aforementioned environment. The thought I have is that each child, regardless of his/her grade level, should know *why* an assignment is assigned/given. What's the purpose of the assignment should be part of their and, of course, the teacher's awareness.

In whatever grade I have taught I have made either a weekly list or semester-graphic organizer type chart of the (1) Assignment, (2) Guidelines for Presentation/Submission of Work, and, (3) Purpose of Assignment. With the IM as the continual mainstay for all assignments, the "Purpose" section for the IBR Assignment reads as follows:

At a minimum, the purpose of this assignment is to call attention to your own thinking process, respective of "what you are thinking." This occurs when or shortly after designing a page for the IBR. As your own awareness of what cognitive and metacognitive skills are used when creating a page, you analyze what ones are used when playing the page.

Additionally, this assignment assists with organization, analysis, scope, and sequencing, as it's designed to be used as a prototype for your student learners. This example you set for your future student learners may develop their cognitive skills using practical hands-on/project- and performance-based work. As such, they'll identify what he/she is thinking, which is empowering and develops self-efficacy while simultaneously addressing creative cognition.

The IBR does the aforementioned by reviewing a piece of literature, addressing a new one in an introductory manner, and/or reviewing or gaining information about a unit of study. These IBRs may be done by working in small groups or partnerships, as the assignment facilitates collaboration and cooperation. While working on this project you build within yourself or with others, a sense of being accepting. Overall, you come to realize that each of us, as we are, is enough.

References

Abedi, J., and O'Neil, H. F. (1996). Reliability and validity of a state metacognitive inventory: Potential for alternative assessment, *Journal of Educational Research*, 89(4), 234–245.

Alongi, A. (2011). *Task cards for IBR on Charlotte's Web: An IBR activity.* EDU506A. Molloy College, Rockville Centre, NY.

Bernard, N., DiBlasio, N., and Gelbart, J. (2012). *How's the weather out there: Task cards & definitions + glossary instructions for making a task card holder and cards: An IBR activity.* Molloy College, Rockville Centre, NY.

Bogner, D. (2008; 2011). Conversations on creativity. In Drew Bogner, Jorun Buli-Holmberg, and M. S. Schiering, *Teaching and learning: A model for academic and social cognition.* Lanham, MD: Rowman & Littlefield.

Borut, C., and Borut, B. (2015, Spring). *Electro-board on European countries and capitals: An IBR activity.* EDU506A. Molloy College, Rockville Centre, NY.

Botte, J. (2015). *An analysis of the IM and IBR.* PS 188. NY.

Bowker, D. (Fall, 2015). *End-of-semester course 506A reflection paper: Personal thoughts on designing, making and using the IBR.* (Unpublished). EDU506A. Molloy College, Rockville Centre, NY.

Burke, K., and Shea Doolan, L. J. (2006). Learning styles and higher education: No adult left behind. In R. Sims and S. Sims (Eds.), *Learning styles and learning: A key to meeting the accountability demands in education* (pp. 163–174). Hauppauge, NY: Nova Science.

Capolongo, D. (2015, Fall). *Electro-board of word opposites.* Tri-fold board. ENG262.03. Molloy College, Rockville Centre, NY.

Carter, K. (2015). *The kindness tree: A morning activity for first-grade.* Robert W. Carbonaro School, Valley Stream, Long Island.

Cedrone, C. (2014). Visit the cradle of western civilization: Ancient Greece: A Webquest. Retrieved from http://ancient-greecequest.weebly.com/.

Cerruto, A. (2013; 2015). *Making interactive posters on recycling, reusing, and reducing: Sustainability.* Lexington School for the Deaf, Queens, NY. Lanham, MD: Rowman & Littlefield.

Classmate photo: A service learning project. Freshmen learning community. (2015, Fall). Tri-fold board. ENG262.03. Molloy College, Rockville Centre, NY.

Collins, D., and Stein, V. (2015, Fall). *Math with Junie B.: An IBR activity.* (Unpublished). EDU506A. Molloy College, Rockville Centre, NY.

Connor, L., and Gerbino, D. (2013). *The how-to of puppetry theater: An IBR activity.* (Unpublished). EDU506A. Molloy College, Rockville Centre, NY.

Croft, D. J., and Hess, R. D. (1980). *An activities handbook for teachers of young children.* Boston: Houghton Mifflin.

D'Amprisi, J. (2015, Fall). *Wrap-around math equations.* Tri-fold board. ENG262.03. Molloy College, Rockville Centre, NY.

Delialioglu, O., and Yildirim, Z. (2007). Students' perceptions on effective dimensions of interactive learning in a blended learning environment. *Journal of educational technology and society*, 10(2), 133–146.

DiBlasio, N., (2015a). *Name that USA state and its capital: Educational gaming activity.* Molloy College, Rockville Centre, NY.

———. (2015b). *Learning standards for 23 (A-W) of the section three activities: A narrative applying the IBR to NYS learning standards.* (Unpublished). Molloy College, Rockville Centre, NY.

Donaldson, J., and Scheffler, A. (2012). *The gruffalo.* London: Macmillan Children's.

Drew, L. (2015, Fall). *Peter Rabbit tri-fold board for service learning.* Tri-fold board. ENG262.03. Molloy College, Rockville Centre, NY.

Dunn, R. (2008). Theory behind the strategies. In R. Dunn and B. E. Blake (Eds.), *Teaching every child to read: Innovative and practical strategies for K-8 educators and caretakers.* Lanham, MD: Rowman & Littlefield.

———. (1992). *Teaching elementary students through their individual learning styles.* Boston: Allyn & Bacon.

Dunn, R., and Griggs, S. A. (2007). *What if? Promising practices for improving education.* Lanham, MD: Rowman & Littlefield.

Falconieri, A., and Gould, M. (2014). *The five senses: Close reading: An IBR activity.* EDU506A. Molloy College, Rockville Centre, NY.

Ferrandino, A. (2015, Spring). *Venn diagram for Mexico and California + venn diagram statements: An IBR activity.* (Unpublished). EDU506A IBR page. Molloy College, Rockville Centre, NY.

Ferrentello, D. (2010). *Recollections and implementation of role-play scenarios.* Croton on Hudson, NY.

———. (2014). *Sequence of events for a high school English class: Solving essay puzzles.* Croton on Hudson, NY.

Fischer, K. (2013). *American revolution: A webquest.* Retrieved from http://sws5thwebquest.weebly.com/.

Fitzpatrick, J. (2015, Fall). *Sink or float science experiment: An IBR activity.* EDU506A. Molloy College, Rockville Centre, NY.

———. (2015). *End-of-semester course 506A reflection paper: Personal thoughts on designing, making and using the IBR.* (Unpublished). EDU506A. Molloy College, Rockville Centre, NY.

Gelbart, J., and Diblasio, N. (2014). *Electro-board of the Empire State Building: An IBR activity.* EDU506A. Molloy College, Rockville Centre, NY.

Gianesses, J. (2015, Fall). *Decision-making graphic organizer: An IBR activity.* EDU506A. Molloy College, Rockville Centre, NY.

Glatthorn, A. (1995). Developing *the classroom curriculum: Developing a quality curriculum.* Alexandria, VA: ASCD.

Herdman, J. (2011). *Chirp Game: An IBR activity.* (Unpublished). Molloy College, Rockville Centre, NY.

Hurley, J., and Nackerson, J. (2014). *The interactive book report on ecosystems: Electro-board: Biodegradable or not?: An IBR activity.* (Unpublished). EDU506A. Molloy College, Rockville Centre, NY.

———. (2014). *Ecosystem math sticks: An IBR activity.* (Unpublished). EDU506A. Molloy College, Rockville Centre, New York.

———. (2014). *Food chain stacking cups: An IBR activity.* (Unpublished). EDU506A. Molloy College, Rockville Centre, New York.

Hurley, J., and Schiering, M. S. (2014). *Your choice ecosystems: Task cards or Pic-a-do: IBR activities.* Molloy College, Rockville Centre, NY.

Interactive book report photo from integrated reading and ELA for the diverse learner in the inclusion classroom. (2015, Fall). (Unpublished). EDU506A. Molloy College, Rockville Centre, NY.

Kaur, K., and Martinez, X. (2013). Wheel of adjectives: An educational game in language arts: An IBR activity. In E. B. Lewis, *From the other side.* Molloy College, Rockville Centre, NY.

Kellegher, C. (2015). *End-of-semester course 506A reflection paper: Personal thoughts on designing, making and using the IBR.* (Unpublished). EDU506A. Molloy College, Rockville Centre, NY.

Korwan, K., and Shea, J. (2013). *Wrap-around weave: Wrap your mind around this timeline: An IBR activity.* In L. Lowry, "Number the Stars." EDU506A. Molloy College, Rockville Centre, NY.

———. (2013). *Flip-chute vocabulary match: An IBR activity.* EDU506A. Molloy College, Rockville Centre, NY.

Laupheimer, L. (2015). *Recycling clothes dryer lint: A participatory teaching project: An IBR activity.* (Unpublished). Molloy College, Rockville Centre, NY.

———. (2014). *An introduction to section two: Interactive method (IM) and four interactive instructional resources.* (Unpublished). Molloy College, Rockville Centre, NY.

———. (2010). *A city of shapes: Geometry and geography, children's literature service learning project.* Tri-fold board. ENG262. Molloy College, Rockville Centre, NY.

Lockwood, A. (2010, Spring; 2015). The interactive word-family house tri-fold board: A personal accounting of using creativity in the classroom. In M. S. Schiering (Ed.), *Learning and Teaching Creative Cognition: The Interactive Book Report* (pp. 162). Lanham, MD: Rowman & Littlefield.

Maloney, C. (2012). *Cutout Velcro story map: An IBR activity.* (Unpublished). EDU506A. Molloy College, Rockville Centre, NY.

———. (2014). *Match that word ELA vocabulary game.* (Unpublished). Molloy College, Rockville Centre, NY.

Marino, A. (2015). Graphic organizer design of the reciprocal creative cognition process. In M. S. Schiering (Ed.), *Learning and Teaching Creative Cognition: The Interactive Book Report* (p. 13). Lanham, MD: Rowman & Littlefield.

Miro, A. (2001–2012). *Designing a pasta skeletal system.* Siwanoy Elementary School, Pelham, NY.

———. (2006). *Interactive phases-of-the-moon identification chart.* Siwanoy Elementary School, Pelham, NY.

Miro, E, Miro, S., and Miro, J. (2015). *Children using interactive instructional resources: Photo.* Stony Point, NY.

Mondesir, M. (2014). *Electro-board: Making connections: An IBR activity.* EDU506A. Molloy College, Rockville Centre, NY.

———. (2014a) *Making compound words: Interactive instructional resource project.* EDU506A. Molloy College, Rockville Centre, NY.

Moroney, E. (2011). *Immigrationopoly: A new twist on an old classic: An IBR activity.* (Unpublished). EDU506A. Molloy College, Rockville Centre, NY.

Moroney, R. (2012). *Long Island during the American revolution: A Webquest.* Retrieved from http://revolutionarylongisland.weebly.com/.

Nackenson, J., and Hurley, J. (2014, Spring). *Biodegradable or not electro-board: An IBR activity.* EDU506A. Molloy College, Rockville Centre, NY.

Negron, G., Cassidy, K., Snell, J., White, B., Wiegman, V., Soldano, A., Drew, L., Miritello, A., Capolongo,m D., D.Amprisi, J., Moore, S., Gardner, B., and Malinowski, M. (2015, Fall). *Photograph of freshmen learning community children's literature course 262.03.* Tri-fold board. Molloy College, Rockville Centre, NY.

Neiman, L. (2012). Creativity at work: What is creativity? [Web log message]. Retrieved from http://www.creativityatwork.com/2014/02/17/what-is-creativity/.

O'Hara-Guerrara, A. (2007). *Decision-making: Finding the best solution: A decision making graphic organizer based on Pipi Longstockings by Astrid Lingren.* (Unpublished). EDU506A. Molloy College, Rockville Centre, NY.

———. (2015). *Character map format for character analysis.* (Unpublished). Ideas for an IBR. EDU506A. Molloy College, Rockville Centre, NY.

Olsen, D. G. (1995). "Less" can be "more" in the promotion of thinking. *Social Education, 59*(3), 130–38. Silver Spring, MD: National Council for the Social Studies.

Pallidino, C. (2015). *End-of-semester course 506A reflection paper: Personal thoughts on designing, making and using the IBR.* (Unpublished). EDU506A. Molloy College, Rockville Centre, NY.

Ressa, W. (2015, Spring). *Math puzzle: Photos.* (Unpublished). Stony Point, NY.

Riba, N. (1985–2015). *Hands on methods of teaching geometry.* A class assignment and idea of an IBR. Retired Mathematics Teacher. New York.

———. (1985–2015). *Ruling with rulers: How to use the ruler.* A class assignment and idea of an IBR. Retired Mathematics Teacher. New York.

———. (1985–2015). *Same size and shape: Congruent triangle activity.* A class assignment and idea of an IBR activity. Retired Mathematics Teacher. New York.

———. (1985–2015). *Plane area activity.* A class assignment and idea of an IBR activity. Retired Mathematics Teacher. New York.

Rochford, K. (2014). *Nouns, verbs, adjectives: A floor game.* EDU506A. Molloy College, Rockville Centre, NY.

Romano, A. (2013). *Spyglass multiplication: An IBR activity.* EDU506A. Molloy College, Rockville Centre, NY.

Rosenberg, D, and Grary-Cruz, J. (2011). *Electro-board map based on In the Year of the Boar Jackie Robinson: An IBR activity.* (Unpublished). EDU506A. Molloy College, Rockville Centre, NY.

Sapienza, L. (2010). *Create a postcard: An IBR activity.* (Unpublished). EDU506A. Molloy College, Rockville Centre, NY.

———. (2015). *Portrait of adjectives: An IBR activity.* (Unpublished). PS 153. Maspeth Elementary School, New York.

Schiering, C. (2015). *Receptive and expressive language through puppetry: Five monkeys on the bed: A bi-lingual approach to teaching speech through puppetry.* (Unpublished). Chula Vista, CA.

Schiering, J. (1997). *Creating a constellation design and narrative on how it came to exist.* Fifth-grade science class assignment. Stony Point Elementary School, NY.

Schiering, J. A. (2012). *Kicking it up a notch!: Addendum to section three.* Vice President of "Linx" Summer Camps and Enrichment Center. Wellesley, MA.

Schiering, J. A., and Schiering, L. (2015). *Daughter's book report: A narrative on my daughter's three-dimensional book report: A possible IBR activity.* Stow, MA.

Schiering, M., and Byrne, J. (2013; 2015). Conversations on the linear process of creativity. In M. S. Schiering (Ed.), *Learning and teaching creative cognition: The interactive book report.* Rowman and Littlefield, Lanham, MD.

Schiering, M., and Marino, A. (2014; 2015). The content and design of the reciprocal creative cognition process. In M. S. Schiering (Ed.), *Learning and Teaching Creative Cognition: The Interactive Book Report.* Lanham, MD: Rowman & Littlefield.

Schiering, M. R. (2014; 2015). Qualities of a leader, from LinkedIn "Princess bride" leadership lessons. In M. S. Schiering (Ed.), *Learning and teaching creative cognition: The interactive book report* (pp. 51–58). Lanham, MD: Rowman & Littlefield. Retrieved from https://www.linkedin.com/pulse/20141014115549-3569415-princess-bride-leadership-lessons.

Schiering, M. S. (1978). *Role-play theater scenarios and decision-making processes.* Farley Middle School, Stony Point, NY.

———. (1983). *Student council project at Farley Middle School on identifying preferences for a "Things-We-Like Quilt."* Farley Middle School, Stony Point, NY.

———. (1999; 2011). *The effects of learning-style instructional resources on fifth grade suburban students meta-cognition, attitudes, achievement, and ability to teach themselves + the reciprocal thinking phases.* EdD dissertation. St. John's University. Lanham, MD: Rowman & Littlefield Publishers.

———. (2000a). *Circle of knowledge and nouns-verbs and adjectives floor game.* Course syllabus. EDU506A. Molloy College, Rockville Centre, NY.

———. (2000b). *The reciprocal thinking phases identification chart.* Molloy College, Rockville Centre, NY.

———. (2000–present). *Course syllabi for integrated ELA and reading (EDU506A) and interdisciplinary methods for the diverse learner in the inclusion classroom.* EDU504. Molloy College, Rockville Centre, NY.

———. (2001). *How to make a puppet theater.* Molloy College, Rockville Centre, NY.

———. (2009). *Allusions to god in children's literature: An interactive book report on you are special.* Oxford Roundtable Conference. Oxford University, England.

———. (2010, March). From equations to letters to message. In *Science and technology and arts and humanities: Two cultures; Real or perceived . . . We're human beings . . . Humans in the act of being.* Oxford, England; Oxford Round Table.

———. (2012). Creative cognition is creative thinking. *Brain world: Humanity's new frontier magazine*, 1(2), 32–33. NY: IBREA Foundation.

———. (2015). The interactive method (IM) and interactive book report (IBR). In M. S. Schiering (Ed.), *Learning and teaching creative cognition: The interactive book report.* Lanham, MD: Rowman & Littlefield.

Schiering, M. S., Bogner, D., and Buli-Holmberg, J. (2011). *Teaching and learning: A model for academic and social cognition.* Lanham, MD: Rowman & Littlefield.

Schiering, S. D. (2008). *Three-dimensional word-search geo-board: Activities for special needs students.* EDU572. Molloy College, Rockville Centre, NY.

Shea Dolan, L. J. (2013). Afterword: Fostering engagement, motivation, and empowerment: Why? In A. Cohan & A. Honigsfeld (Eds.), *Breaking the mold of education.* Lanham, MD: Rowman & Littlefield.

———. (2015). *Intertwining creativity and innovation for classroom success: The IBR as inspiration for learning achievement.* (Unpublished). Garden City, NY.

Speirs, C. (2013, Fall). *Sailboat with geometrical shapes: An IBR activity.* (Unpublished). EDU506A. Molloy College, Rockville Centre, NY.

Spotkov, L. (2014). *Presentation of educational games for everyday learning: Metamorphosis of a butterfly and literary elements of a story.* (Unpublished). Molloy College, Rockville Centre, NY.

———. (2015). *Literary elements: Story map: Rainbow fish: Activities for an IBR.* (Unpublished). Molloy College, Rockville Centre, NY.

———. (2015). *Let's keep our earth clean: An IBR activity.* (Unpublished). Molloy College, Rockville Centre, NY.

———. (2015). *End-of-semester course 506A reflection paper: Personal thoughts on designing, making and using the IBR.* (Unpublished). EDU506A. Molloy College, Rockville Centre, NY.

Stein, V. (2015). *End-of-semester course 506A reflection paper: Personal thoughts on designing, making and using the IBR.* (Unpublished). EDU506A. Molloy College, Rockville Centre, NY.

Struzzieri, E. (2015, Fall). *The complete interactive book report on "The Gruffalo (Donaldson)" from title page, reciprocal thinking skills, welcoming page, author study, story summary, and 12-activity pages to references and congratulations.* (Unpublished). EDU506A. Molloy College, Rockville Centre, NY.

Struzzieri, E. M., and Schenne, G. (2015, Spring). *Integrated reading and ELA for the diverse learner in the inclusion classroom.* (Unpublished). Molloy College, Rockville Centre, NY.

Sullivan, A. (1996). *Using the kinesthetic modality/perceptual preference to address learning styles: Sandwich boards for types of weather.* Thiells Elementary School, NY.

Sullivan, M. (2013). *Math flash cards using a deck of playing cards: An IBR activity.* EDU506A. Molloy College, Rockville Centre, NY.

Tobias, S., and Everson, H. T. (1995, April). *Development and validation of an objective measure of metacognition appropriate for group administration.* Paper presented at a symposium on "Issues in Metacognitive Research and Assessment," at the annual convention of the American Educational Research Association, San Francisco, CA.

Tomlin, D., and Gaynor, K. (2014). *Necklace sequence of events game: An IBR activity.* (Unpublished). EDU506A. Molloy College, Rockville Centre, NY.

Treffinger, D. J, Schoonover, P. F., and Selby, E. C. (2013). *Educating for creativity & innovation.* Prufrock Press, Waco, TX.

Voltmer, D., and Defliese, D. (2014). *IBR on The Four Seasons.* Seasons electro-board. Molloy College, Rockville Centre, NY.

———. (2014). *Weather wheel: Identifying seasons by months and events: IBR on The Four Seasons.* EDU506A. Molloy College, Rockville Centre, NY.

———. (2015). *Seasons of the year dress-up.* EDU506A. Molloy College, Rockville Centre, NY.

Wandberg, R., and Rohwer, J. (2003). *Teaching to the standards of effective practice: A guide to becoming a successful teacher.* Boston, MA: Allyn & Bacon.

About the Author

Marjorie Schiering is a professor of children's literature, interdisciplinary methods, integrated reading, and ELA at Molloy College. She has devoted her career as a classroom teacher to creating a comfortable and safe environment where children want to learn. In so doing, she addresses the social and academic components of teaching by focusing on two basic life statements/in-action rules. These imperatives are: "No Put Downs . . . Only Lift Ups!" and "I Am Enough!" Schiering obtained her BS in education from Ohio State University, her MS in reading from the College of New Rochelle, and her doctorate in instructional leadership from St. John's University. Prior to teaching graduate school she taught grades 1, 3, 5, and 6. She has presented extensively and been published on children's literature, character development, motivation, creativity, critical thinking techniques, linking the cognitive collective (thinking and feelings), "who" one is as a teacher and learner, and inspiration as a baseline for stimulating one's imagination. Her philosophy of education is: "We are all teachers of something . . . be engaged, physically/emotionally/mentally in the learning and teaching process. Caring about ourselves so we may care about others is important because we are responsible, as educators, for someone else's children."

Made in the USA
Middletown, DE
03 September 2017